DISCARDED

Law Enforcement, Communication and Community

Law Enforcement, Communication and Community

Edited by

Howard Giles
Center on Police Practices and Community
University of California, Santa Barbara
and Santa Barbara Police Department

John Benjamins Publishing Company
Amsterdam / Philadelphia

The paper used in this publication meets the minimum requirements of American National Standard for Information Sciences – Permanence of Paper for Printed Library Materials, ANSI Z39.48-1984.

Library of Congress Cataloging-in-Publication Data

Law Enforcement, Communication and Community / edited by Howard Giles.
    p. cm.
Includes bibliographical references and indexes.
    1. Communication in law enforcement. 2. Police-community relations. 3. Communication in law enforcement--United States. I. Giles, Howard.

HV7936.C79 L38 2002
363.2´4-dc21   2002025405
ISBN 90 272 2589 3 (Eur.) / 1 58811 201 2 (US) (Hb; alk. paper)
ISBN 90 272 2592 3 (Eur.) / 1 58811 255 1 (US) (Pb; alk. paper)

© 2002 – John Benjamins B.V.
No part of this book may be reproduced in any form, by print, photoprint, microfilm, or any other means, without written permission from the publisher.

John Benjamins Publishing Co. · P.O. Box 36224 · 1020 ME Amsterdam · The Netherlands
John Benjamins North America · P.O. Box 27519 · Philadelphia PA 19118-0519 · USA

Dedicated to the Uniformed Heroes of September 11, 2001 and to Jane and Robbie who always live through the fear of tragic outcomes every time I go out on patrol.

Table of contents

Foreward *Camerino (Cam) Sanchez*	IX
1. Revoking Our right to remain silent: Law enforcement communication in the 21st century *Michelle Chernikoff Anderson, Thomas Knutson, Howard Giles and MaryLinda Arroyo*	1
2. Community policing as communication reform *Edward R. Maguire and William Wells*	33
3. Attitudes, culture and emotion in police talk *Keith Tuffin*	67
4. The impact of contemporary communication and information technologies on police organizations *Andrew J. Flanagin*	85
5. Fictional Cops: Who are they, and what are they teaching us? *Jan J. M. Van den Bulck*	107
6. Communication issues in policing family violence *Mary Anne Fitzpatrick*	129
7. The discourse of police interviews: The case of sexually abused children *Ann-Christin Cederborg*	155
8. In the shadow of the stalker: The problem of policing unwanted pursuit *Brian H. Spitzberg*	173
9. Signs and cultural messages of bias motivated crimes: Analysis of the hate component of intergroup violence *Edward Dunbar*	201
10. Crisis/hostage negotiations: A communication-based approach *Randall Gage Rogan and Mitchell R. Hammer*	229
Index	255

Foreward

Camerino (Cam) Sanchez
Chief of Police
Santa Barbara Police Department

In a world where clear and effective communication is essential at all levels of life in order to accomplish personal and professional goals, it is extremely critical that one focus on not just communication gaps being filled in society, but in fact should include an exclusive study on the desire to truly understand another person's prospective and needs.

In the complicated world of law enforcement, one must always remember that the goal is to always look for strategies that will improve how we serve our constituency. Assisting others with their needs, be it through the enhancement of routine services or through examining ways in which to improve communication within a police organization as well as within the communities we serve is essential.

This outstanding text will assist us all in examining further the need to establish collaboration that will improve communication in order to succeed in the establishing of clear understandings between various groups of individuals who rely on law enforcement as an essential tool to solving problems.

What this text will bring out time and time again, is that the need to enhance all of our abilities to communicate in a variety of ways is a continuous process. That establishing clear communications verbally or by listening will require our complete attention if we are to succeed in learning what to do next as a problem-solver.

Establishing outstanding communication will allow us to help others, plain and simple. It will allow not only law enforcement personnel to solve crimes and provide proactive options to keep crime rates down, but will give ample opportunity for our constituency to understand how policing in partnerships work, whether or not we speak each other's language or not, or whether we fully understand the possible cultural barriers which in the past have become stumbling blocks for problem-solving.

Together, as both a speaking and listening audience we can in a large manner improve how we grow in the understanding of clear communications and partnership building.

CHAPTER 1

Revoking our right to remain silent

Law enforcement communication in the 21st century

Michelle Chernikoff Anderson, Thomas Knutson,
Howard Giles and MaryLinda Arroyo
University of California, Berkeley, USA (Anderson)
California State University, Sacramento, USA (Knutson)
University of California, Santa Barbara, USA (Giles)
Santa Barbara Police Department, USA (Arroyo)

Law enforcement is a profoundly important institution in our society given its critical role in maintaining legal and social order, topics especially salient in times of global unrest. Our quest in this book is to underscore that Communication research has considerable potential to benefit law enforcement and that policing is a domain of critical importance to the Communication discipline. Yet, until now, Communication scholars have only afforded matters of law enforcement sporadic attention at best. For these reasons, we have written this book to be accessible to both academic and law enforcement audiences.

The chapters assembled for this volume display a wide range of topics relating to law enforcement. They address significant communication issues pertaining to the improvement of both public harmony and officer safety. Although law enforcement has undergone considerable changes over the years, the continuing essence of an officer's job involves communicating with people. Successful law enforcement depends on the vital ability to communicate capably and competently not only on the street, but also within the police organization and other branches of the government, such as the courts. Indeed, the ability to communicate appropriately represents an officer's prime worth in terms of safety and the community good.

Law enforcement is ubiquitous in widely-absorbed fictional drama and standard fare in news-reporting. Few Americans, however, have much direct contact with law enforcement officials apart from when they occasionally invite service or are pulled over for a traffic violation, though at times such as September 11, 2001, the media coverage aids the public in understanding some of the risks and dangers officers willingly undertake for the sake of their communities. As such, the ordinary citizen has little understanding of the reality of this unique occupation (see Perlmutter 2000), let alone the role of communication in law enforcement. While one distinguishing aspect of law enforcement is the institutionally-endorsed ability to engage in lethal force when absolutely necessary (a feature clearly announced communicatively on the persona of uniformed officers in the United States and elsewhere), an under-appreciated fact is that law enforcement officers are an integral part of, and not separate from, the community — citizens when off-duty. Also poorly understood are the uncertainties, emotions and parameters of discretion that affect an officer's choice and use of communication, discretion which is frequently necessary to accommodate a wide range of humanity (including victims, those falsely claiming to be victims, witnesses and alleged criminals), some of whom are in dire and/or stressed psychological states. Furthermore, one of the infinite number of challenges to which law enforcement communications must adjust (see Chapter 2) is the constant ebb and flow of public tastes, municipal pressures, governmental edicts, legal requirements, and ever-changing forms of new criminal activity (Seave 2001).

Given this collection is really the first of its genre, we cannot cover every captivating topic at the interaction of law enforcement, communication, and community. Even if we had the scope to do so, with the current state of embryonic research data, that would be impossible to accomplish and we are at the mercy of what can be garnered. Encouragingly, there are, as this volume attests, committed and high caliber scholars mining this research arena. Hence, through the following topics we provide what we hope is an intriguing and wide-ranging sample of important issues addressing law enforcement, community and communication: community policing; police talk; new technologies and policing; media images of police; and the policing of domestic violence, child sexual abuse, stalking, hate crimes, and hostage negotiation crises. We have tried to provide, where feasible in terms of extant research, an international flavor by including contributors (see Chapters, 3, 5 & 7), and data in other chapters (see Chapter 9), from other than the United States. Clearly, the communicative practices of law enforcement are a function of the historical, political, and ideological contexts in which they are embedded. Methodologically, there is an eclectic blend of qualitative (see Chapters 3 & 7) alongside quantitative data (e.g., Chapter 9). In addition, contributors have, where feasible, provided guidelines — non-prescriptively — for applying their approaches for the consideration of professionals in the field (see Chapters 6–10). And finally, new theoretical models are introduced, giving this enterprise theoretical teeth as well (e.g., Chapter 5, 9 & 10).

In this opening chapter, we provide the reader with an overview that attempts to capture the essence of each chapter. Moreover, we contextualize each one in broader terms if and where each might align with relevant communication models, and especially as each aligns with legal ones. We do this acknowledging that all contributions, to varying degrees (but especially Chapter 6–9) recognize the important relationships between law enforcement and the judiciary, connections incidentally that are rarely portrayed in the media (Perlmutter 2000). The law both proceeds and frames police–citizen communications; the law also follows law enforcement actions into the courts and elsewhere. In so doing, we attempt to raise pertinent questions beyond those constituting the authors' own proposed research agendas for the future. In addition, we proffer constructs and processes (particularly as they relate to *intergroup* matters) where Communication research can be informative to law enforcement.

But before engaging on this path, it is important to underscore the fact that law enforcement has, for the longest time, understood the value of communication; indeed, Santa Barbara Police Chief Sanchez's Foreword expresses this sentiment well. Recognizing this, we first overview communication training for law enforcement in our own region: California, U.S.A.

The POST mandate

The emphasis placed on peace officer communication is evident in California's Peace Officers Safety and Training (POST) Basic Academy and in a variety of other programs, workshops, and seminars. All law enforcement officers in California must complete this Basic Academy prior to exercising peace officer powers and responsibilities. POST reflects California Law Enforcement's understanding that the vast majority of law enforcement responsibilities involve effective communication.

Even though discussions of violence are an integral component of many of the chapters herein (e.g., Chapters 9 & 10), much of law enforcement does not involve crime and danger. Most peace officers report upon retirement, for example, that they have never used lethal force in the performance of their legal responsibilities. POST clearly recognizes this situation, as well as the necessity for officers to take proactive steps to promote positive interactions with community members. The vast majority of an officer's work requires an ability to improve community relations. The POST Basic Academy devotes considerable time to training officers in techniques to give them "... an active knowledge of the perceptions and expectations the members of the community in which officers serve have toward law enforcement in order to promote positive officer interactions with members of that community" (California Commission on Peace Officer Standards and Training [CCPOST] 1999:1–1). The POST Community Relations course strongly emphasizes a proactive approach to enlist citizen support in all aspects of law enforcement. Officers must maintain order, enforce the law, and prevent crime, but they are also called upon to deliver service and to educate the public.

Communication is seen as the basic tool to accomplish these goals and to ensure that the public perceives officers as a *part* of the community. Accordingly, the POST Basic Academy stresses the benefits of tactical communication to reduce the likelihood of physical confrontation (CCPOST 1998). Improved communication is also aimed at improving community relations and decreasing citizen complaints and civil liabilities. POST maintains that physical force should be avoided except under specific circumstances where communication through words is not effective.[1] While peace officers in California are required to use force under some circumstances, the overriding goal of law enforcement communication is to generate voluntary compliance with reasonable conversations and lawful commands (CCPOST 1998:2–10).

The POST Basic Academy courses summarize basic communication theory as applied to law enforcement responsibilities. Elements include concepts that will be familiar to many readers of this book as well as other factors found in subsequent contributions to this book: source; message; noise; channel; receiver; feedback; listening; nonverbal cues; empathy; radio and telephone demeanor; and cultural influences. These concepts are taught as methods to improve law enforcement communication with the community by focusing upon the following:

- always treating people in a professional manner;
- responding promptly to any calls;
- being courteous to all persons contacted;
- avoiding pre-judging individuals based on previous experience;
- remembering not to underestimate individuals based on their appearance;

- maintaining self-control at all times; and
- becoming familiar with cultural customs of different community groups (CCPOST 1999: 2–32).

Beyond these basic interpersonal communication applications, officers also receive instruction in applied communication techniques in the following areas:

- components of crime prevention;
- crime risk factors;
- crime prevention techniques;
- basic problem solving strategies; and
- community-oriented policing.

The POST Commission recently declared that personal and tactical communication is a perishable skill (CCPOST Regulations 2001) and thus requires officers, beginning in January 2002, to engage in Continued Professional Training in communication skills. POST (both through basic academy and the continued professional training) is one of the ways in which California's law enforcement officials have demonstrated persistent and reassuring determination to improve the quality of interpersonal communication which provides for public safety and professional credibility — and may act as a model for other agencies throughout the United States. Indeed, constructs related to professional credibility such as legitimacy, trust, cooperation, rapport, and empathy are frequently encountered in subsequent chapters. We return now to what scholars have to report on topics at the interface of law enforcement, communication, and the community, beginning with community policing.

Chapter overviews

We begin the chapters with a satellite view of the landscape which maps the many junctions between community policing and communication research. We end the chapters with a powerful zoom lens focusing on specific intersections of law enforcement and the community in which the authors demonstrate the critical role of communication and thus communication research. In Chapter 2, Maguire and Wells lay the groundwork for demonstrating the benefits of applying communication research and theory to improving and assessing community policing programs. The authors point out that many community policing reform efforts are intended to improve communication at many levels.

To date, however, few studies have addressed whether such policies actually improve community policing. After beginning with a history of the community policing movement, the authors discuss the role of community policing reforms in external communication, that is, communication between the police and the communities they serve. The authors apply public relations theory to analyze how the police communicate with citizens and the purposes and effects of such communication. Externally-improved police–community relations are intended to result in safer, less fearful, and more satisfied communities. Chapter 2 also examines internal communication reforms, i.e., within the organization itself, such as changing vertical, functional, spatial and/or temporal organizational structures. Internal community policing reforms are intended to reduce bureaucracy and, thus, to allow the law enforcement agency to respond more flexibly and creatively to problems in the community.

Maguire and Wells point out that the assumptions underlying such reforms and the effectiveness of specific implementation approaches, however, are almost completely untested. They suggest that recent corruption scandals and allegations of police violence raise tensions between the police and communities. They argue accordingly that the need for a framework to view the role of communication reform in community policing, particularly to test proposed reforms, is only increasing. By integrating theories and concepts from public relations, organization theory, and policing, the authors have established such a framework for viewing the role of communication reform in community policing.

Maguire and Wells' welcome approach notwithstanding, we add that changes to both the external and internal communications of the police also have *legal* ramifications. External communication raises legal concerns of the sort the public is most accustomed to hearing: those between the police and the community. Maguire and Wells, for example, refer to Los Angeles' then Mayor Riordan's suggestion that the city set aside up to $300 million worth of tobacco settlement money to pay for the lawsuits stemming from the Los Angeles Police Department's Rampart Division corruption scandal. Any communication reform measure will need to be assessed for its impact on preventing these kinds of illegal actions by the police, from drug smuggling and civil rights violations to assault and even murder. In addition, communication reforms should be assessed for how well they will lead to a swift and just resolution to any future breaches of trust between the police and the community, in order to avoid the scandals from mushrooming to the magnitude recently seen in several large metropolitan police departments.

Internal communications, on the other hand, raise employment law issues similar to those of any large organization which, of course, can also have a significant economic impact on the deep pockets of the government. Maguire and Wells, for example, refer to a *Law Enforcement News* (2001) report that a quarter of the four million e-mails sent by officers to one another within one year in the Washington, DC Metropolitan Police Department contained either hate filled language or obscenity. If any of these e-mails, whether as a single incident or a pattern and practice, raises to the level of harassment barred by employment law in the jurisdiction (such as race, ethnicity, gender, disability, age, religion or national origin and, in many jurisdictions, sexual orientation), the offending officer(s), the department itself, and others may be liable. Accordingly, proposed communication reforms need to be assessed as to their effect on such forms of harassment. Does the proposed reform prevent such incidents? Does the proposed reform improve the timeliness and accuracy in reporting such incidents? Or does the proposed reform impede modes of communication originally aimed at hindering harassment?

Chapter 3 also employs a widescreen lens to communication, law enforcement and the community by employing discursive methods to understanding police talk. In Chapter 3, Tuffin argues from the viewpoint that language is constructive, not merely descriptive. For this reason, he considers three separate studies of the language used in three different contexts of police work in New Zealand. These discursive studies involved interviews with the police and analyses of the common language used in police settings. First, Tuffin considers attitudes towards gay cops. The 1986 change in the legal status of gays and lesbians as a result of New Zealand's Homosexual Law Reform Act meant that police officers who once regarded gays and lesbians as *criminals* under New Zealand law now found themselves unable to discriminate against gays and lesbians with whom they were *working*. Interestingly, Tuffin found that police officers constructed their unfavorable reactions to gay officers as reflecting prejudice outside their control, that is, prejudice which impacted all of society, including the police. They blamed a negative reaction to gay cops as stemming from internal pressures from *others* on the force, not themselves, and on a presumed negative public reaction which, in turn, would have a denigrating impact on the reputation of the police. In this way, the police justified their negative reactions to gay officers by suggesting that they were not the enforcers of prejudice, but rather, victims themselves of much wider forces of bias.

Second, the author examines internal pressures operating within police culture. Tuffin discusses three kinds of police discourse which contribute to an overall police culture supportive of conformity to, and maintenance of, the status quo: (a) police status (the reputation of the police in society); (b) adherence to standards upon which the reputation of the police rests; and (c) internal pressure, such as peer monitoring and threats to job safety through a failure of fellow officers to assist noncompliant officers in need.

Third and lastly, Tuffin examines the complex set of rules by which police speak or choose not to speak of their emotions following a traumatic event. Though officers will openly state that discussing such events can be helpful given that the emotions are natural human responses, emotion is also seen as highly irrational — and thus dangerous — in a job requiring firm, decisive, rational, and controlled actions. Accordingly, fearing repercussions to their careers, officers have developed a carefully chosen set of circumstances under which it is acceptable, indeed actually encouraged, to share such emotional discourse.

Similar to our discussion above of Maguire and Wells' chapter, in which we considered the effect of communication reform on police employment law issues, the discursive methods applied by Tuffin could be applied to reduce and/or prevent violations of employment law via a better understanding of the constitution of bias within the police force. With this improved understanding of the construction of negative attitudes, of gay law enforcement officers for example, more effective policies could be implemented to prevent sexual orientation discrimination. Because the biased attitudes and the conformity culture to which Tuffin refers raise the legal issues we touched upon in discussing harassment law issues implicated in Chapter 2, proposed communication reforms also need to be assessed as to their effect on such forms of harassment.

Discursive analysis of police culture also provides a means to recognize problems of officer safety, such as where fellow law enforcement officers threaten to purposely fail to assist noncompliant officers, threats which might go unnoticed to the lay ear. Might similar discourse patterns be observed in law enforcement officers who fail to respond to the needs of particular individuals or segments of the community? Such analyses open the door for recognizing and preventing officer threats and/or acts for which the police may be criminally or civilly liable. Gerber's (2001) model of cross-gendered patrol partnerships, also, might be a fruitful way of theorizing further this important affective arena (see also, Boggs and Giles' [1999] model of miscommunication in the gendered workplace).

Lastly, Tuffin's discussion of emotional discourse leads us to suggest that the military's experience may provide some worthwhile lessons. The Marine Corps and the Air Force have responded differently to suicides in the services and have had different results as well. The Air Force has focused on early therapeutic outreach to troops, protection of confidentiality and the separation of therapy from one's career. The Air Force's record low level suicide rate suggests this is working. In contrast, the Marine Corps offers very little confidentiality and their suicide rate has remained much higher than that of the Air Force (even accounting for the fact that is was higher than that of the Air Force prior to the Air Force's new confidentiality policies). When asked why none of the Marine Corps suicide victims had sought counseling, the Marine Corps psychiatrist, Captain Scott McClelland, answered, "I think they're afraid for their careers. I think they fear that it will be discovered" (ABC News (Nightline) 1999). These sentiments differ little from those Tuffin discusses regarding "emotion in police talk." Accordingly, Communication research from one service, whether law enforcement or the military, may be useful in understanding and improving the others. Fortunately, more research will soon be available to help develop a firmer understanding of the effects of police emotional discourse. For example, the National Institute of Justice has funded a research project to determine if the availability of psychological counseling increases police officers' resistance to stress and if it is related to relational communications (S. Chadwick, Iowa State University, personal communication, 29 June 2001).

In the next set of chapters we turn to specific issues at the intersection of police communication and community. In Chapter 4, Flanagin asserts that while modern technology has fundamentally altered communication between and among institutions and has resulted in improvements in organizational efficiency and effectiveness for many institutions, one does not find many of these benefits in police organizations. Flanagin argues that barriers which are specific to police organizations, such as the bottom-up flow of information, have prevented police organizations from fully embracing many of these new communication technologies.

The author argues that many of these technologies provide a lower return for police organizations than for other organizations. He suggests that explanations lie in the nature of police organizations, the work they perform, and the conditions necessary for effective information processing. He also recommends ways in which the police may be able to take advantage of some of these technological tools that, until now, have failed to benefit them.

We concur that there is a need for law enforcement to be well-versed in new technologies and suggest the need spans beyond any advantages the devices may serve for law enforcement's own use. If law enforcement is not familiar with modern communication technology, how will it be able to address old wine (old crimes) in new bottles (cloaked in new technology), some of the more recent examples being identity theft, child endangerment via the web, and bioterrorism?

In addition, our jurisprudence needs to be flexible in order to respond to the issues raised by technological advances. Just as intellectual property jurisprudence has had to adjust to reflect the reality of globalization and the internet, so too will our constitutional jurisprudence need to reflect the reality of modern communication technologies. Moreover, each new device that enables law enforcement greater access to otherwise private information about civilians, raises constitutional right to privacy issues. Indeed, technological advances such as flight and heat sensing have raised new 4th Amendment questions where law enforcement has sought to apply such technology to searches. For example, the plain view doctrine holds that "what a person knowingly exposes to the public, even in his own home or office, is not a subject of Fourth Amendment protection" (Katz v U.S. 1967:351). The Court has applied this doctrine to allow electronic tracking beepers, pen registers, hidden microphones and flight surveillance of back yards without a warrant (Harvard Law Review 1986).

The Court has, however, drawn a line such that warrantless surveillance is not, in all cases, as open as the latest technology. For example, this year the Court held that the use of thermal imaging to detect high heat inside a house (as an indicator of the cultivation of marijuana) constitutes a "search." That is, "obtaining by sense enhancing technology any information regarding the interior of the home that could not otherwise have been obtained without physical intrusion into a constitutionally protected area" (Kyllo v U.S. 2001:15) is a search and thus requires Fourth Amendment protection.

Where the searches or seizures pass constitutional muster, they may still raise other evidentiary issues for the court. The prejudicial value of evidence bearing the authoritative mark of "advanced technology," which may not accurately reflect the validity of the device in question, still needs to be weighed against its probative value in assessing its admissibility in court. Lastly, in light of the tragedies of 11 September 2001, the United States Congress has just passed legislation expanding law enforcement's potential uses of communication technologies such as wire-tapping (USA Patriot Act 2001). Not surprisingly, the debates preceding the votes on this legislation revolved around constitutional issues such as those raised here and no doubt some of them will be tested in the courts. Next we focus on what we can learn from another set of communications involving law enforcement — the media's fictional cops.

"You have the right to remain silent. Anything you say can ...." Why is it that so many of us can complete this phrase verbatim? Perhaps years of hearing fictional cops repeat these lines have affected our perceptions about our criminal justice system and the role of law enforcement in it. Indeed, in a recent argument to the United States Supreme Court, a party seeking to have the Court uphold the *Miranda* decision (the case from which the recitation of these rights stems, *Miranda v. Arizona* 1966), remarked on the influence of fictional cops in the media and even suggested that these images have served to legitimize the real criminal justice system: "*Miranda's* specific holdings have been widely popularized through the media and accepted in the legal culture. Departing from them would erode public confidence in the legitimacy of the criminal justice system" (Petitioner's Brief 2000).

American fictional cops are available in the media all over the world and many chapters herein address the ways police agencies can frame understandings of broadcast news events as well as the public's perceptions of police actions (e.g., Chapters 2 & 4). In Chapter 5, Van den Bulck asks whether or not fictional cops are relevant to understanding the nonfiction police and community. What, if any, affect do these fictitious cops have on the criminal behavior of viewers, on viewers' expectations of law enforcement, and on the perceptions and expectations held of and by real law enforcement officers? Van den Bulck first reviews the demographics of fictional crime shows and how well, if at all, they represent reality. The author then examines the literature on the imitation of television violence versus contagion, meaning the removal of inhibitors to create new or increase existing violent tendencies. Van den Bulck next accesses literature on whether crime fiction causes aggression, discusses hypotheses on what and how fiction may teach about reality, and looks at whether the lives of viewers and/or the lives of law enforcement imitate the art of fictional cops.

We feel it is important here to note that there exist large differences in the policies and procedures of East versus West coast American police agencies. While one is not better than the other, most current TV cop shows are based on the former model. Indeed, it would be intriguing to map out the communication styles and procedures that differentiate the two coasts and determine what audience effects are instilled in those who view one or the other. It is also important to acknowledge that these shows very often have police officers as consultants. Nevertheless, our anecdotal experience suggests that most police officers believe that were they to do the same as fictional cops, they would be fired, sued, or reprimanded in some manner. Given these reality gaps, we would hope that police personnel are skeptical of potential recruits who pursue a law enforcement career on the basis of identifying with fiction cops, particularly those who might pursue what could be framed as "vigilante justice".

Van den Bulck refers to how television and movies have made *Miranda* rights a part of society's legal lexicon. As mentioned briefly above, the U.S. Supreme Court recently took up the issue of retaining or relinquishing *Miranda*. Some legal scholars argued that even if one could constitutionally justify removing the requirement to Mirandize confined suspects, the Court should not risk removing the perception held by the public that its rights are protected, a perception which they believe numerous cop shows have produced by reciting the *Miranda* rights. Indeed, some legal scholars suggest that *Miranda* may not be the best solution to the issue of involuntary confessions but that it has acquired such symbolic value in our society, via the media, that to remove it would be to remove an important symbol of the rights our society holds dear (Leo 1996).

If, as Van den Bulck asserts, both the public at large and law enforcement (see Perlmutter 2000) itself "learns" of the public's expectations of law enforcement through fiction and the news — and certainly we need more rigorous research to test this assertion and the doubtless complex relationships attending it (see Bruschke & Loges 1999; Mares 1996) — might this "learning" (if it is, indeed, widespread) be true regarding other legal figures? For example, how do lawyers and judges on *The Practice, Ally McBeal, Law and Order, NYPD Blue, Philly, The Sopranos,* and numerous other shows, affect the public's, lawyers' and judges' perceptions of the roles of each in society? Similarly, might law enforcement officers also "learn" what to expect of lawyers and judges from fictional lawyers and judges? Accordingly, might law enforcement personnel who consume such media have an increased likelihood of expecting lawyers to circumvent the truth and to win at all costs as is often portrayed on screen? Moreover, might law enforcement officers who consume such media, be more likely to perceive judges and juries as pro defense given the seemingly disproportionate number of criminal defense victories in shows such as *The Practice*? Finally here, it is important to recognize that police officers now feature in non-fictional, albeit usually action-oriented, reality-shows. The kinds of officers and their behaviors so depicted and the social consequences of these popular shows should attract media effects studies as well.

In the next set of chapters, we focus on communication issues at the intersection of law enforcement and the community where the perpetrator and the victim normally know each other, beginning with domestic violence. In the conclusion to Chapter 6, Fitzpatrick refers to a line from the Chicago Police

Department training program on domestic violence which states that the best way for the police to stop crime is to concentrate on family violence. Not only is this true because, as the author notes, 10–15% of all homicides are caused by domestic violence but, for years, criminologists have found that both children who are direct victims of domestic violence and those who "merely" witness domestic violence, are more likely to be involved in crime as juveniles and as adults (Currie 1985). Fitzpatrick looks at the nature of family violence, the range of definitions used by different jurisdictions to identify this crime, and the myths surrounding these old acts criminalized by relatively new laws. The author also explores the socio-legal environment of domestic violence — from mandatory arrest policies to restraining orders and treatment programs (see Trinch 2001). From the literature on social interaction dynamics, the author then draws recommendations to improve interactions between law enforcement and families. Her theoretical position might well profit from notions represented in Le Poire, Prescott and Shepard's (in press) inconsistent nurturing as control theory that examines couples-at-risk, one member of which inadvertently reinforces malfunctional behaviors of the other.

Some of the most interesting new legal issues in policing domestic violence involve allegations of the discriminatory application (i.e., abuse of discretion) in policing domestic violence. For example, in Texas, the parents of a man shot by his ex-boyfriend are suing the city claiming that the police ignored their son's repeated requests for help in response to threats from his ex-boyfriend. His parents are claiming that the police's failure to act was based upon their son's sexual orientation (ACLU 2001; Fleck 2001; Grossman 2000).[2] At the same time, looking outside the United States, Miccio (1998) points out that a Human Rights Watch report on Brazil is the first to hold a nation state accountable for the harms of private actors due to discriminatory state action in violation of international law. Miccio (1998) notes that this report demonstrates wide-spread abuse of police discretion in domestic violence cases, finding that the gender and status of the actor and victim were critical factors in law enforcement deciding whether or not to pursue a case. Some law enforcement agencies have attempted to prevent such abuses of discretion through mandatory arrest laws. For example, California has a mandatory arrest law for domestic violence with visible injury, regardless of the gender of the two partners.

Another issue in domestic violence law is self-defense. Some feminists argue that the jurisprudence of self-defense is based upon a male model of, and responding to, threat (e.g., Hunter 1996; Miccio 1998). They argue that the self-defense requirement — that a reasonable person in the victim's shoes must have felt in danger of great bodily harm — often fails to protect a victim who kills the abuser (where the criminal justice system has failed to protect the victim). As a result, some argue that the law unfairly punishes the victim who, feeling with certainty that the abuser will eventually kill her/him, ultimately kills the abuser at an opportune moment, and then ends up imprisoned for manslaughter or murder. Indeed, the diagnostic importance of subjective fear levels is poignantly drawn out in Chapter 8.

Continuing the focus on law enforcement communication issues where the perpetrator and victim generally know each other, we direct our lens to the sexual abuse of children. How the interview between the police and allegedly abused children proceeds can have a profound impact on the accuracy of the child's description of abuse, with incorrect interviewing infecting the accuracy of the child's descriptions of the abuse event, regardless of whether the abuse actually occurred. For example, where police investigators rely on option-posing and suggestive utterances, rather than open-ended invitations, the accuracy of the story may easily be flawed. Accordingly, the rights of the child to be raised by his/her parents and the rights of the alleged abuser(s) may be wrongfully terminated. In Chapter 7, Cederborg seeks to explore and analyze the discourse patterns in police interviews of children allegedly sexually abused. The data include 193 videotaped interviews from 1986 to 1995 of child witnesses in cases of child sexual abuse. Cederborg focuses on the discourse patterns in police interviews of children to analyze how the child and the officer co-produce the report of the alleged abuse (see also Davies, Westcott & Horan 2000).

Interestingly, the effect on discourse of power and status differentials (see Ng & Bradac 1993) between the police and child, which Cederborg discusses, is not unique to the police interview. Jury researchers have studied such differences in the jury room. They have found that "status in the jury room mirrors status in the outside world" (Hans & Vidmar 1986: 100–101). That is, higher status jurors (e.g., more highly educated and with a high status occupation) and male jurors speak more during deliberations and are more likely to be selected as the foreperson. Indeed, might these power and status discourse patterns within the jury room itself affect the jury's assessment of the evidence in a child abuse case in which the child and police witness testimony is also the product of similar power and status discourse patterns?

It is important for us to point out that several law enforcement agencies in the U.S.A. do not conduct interviews of child abuse victims. Rather, they schedule the interviews to be undertaken by qualified "experts" with law enforcement officials observing from a separate room. Future research should compare the discourse patterns of "expert interviewers" with police interviewers as well as determine the validity of the outcomes of both processes. Moreover, it is important to carefully define what actually constitutes an "expert" in these cases, and to what a given expert may testify in court, prior to making any comparisons between law enforcement and expert interviewers.

The legal battleground is in balancing the rights of the accused with the rights of children not to be abused. The infamous McMartin Preschool case is a frightening example of the horrendous errors (and lives destroyed) by the misuse of power in which law enforcement and others suggestively interviewed children about alleged sexual abuse (Humes 1999). The constitutional issues revolve around the defendant's 6th Amendment right to be confronted with the witnesses against him/her and the defendant's 5th and 14th Amendment rights to due process. Social science research in this area often seeks to inform the legislature and courts of the actual effects of various legal practices so that new legal policies, including the acts of law enforcement in accord with such laws, can consistently balance the rights of the accused with the State's obligation to ensure the welfare of its children.

Carrying on the focus on law enforcement communication issues where the perpetrator and victim generally know each other, we again move our lens, this time to stalking. In Chapter 8, Spitzberg examines this very old behavior consisting of "stealthy, unwanted pursuit and harassment", but which did not become a crime in the United States until 1990 when California's first anti-stalking statue took effect. By the end of the 1990s, however, all 50 States and the federal government had some form of anti-stalking legislation on the books. Spitzberg carefully examines the concept of stalking, including the commonalties amongst the various jurisdictions' legal definitions, the typologies of stalker types, profiles of the tactics used by stalkers, and the prevalence and seriousness of stalking in society.

The author then discusses the obstacles the police currently face in trying to address this crime. These include victims' tendencies to turn to the police only as a last resort; the lack of an obvious injury such as one might expect in a theft or assault; a lack of police officer training in the specifics of stalking; officers' lack of clear jurisdiction; and law enforcement's failure to identify stalking because of a propensity to identify only those crimes most familiar, such as trespassing, harassment, or assault, but which are "merely" incidental to stalking. Not only might the police benefit from a better understanding of the coping mechanisms commonly found amongst stalking victims, but such an understanding might enable the police to assess if, and when, to recommend various other sources of victim assistance, including protective orders. Spitzberg cautions that the police and victims of stalking can expect to continue to face these obstacles until a sufficient amount of sound social science accumulates to replace current policies which generally stem from anecdotal experience. Spitzberg notes that many stalking laws have been or are facing constitutional challenges, generally for being vague or overbroad. While he states that most stalking legislation has been upheld, we caution that borderline vague or overbroad statues may provide ample wiggle room to open the door to law enforcement abuses and harassment under the veil of pursuing an alleged stalker.

Like the commonly nonstranger crimes of Chapters 6, 7 and 8, hate crimes are another relatively new set of crimes, however, the victim and perpetrator do not necessarily know each other. Law enforcement is only just beginning to grapple with the issues of understanding, detecting, and enforcing hate crime statutes, which is the focus of the penultimate chapter. In Chapter 9, Dunbar considers the symbolic components of intergroup violence to provide an analysis of hate crime. Dunbar looks at how intergroup violence incorporates attributional signs, which reveal the hate motivation of the offense, and the cultural meta-messages demonstrating ingroup bias. In addition, he empirically assesses behavioral and cognitive elements of hate crimes in different cultural contexts. In so doing, the author seeks to address the concerns of hate crime legislation critics who ask why victims are selected, what motivates the offender, how best to demonstrate this motivation, and how to uniformly enforce laws which are seemingly ambiguously defined.

Dunbar first reviews the literature on: the attributional signs of bias; the cultural message being sent by the offender; and factors used to classify a crime as bias motivated, including hate speech, articulated hate ideology, and so forth. Second, he develops a typology of seven meta-messages of bias and tests this typology by applying it to an analysis of 518 bias crimes reported to a metropolitan law enforcement agency in California in 1999. The author found that for those persons identified as hate crime perpetrators,[3] bias aggression included more than hate speech, however, such hate utterances were the most common indicator of bias motivation.

Dunbar argues that law enforcement can effectively assess and evaluate bias aggression using the multi-dimensional approach incorporating both the behavioral and meta-communicative elements which he has discussed in describing the attributional signs of bias aggression. He also looks at factors that affect the reporting of hate crimes, including the perception of police bias. Finally, Dunbar proposes a model of expertise in bias crime response that might align well with communication models of "harmful speech" more generally (see Leets & Giles 1999). The author suggests that through an improved understanding of the differences in bias offenders, victims and respondents, communities will be better equipped to target prevention efforts as well as rehabilitative measures.

Hate crimes raise several socio-legal issues. First, mental state (particularly as it relates to the *intent* of the subject) is a vital component of our criminal law. Some critics ask why the same act, such as a punch in the face, can constitute two distinct crimes, depending upon whether or not the perpetrator's act stemmed from hate of a protected class. These critics may overlook that such distinctions are far from novel in our criminal jurisprudence. For example, an actor's mental state will determine if a dead body is the result of criminal guilt, civil negligence, or no legal liability at all. Within the criminal law, the actor's mental state will determine whether s/he is guilty of no crime, manslaughter, second degree murder, or first degree murder.[4]

In this chapter, Dunbar discusses bias in the enforcement of hate crime laws as reflective of the biases existing in the culture at large, from which law enforcement is not insulated. Similar research exists in the field of Law and Society finding bias effects in jury decision-making and judicial decision-making which reflect the biases held in much of the culture at large in civil cases (e.g. Title VII, sexual harassment) and in the prosecutorial discretion exercised in criminal cases (e.g., the determination to charge a defendant with capital murder). The author, a social scientist and not a lawyer, also refers to "the probability of the bias-motivation of the offense." This kind of assessment highlights a recurring tension between the social sciences and the law. Social scientists measure in probabilities. The law, however, is intended to focus almost exclusively on the case at hand and evidence of similar prior occurrences generally is not to be used to measure a defendant's propensity to have committed or to commit in the future the crime in question.[5] Finally, Dunbar's discussion of "prior enactment of bias motivated aggression" as an "attributional sign" of hate motivation demonstrates the same tension between social science and the law. He states, "As the familiar adage in psychology goes 'past behavior is a good predictor of future behavior.'" In contrast, in the law, evidence of a defendant's prior criminal behavior is often considered irrelevant to the case at hand and/or too prejudicial to be admitted.

In the final chapter, Rogan and Hammer focus on an extremely dangerous and volatile situation that is uniquely fitted to the application of Communication research: communicating in a crisis or hostage negotiation. Much of the crisis/hostage negotiation literature has focused either on the psychology of the perpetrator, the effects on the hostages, or the emotional effects of crisis management for negotiators. Prior to the authors' own research, however, relatively little had been written on the interaction dynamics of crisis/hostage negotiations. What guidelines exist have been developed from practitioner experience, not scientific methodology. In Chapter 10, Rogan and Hammer seek to address the absence of such research by conceptualizing crisis/hostage negotiation as an interactive social phenomenon. They have developed a model which represents the following four interpretive frames through which interactants shape the discourse of their negotiation. The face frame is the sense of self and one's relation to the world which is tied to the social exchange. The interest frame reflects individual concern for objective, tangible demands. The relational frame refers to relations between the suspect and the negotiator, involving factors such as trust, power, control, intimacy and empathy. And the emotion frame refers to the expressive motivation of the suspect. The acronym for *f*ace, *i*nterest, *r*elational and *e*motion frames gives the model its name: the FIRE model. Through the use of this new heuristic, the authors hope to prevent more Ruby Ridges, Wacos, and Munich Olympics by aiding law enforcement in realizing nonviolent resolutions to crisis negotiations.

We believe this model has implications and potential applicability for many legal contexts, from negotiations between divorcing clients to business/labor relations to international law and diplomacy. In these other legal contexts, the FIRE Model may prove eventually useful in understanding the role of emotion and interaction where less costly, particularly nonviolent, resolutions are also the goal. For example, where there is a conflict in international law, there are often very high stakes (e.g., the Cuban Missile Crisis) with demands for face saving opportunities and other negotiation tactics similar to hostage negotiations. Accordingly, it will be particularly important in proposing applications of the FIRE Model to first research the role that different cultural identities may play in the interactions. Lastly, Tracy and Tracy's (1998) notions of "face attack" in their analysis of citizens' calls to a 911 (emergency telephone) center could be relevant here. They suggest ways to generate alternative strategies for people who report no sense of control, ideas that may augment and reinforce the FIRE model.

Law enforcement, communication, and the future

As stated in the opening of this chapter, Communication as a discipline has not been significantly involved in police/citizen relations, police training (see, however, Gundersen & Hopper 1984), or law enforcement/community policies — nor has the Communication discipline developed contexts within which scholars could engage law enforcement. In tandem, research and thinking in police science has rarely drawn on communication theory and research to assist its insights and approaches. As such, and in considering the extensive number of references included to support the positions of the respective authors, it is intriguing to note that the majority of citations appear from sources *outside* the Communication discipline. Less than 12% of the sources come from journals and publications issued by professional Communication associations, a condition justifying a prima facie observation that Communication scholars must be more assertive in translating their work to the benefit of our communities. We are a broad and diverse group of scholars contributing substantial knowledge to our field, but we must devote more efforts to applying our contributions. We find ourselves agreeing with another Communication scholar, Daly (2000: 335), when he writes about a different publication, "Reading these articles made me wonder how we might use our research to help people improve their communication skills".

That notwithstanding, the chapters that succeed ours represent a cogent and unique contribution to continuing discussions of the role of communication and community in law enforcement. Indeed, the book may likely inspire more scholarly investigations due to the heuristic value of the chapters herein. As mentioned above, this volume, necessarily, represents only a cursory look at some of the elements. Hence, it is important to provide a flavor of some of the many important topics and sources not addressed by authors herein. They open the door to a wealth of follow-up discussions, questions, data gathering, and theoretical development. The application of rigorous communication research to law enforcement represents a tremendous opportunity to deliver substantial advice. Kidd and Braziel (1999) display the benefits of collaboration between a communication professor and a police captain in their book, a volume that blends communication theory with practical police behavior. The most recent issues of *Human Communication Research* contain many articles relevant to law enforcement communication practices. Olekalns and Smith's (2000) work on strategy sequences in competitive negotiations offers considerable material of interest to those engaged in hostage negotiation. Goldsmith and MacGeorge

(2000) contribute to an understanding of possible ways in which peace officers can adjust interviewing strategies. White and Burgoon's (2001) study, part of a patterned research strategy in deception, would be applicable to understanding a wide variety of law enforcement communication not limited to the obvious interrogation episodes, but expanded to work-related police language. These examples are admittedly selective, but they do serve as a foundation upon which to build sound prescriptions for proficient law enforcement communication.

Of course, other topics traditionally included in the field of Communication also provide assistance in grappling with law enforcement issues. Littlejohn's (1999) description of the nature of scholarly communication inquiry and the subsequent theoretical findings suggests a wide variety of topics related to law enforcement. The behavioral theories are uniquely compatible with law enforcement's concern for the observation and empirical verification of conduct in a variety of settings, not exclusively crime-related. Research investigating cross-cultural communication values can lead to law enforcement sensitivity in intercultural encounters (Knutson, Hwang & Deng 2000). The notion of communication apprehension (Daly, McCroskey, Ayres, Hopf & Ayers 1997) applies to a breadth of law enforcement communication episodes. The nonverbal immediacy research likewise contains considerable application to law enforcement, both in the field and within the organization (Baringer & McCroskey 2000). The continuing examination of rhetorical sensitivity may also provide considerable value to law enforcement communication development and practice (Hart & Burks 1972; Ward, Bluman & Dauria 1982; Knutson, Komolsevin, Chatiketu & Smith 2000). Buttny's (1997) work on reported speech in talking about racial matters applies directly to most of the chapters in this book.

Just as all contemporary organizations have changed, so too have those in law enforcement. Major law enforcement organizational communication difficulties involve such issues as labor-management disputes, organizational restructuring, and information distribution. To that end, the work of Cheney et al. (1998) and Lewis and Seibold (1998) are recommended as examples of the type of communication research that could provide practical benefit to the increasingly complex changes occurring in law enforcement organizations. It is just possible that the excitement and emotional drama associated with law enforcement crime and crime prevention duties may draw attention away from other significant organizational communication problems. There are many other areas of communication research too numerous to list here with applications to law enforcement and we shall focus on just one more in the next section.

Intergroup communication

On August 14, 1998, ABC news reported the story of a Los Angeles police officer, shot through the head as he sat in his patrol car. Wearing a uniform showing his identity as a police officer was his only crime and, in certain circles, killing a cop earns one much envied status. But to kill the police officer, the shooter had to kill the other social identities attached to the human being wearing the uniform (e.g., son, husband, father, basketball fan, etc). Social identity theory (SIT: see Tajfel & Turner 1986) suggests that different processes are involved when two people deal with each other in terms of their social group memberships than when they communicate with each others as individual personalities, temperaments, and so forth (where their social categories are irrelevant). In particular, SIT suggests that when individuals converse with each other and manage the interaction based on their social group identities — and many police officer-with-citizen encounters can be construed by participants in these very terms — they will differentiate from, rather than accommodate to, each other (as a means of achieving a positive identity). These processes are most likely to be evoked when the intergroup identities are embedded in their own longstanding "cultures" as well, be they gang, ethnic group, police, community, etc. (see e.g. Chapters 3, 6 & 9). The aforementioned ABC News example — albeit extreme — is but one of many involving charged police/citizen interactions that are principally "intergroup" and communicative in nature. In Chapter 9, we also see how victims of hate crimes are usually randomly chosen as outgroup members *per se* and not selected on the basis of personal characteristics.

But beside the large-scale dichotomy between law enforcement vis a vis "the community", the chapters that follow ours allude to the many social categories interlaced within each of these, thereby making interpersonal communications very often "intergroup" in nature. In Chapter 5, an important distinction is made between federal officers on the one hand and local cops on the other. In California, for example, the latter can be further divided into Police Departments, the Sheriffs, and the Highway Patrol, each communicatively marked by their distinctive uniforms, ethos, values and so forth. Even within any of these, we can locate further group identities in terms of Detectives, Reserve Officers, and Supervisors (see Chapter 2), and so it goes. In other words, police organizations — like many other occupations — are replete with group boundaries (Petronio, Ellemers, Giles & Gallois 1998) and become all the more complex — positive notions of their fusion notwithstanding — when valued multi-agency task forces are established (see Chapter 8). Intergroup theory has a lot to say about the creation, maintenance, and dissolution of group boundaries in the workplace (Gardner, Paulsen, Gallois, Callan and Monaghan 2001) that could well be informative to police culture and organizations.

The community (or "publics", see Chapter 2) is also divided up (by police officers and others) according to many group criteria, not least of which is the proverbial "good guys-bad guys". A number of the chapters herein caution against over-inclusive categorizations of perpetrators into criminal types. For instance, Chapters 6, 8, 9 and 10 afford analytical attention to the critically different motivations underlying various forms of domestic abuse, stalking, hate crimes, and hostage-taking, respectively. The authors point out that over-categorizing — and hence side-stepping important within-group differences — can impede interrogations, detection, conviction, and rehabilitation. Of course an important distinction in the community is that of ethnicity. Given that policing frequently occurs in diverse multicultural (as well as multilingual) settings, the authors in this volume, to varying degrees, have addressed ethnic parameters raised by their respective topics (e.g., Chapter 2, 5 & 9). Recent research by Huo and Tyler (2000) demonstrates the importance of considering ethnicity when researching and implementing the kinds of policies suggested in the chapters that follow.

These scholars conducted telephone interviews with samples from Los Angeles and Oakland, California, from three ethnic groups, African American, Latino and Caucasian (referred to by Huo and Tyler and thus hereinafter as "White") about their most recent encounter with a legal authority. They were interested in understanding how different ethnic group members experienced face-to-face interactions with the police, judges, and other court officials, and how their perceptions of those experiences affected both their evaluations of those authorities and their likelihood of compliance with directives from them. The bad, though not surprising, news which these scholars identified was that African Americans and Latinos report more negative treatment from legal authorities than do Whites.

But there is good news too. First, while people cared about the outcomes of their experiences with legal authorities, all ethnic groups cared *more* about being treated fairly by legal authorities than they cared about the outcomes of their given experiences. Second, African Americans, Latinos and Whites shared a common set of criteria for assessing how fairly they had been treated by a legal authority. Huo and Tyler's findings suggest that focusing on ensuring fairness in police responses to community members of all ethnicities will result in a more positive response to and higher compliance with the police. Accordingly, any communication reform proposal, such as those addressed in Chapter 2 by Maguire and Wells, should be assessed less so for its effect on the *outcome* that a specific ethnic community may receive, and more so in terms of its effect on the *perception* by each community that it is being *treated fairly*. By ensuring that the community perceives it is being justly treated, the reform is more likely to result in a positive response to, and higher compliance with, the police.

Huo and Tyler also found that African Americans and Latinos reported more negative reactions to all types of experiences with the police than Whites reported. For example, whether or not the respondent initiated the contact with the police or was stopped by the police, African American and Latino respondents, when compared to Whites, reported lower levels of satisfaction. It is interesting to note, however, that these differences in levels of satisfaction with the police based on ethnicity were not the case for experiences with legal authorities in the courts. In addition, Huo and Tyler found that African Americans and Latinos were less willing than Whites to comply with police directives. Again, however, there were no differences among the three ethnic groups regarding willingness to comply with court directives. Reflecting on Van den Bulck's fictional cops, it would be interesting to note if this mirrors the experiences portrayed in fiction. For example, in *NYPD Blue*, are African Americans and Latinos more likely than Whites to be harassed by the police, while all three ethnicities are treated similarly by the courts in *The Practice*? If so, how might such portrayals be constructing perceptions of the police, particularly as opposed to the courts? Under what conditions do different ethnic groups identify with police officers of their own ethnicity as part of their ingroup, and under what conditions do they not? Moreover, when is ethnic profiling presumed to be in operation in the eyes of which members of the public and why? Similar questions could be posed regarding gender, all of which are related to recruitment policies and could be informed by SIT.

Clearly a myriad of intergroup-oriented questions can be raised, and it is our conviction that using intergroup communication theories can contribute to a much fuller and pragmatic understanding of policing effectiveness, from the interpersonal to the organizational level. And to be truly effective, public relations policies must not only improve citizens' attitudes toward particular and specific local officers, but law enforcement *in general*. Interestingly, Community Oriented Policing (COPs) programs typically reveal an unreferenced reliance on encouraging very favorable contact between officers and civilians. This notion plays off traditional intergroup contact theory (see

Hewstone & Brown 1986) which suggests that positive interpersonal contact between members of groups can lead to liking between the individuals involved (e.g., having officers be plainclothed and talking about their own personal lives as citizens too). Program implementers assume and trust that citizens' newly-acquired positive feelings towards COP officers will carry over to all officers in their department. However, to be truly effective in changing attitudes towards "the police" *per se*, positive contact must be combined with citizens' beliefs that the target officers are typical representatives of the social category "police." Otherwise, citizens can either discount such contacts as individual exceptions or confine them to a unique *sub*category while leaving their previous attitudes toward officers in general intact (see Hewstone, Hopkins & Routh 1992). Indeed, the need to build strong personal relations between civilians and officers (so-called "high interindividual contact") while not underplaying or camouflaging the fact that two distinct groups with their own codes and values are actually engaging each other ("high intergroup contact", see Tajfel & Turner 1986) is often neglected in the community policing literature (see also, Pettigrew 1998).

Contact (and hence communication) between groups can then bring both our personal and our social identities into play. The essence of Tajfel and Turner's (1986) social identity theory — also referred to in Chapters 9 and 10 — suggests that we define ourselves as individuals in terms of our membership in various social groups. These groups of ours can range from being a police officer, female, Asian American, gay, etc. As indicated above, the authors argue that we constantly strive to feel good about our membership in our social groups in order to maintain a positive self-image. In effect, we feel good about ourselves when we have achieved a positive group identity. Knowing whether these social identities are positive or not depends on where our particular social groups stand in comparison to other social groups in society. Negatively stereotyping other groups (i.e., through the use of taunts and slurs) is a common means of feeling good about one's own group membership and obtaining a feeling of positive distinctiveness (see Chapter 9). Such differentiation between self and others is readily apparent in an examination of the stigma sometimes associated with policing (Molloy & Giles in press).

An important feature of SIT is the so-called "social creativity strategies" which members adopt in order to assume a more positive identity (e.g., adopting more positive group labels; developing new, valued art forms including dance and music). A further set of "social competition" strategies are invoked, under certain psychological conditions, when a group vocally, and sometimes with civil actions, questions the status and power of another, more dominant, outgroup. The *communicative* parameters of the processes (Giles & Coupland 1991) involved have been applied to a number of different intergroup settings, such as between: the genders (Boggs & Giles 1999); ethnic groups (Giles 1979); persons with and without physical disabilities (Fox & Giles 1996); gay communities (Hajek & Giles in press) and the generations (Harwood, Giles & Ryan 1995) as well as in critically examining training and social policies designed to engender healthy intergroup contact (e.g., Cargile & Giles 1996; Fox & Giles 1993).

In all of these, moves to nonaccommodate to, or diverge from, the speech and nonverbal styles of outgroup members (Giles, Coupland & Coupland 1991) are fundamental strategies of social differentiation by people in search of a sustained or enhanced positive identity. To date, however, intergroup communication theory has only just been invoked (Molloy and Giles in press) with regard to police/citizen relations where the creation of communicative distances from both parties are rational tactics leading to misattribution, miscommunication, or even worse. With national attention being brought to this issue by former President Bill Clinton and a number of high profile cases involving the charge of police brutality (see Lawrence 2000; Ross 2000), a clear need exists for a better *theoretical* understanding of how to best improve police/citizen relations and communication through community policing. Interestingly, the last two citations are, in some ways, concerned with the conditions under which the community will take vociferous social and vocal action in reaction to police use of force. The complementary question as to when the community becomes outraged (or even voices collective concern) by violence against police officers (as in the case study opening this section) is, however, very rarely raised.

Returning to SIT, community policing efforts are socially creative because they demonstrate an innovative, repackaging of the police image (see Chapter 2). Examples also come in the form of having law enforcement refer to themselves as "peace" officers and using negative terms to their advantage (as in adopting the negative slur for an officer, "pig," and changing the meaning with the acronym, Pride-Integrity-Guts). Indeed, Weatheritt (1988) notes that the nebulously-defined COP (i.e., community-oriented policing) was actually used by British police to raise their public image without making substantive behavioral or organizational changes. Although the typical goals of COP appear to be legitimate and admirable, it is an attempt, in effect, to make policing palatable to the public by challenging negative media images and stereotypes about the police.

Indeed, much of citizens' (oftentimes negative) attitudes toward the police (see, for example, Ennis 1967; White & Menke 1982) are not based on personal experience (e.g., with COP programs, traffic stops) but, instead, may be informed substantially by media influences. However, to combat negative media images of the police is not an easy task. According to Van den Bulck (1998:1), "... in almost every movie or television series — be they serious or comic, action oriented or romantic, mainstream or alternative — there is at least one cop". Furthermore, stereotypical images of the police characteristic of the U. S. media are exported throughout the world. In fact, Arcuri (1977) argues that even television shows that help the police image by portraying officers as competent, well-trained, dedicated, and professional — qualities that are valued in our culture — "may, ironically, lead the public to expect too much" (p. 237). Combined with the taunts and slurs often lobbied at the police, all of this makes it difficult for officers to be treated fairly in society, a characteristic shared by stigmatized, and stigmatizable, groups. We recognize, of course, that one substantial difference between law enforcement and the latter is that the former reflects or, rather, is government; that is, we as a society employ law enforcement and their officials volunteer to serve. Accordingly, in discussing the benefits of fair treatment for all, it may be useful to note where fair treatment of law enforcement better allows law enforcement to do the job "we" have hired them to do.

In sum, we feel that intergroup theory has enormous potential for elaborating our understanding of law enforcement, communication, and community, both inside and outside the precincts of the police station. The ability not to take slights or even abuse from the public *personally* as a police officer should be an important attribute for being able to manage the public effectively; indeed, it is a compelling empirical question as to how many encounters in which police officers are engaged involve communicative distance, disdain, abuse and so forth by whom, when, where (and obviously, why). Such occasions undoubtedly breed unpredictability and arousal and a large number of the chapters that follow focus to varying degrees on these two constructs (viz., Chapters 3–6 & 8–10). Relatedly, Gudykunst's (1995) theory of anxiety-uncertainty-management articulates the conditions which give rise to, as well as the outcomes flowing from, such psychological states. Sidanius and Pratto's (1999) theory of social dominance highlights the role of myths associated with the feelings, habits, and behaviors of outgroups and the roles these have in sustaining and legitimizing intergroup actions; the need to challenge and deconstruct myths is an element of both Chapters 6 and 9. In other words, an array of intergroup theories beyond those of SIT (highlighted above) could be invaluable for further developing vibrant theoretical frames for future work (see also, Hecht 1998; Nelson 2001).

Epilogue

At the risk of oversimplifying the authors' contributions, several principles emerge from the collected chapters:
- The vast majority of law enforcement time is spent in communication-related activities;
- The effectiveness of law enforcement communication can, and is, being improved;
- Communication is *behavior*, consistent with the emphasis of law enforcement;
- Creation of data, documentation and storage of information, and retrieval of reports, are all extraordinarily important functions of law enforcement;
- The establishment of rapport with diverse constituencies will enhance public safety and officer security;
- Expansion of law enforcement communication to areas beyond crime prevention, detection, and apprehension is critical to agency success;
- Examination of the multitude of pressures under which law enforcement officials work can lead to increased competency and efficiency;
- Communication scholars can contribute significant advice to enhance law enforcement competence, not least of which would be an understanding of its intergroup dynamics.

The contributions contained in this book validate these principles and contribute considerable information for the use of law enforcement agencies. The issues raised by the authors are important and should generate future research into all areas of law enforcement communication. In this vein, it is important to point out that there is very little overlap among the bibliographies of the different chapters. Particular policing of crimes and policing policies appear to have mutually exclusive literatures. It seems important to invest in cross-fertilization across these domains, as many principles, communicative processes, and intervention strategies are common to them. It is time, therefore, to chart a coherent and integrative *communication* science of law enforcement. While some of us occasionally encounter prejudice toward the academy from certain law enforcement personnel (as we sometimes do from some other sectors of society), it is important not to overlook many law enforcement agencies' desire to learn from us and their equally strong desire to improve communication effectiveness in every aspect of their profession. May this book be the first of many containing the results of strong and rigorous communication research for the benefit of our communities.[6]

Notes

1. Officers become familiar early in their training with "SAFER," an acronym summarizing the five conditions for the use of force. Security refers to conditions whenever others are in imminent jeopardy. Attack designates circumstances whenever the officer's personal danger zone is violated. Flight indicates conditions whenever a suspect unlawfully flees from the officer's presence. Excessive repetition means that voluntary compliance is not forthcoming and all verbal options have been exhausted. And, Revised priorities describes whenever a matter of higher priority requires immediate attention.

2. The district court dismissed the law suit saying that the victim was not a member of any class protected by the Equal Protection Clause of the 14th Amendment. The parents and the American Civil Liberties Union (ACLU) are currently appealing the case.

3. This of course does not address those perpetrators of hate violence whom law enforcement has failed to identify as such (Type II errors). Dunbar's appendix on "Erin's Story" demonstrates one way in which Type II errors can occur in detecting hate crimes.

4. Many jurisdictions have created an exception to this common-law rule which does not require the same mental state as is otherwise required for first degree murder: the felony murder rule.

5. Well known exceptions to this legal rule are the assessment of bail and parole.

6. We acknowledge and appreciate the input, patience, and support of Kees Vaes, Editor at John Benjamins, for his encouragement of this book project.

References

ABC News 1999. "Even warriors cry: Suicide in the military". *Nightline* December 23: Transcripts.
ACLU Lesbian and Gay Rights Project 2001. *News from the ACLU Lesbian and Gay Rights Project*, July 5.
Arcuri, A. F. 1977. "You can't take fingerprints off water: Police officers' views toward "cop" television shows". *Human Relations* 30: 237–247.
Baringer, D. K. and McCroskey, J. C. 2000. "Immediacy in the classroom: student immediacy". *Communication Education* 49: 178–179.

Boggs, C. and Giles, H. 1999. "" The canary in the cage": The nonaccommodation cycle in the gendered workplace". *International Journal of Applied Linguistics* 22: 223–245.
Bruschke, J. and Loges, W.E. 1999. "Relationship between pretrial publicity and trial outcomes". *Journal of Communication* 49: 104–133.
Buttny, R. 1997. "Reported speech in talking race on campus". *Human Communication Research* 23: 477–506.
California Commission on Peace Officer Standards and Training (CCPOST) 1998. *Basic Course Workbook Series: Use of Force* (Learning Domain 20). Sacramento, CA: Office of State Publishing.
California Commission on Peace Officer Standards and Training (CCPOST) 1999. *Basic Course Workbook Series: Community Relations* (Learning Domain 3). Sacramento, CA: Office of State Publishing.
California Commission on Peace Officer Standards and Training (CCPOST) 2001. *Commission Regulation 1005 (D)*. Sacramento, CA: Commission procedures D-2.
Cargile, A. and Giles, H. 1996. "Intercultural communication training: A critical review and new theoretical perspective". In *Communication Yearbook 19*, M. Roloff (ed.), 385–423. Thousand Oaks: Sage.
Chadwick, S. 29 June 2001. Iowa State University, personal communication.
Cheney, G., Straub, J., Speirs-Gelbe, L., Stohl, C., DeGooyer, D., Whalen, S., Garvin-Doxas, K. and Carlone, D. 1988. "Democracy, participation, and communication at work: A multidisciplinary review". In *Communication Yearbook 21*, M. Roloff (ed.), 35–91. Thousand Oaks, CA: Sage.
Currie, E. 1985. *Confronting Crime: An American Challenge*. New York, NY: Pantheon.
Daly, J.A. 2000. Colloquy: "Getting older and getting better." *Human Communication Research* 26: 331–338.
Daly, J.A., McCroskey, J.C., Ayres, J., Hopf, T. and Ayres D. 1997. *Avoiding Communication: Shyness, Reticence, and Communication*. Cresskill, NJ: Hampton Press.
Davies, G.M., Westcott, H.L. & Horan, N. 2000. "The impact of questioning style on the content of investigative interviews with suspected child sexual abuse victims". *Psychology, Crime and Law* 6: 81–98.
Ennis, P.H. 1967. *Criminal Victimization in the United States*. Washington, DC: U.S. Government Printing Office.
Fleck, T. 2001. "Going both ways? A step toward addressing the lack of legal protection for gays". *Houston Press*, July 12.
Fox, S. and Giles, H. 1993. "Accommodating intergenerational contact: A critique and theoretical model". *Journal of Aging Studies* 7: 423–451.
Fox, S. and Giles, H. 1996. "Let the wheelchair through! An intergroup approach to interability communication". In *Social Groups and Identities: Developing the Legacy of Henri Tajfel*, W.P. Robinson (ed.), 215–248. Oxford: Butterworth-Heinemann.
Gerber, G.L. 2001. *Women and Men Police Officers*. New York: Praeger.
Gardner, J., Paulsen, N., Gallois, C., Callan, V. and Monaghan, P. (2001). "An intergroup perspective on communication and organizations". In *The New Handbook of Language and Social Psychology*, W.P. Robinson and H. Giles (eds), 561–84. Chichester: Wiley.
Giles, H. 1979. "Ethnicity markers in speech". In *Social Markers in Speech*, K. Scherer and H. Giles (Eds.), 251–289. Cambridge: Cambridge University Press.

Giles, H. and Coupland, N. 1991. *Language: Contexts and consequences*. Pacific Grove, CA: Brooks/Cole.
Giles, H., Coupland, N. and Coupland, J. (eds) (1991). *The Contexts of Accommodation*. New York: Cambridge University Press.
Goldsmith, D. J. and MacGeorge, E. L. 2000. "The impact of politeness and relationship on perceived quality of advice about a problem". *Human Communication Research* 26: 234–263.
Grossman, W. 2000. "Bullets after brunch". *Houston Press*, May 4.
Gudykunst, W. B. (1995). "Anxiety/uncertainty management (AUM) Theory: Current status". In *Intercultural Communication Theory*, R. L. Wiseman (ed.), 8–58. Thousand Oaks, CA: Sage.
Gundersen, D. F. and Hopper, R. H. 1984. *Communication and Law Enforcement*. New York: Harper & Row.
Hajek, C. and Giles, H. in press. "The old man out: An intergroup analysis of intergenerational communication". *Journal of Communication*.
Hans, V. P. and Vidmar. N. 1986. *Judging the jury*. Reading, MA: Perseus Books.
Hart, R. P. and Burks, D. M. 1972. "Rhetorical sensitivity and social interaction". *Speech Monographs* 39: 75–91.
Harvard Law Review. 1986. "The Supreme Court, 1985 Term: Leading Case. I: Constitutional Law". *Harvard Law Review* November 100:100.
Harwood, J., Giles, H. and Ryan, E. B. 1995. "Aging, communication, and intergroup theory: Social identity and intergenerational communication". In *Handbook of Communication and Aging Research*, J. F. Nussbaum & J. Coupland (eds), 133–159. Hillsdale, NJ: Erlbaum.
Hecht, M. L. 1998. *Communicating prejudice*. Thousand Oaks: Sage.
Hewstone, M. and Brown, R. 1986. "Contact is not enough: An intergroup perspective on the "contact hypothesis"". In *Contact and Conflict in Intergroup Encounters*, M. Hewstone & R. Brown (eds), 1–44. Oxford: Blackwell.
Hewstone, M., Hopkins, N. and Routh, A. 1992. "Cognitive models of stereotype change: (1) Generalization and subtyping on young people's views of the police". *European Journal of Social Psychology* 22: 219–234.
Humes, E. 1999. *Mean Justice*. New York, NY: Simon & Schuster.
Hunter, R. C. 1996. "Gender in evidence: Masculine norms v. feminist reforms". *Harvard Women's Law Journal*, 19: 127–167.
Huo, Y. J. and Tyler, T. R. 2000. *How Different Ethnic Groups React to Legal Authority*. San Francisco: Public Policy Institute of California.
Katz v U. S. 1967. 389 U. S. 347.
Kidd, V. and Braziel, R. 1999. *Cop Talk: Essential Communication Skills for Community Policing*. San Francisco, CA: Acada Books.
Knutson, T. J., Hwang, J. C. and Deng, B. C. 2000. "Perception and management of conflict: A comparison of Taiwanese and U. S. Business employees". *Intercultural Communication Studies* 9: 1–31.

Knutson, T. J., Komolsevin, R., Chatiketu, P. and Smith, V. 2000. "Rhetorical sensitivity and willingness to communicate: A comparison of Thai and U. S. American samples with implications for intercultural communication effectiveness". Paper presented at the annual meeting of the International Communication Association, Acapulco, Mexico.

Kyllo v U. S. 2001 US Lexis 4487 (No: 99–8508).

Lawrence, R. G. 2000. *The Politics of Force: Media and the construction of police brutality*. Berkeley, CA: University of California Press.

Leets, L. and Giles, H. 1999. "Harmful speech: An organizing framework for communication research". In *Communication Yearbook 22*, M. Roloff (ed.), 90–137. Thousand Oaks: Sage.

Leo, R. A. 1996. "The impact of *Miranda* revisited". *Journal of Criminal Law and Criminology* 86: 621–692.

Le Poire, B. A., Prescott, M. and Shepard, C. in press. "Understanding the role of the helper: Codependency in three types of health relationships". In *The Management of Health and Illness*, D. Brashers and D. Goldsmith's (eds), Boston, MA: Harvard University Press.

Lewis, L. K. and Seibold, D. R. 1998. "Reconceptualizing organizational change implementation as a communication problem: A review of literature and research agenda". In *Communication Yearbook 21*, M. Roloff (ed.), 93–151. Thousand Oaks, CA: Sage.

Littlejohn, S. W. 1999. *Theories of Human Communication* (6th ed.). Belmont, CA: Wadsworth.

Mares, M. 1996. "The role of source confusions in television's cultivation of social reality judgments". *Human Communication Research* 23: 278–297.

Miccio, G. K. 1998. "With all due deliberate care: Using international law and the federal violence against women act to locate the contours of state responsibility for violence against mothers in the age of Deshaney". *Columbia Human Rights Law Review* 29: 641–685.

Miranda v. Arizona. 1966. 384 U. S. 436.

Molloy, J. and Giles, H. In press. "Communication, language, and law enforcement: An intergroup communication approach". In *Excavating the Taken-for Granted: Essays in Social Interaction*, P. Glenn, C. LeBaron, C. and J. Mandelbaum (eds), Mahwah, NJ: Lawrence Erlbaum.

Nelson, T. D. 2001. *The Psychology of Prejudice*. Boston: Allyn and Bacon.

Ng, S. H. and Bradac, J. J. (1993). *Power in Language*. Thousand Oaks, CA: Sage.

Olekalns, M. and Smith, P. L. 2000. "Understanding optimal outcomes: The role of strategy sequences in competitive negotiations". *Human Communication Research* 26: 525–557.

Perlmutter, D. D. 2000. *Policing the Media: Street Cops and Public Perceptions of Law Enforcement*. Thousand Oaks, CA: Sage

Petitioner's Brief 2000. Dickerson v. United States, 530 U. S. 428 (No. 99–5525).

Petronio, S., Ellemers, N., Giles, H. and Gallois, C. 1998. "(Mis)communicating across boundaries: Interpersonal and intergroup considerations". *Communication Research* 25: 571–595.

Pettigrew, T. F. 1998. "Intergroup contact theory". *Annual Review of Psychology* 49: 65–85.

Ross, J. I. 2000. *Making News of Police Violence: A Comparative Study of Toronto and New York City*. Westport, CT: Praeger.

Seave, P. (2001). "California's new crime wave: How to prevent identity theft". *California Sheriff Magazine* 16: 8–9.

Sidanius, J. and Pratto, F. (1999). *Social Dominance: An Intergroup Theory of Social Hierarchy and Oppression*. Cambridge, UK: Cambridge University Press.

Tajfel, H. and Turner, J.C. 1986. "The social psychology of intergroup behavior". In *Psychology of Intergroup Relations*, S. Worchel and W.G. Austin (eds), 7–24. Chicago: Nelson-Hall.
Tracy, K. and Tracy, S.J. (1998). "Rudeness at 911: Reconceptualizing face and face attack". *Human Communication Research* 25: 225–251.
Trinch, S. 2001. "The advocate as gatekeeper: The limits of politeness in protectice order interviews with Latina survivors of domestic abuse." *Journal of Sociolinguistics* 5: 475–506.
USA Patriot Act (2001). "United and strenghting America by providing appropiate tools required to intercept and obstruct terroism, Act of 2001". *United States Congress*, H.R. 3162.
Van den Bulck, J. 1998. " 'Sideshow Bobby:' Images of the police in Flemish film and television". *Public Voices* 4: 1–8.
Ward, S.A., Bluman, D.L. and Dauria, A.F. 1982. "Rhetorical sensitivity recast: Theoretical assumptions of an informal interpersonal rhetoric". *Communication Quarterly* 30: 189–195.
Weatheritt, M. 1988. "Community policing: Rhetoric or reality". In *Community Policing: Rhetoric or reality?* J.R. Greene and S.D. Mastrofski (eds), 225–238. New York: Praeger.
White, C.H. and Burgoon, J.K. 2001. "Adaptation and communicative design: Patterns of interaction in truthful and deceptive conversations". *Human Communication Research* 27: 9–37.
White, M.F. and Menke, B.A. 1982. "Assessing the mood of the public toward the police: Some conceptual issues". *Criminal Justice* 10: 211–230.

CHAPTER 2

Community policing as communication reform

Edward R. Maguire and William Wells
George Mason University, USA /
Southern Illinois University at Carbondale, USA

The community policing movement represents the most significant era in police organizational change since the introduction of the telephone, automobile, and two way radio (Reiss 1992). In the United States and abroad, community policing is influencing the way police professionals, scholars, policy makers, and citizens think about the role of police in society. While community policing is a complex movement with multiple goals voiced by a diverse array of reformers and supporters, implicit in much of the reform rhetoric is the need to improve communications in the internal and external environments of police organizations. This chapter begins by providing a brief introduction to the community policing movement. Next, it shows how communication themes play an implicit or explicit role in much of the reform rhetoric. It then examines community policing within a conceptual framework forged from three related lines of research and theory: organization theory, organizational communications, and public relations. The chapter concludes by assessing the available evidence on the influence of community policing on internal and external communication patterns in police organizations.

A brief history of community policing

While the roots of the community policing movement extend throughout the history of police (Greene, 2000; Walker 1980), most analysts attribute its birth to the convergence of several prominent social forces in the United States during the 1960s (Greene, 2000). Police historians have noted that until the early 1960s, American policing was a somewhat "closed" institution. State and federal politicians did not routinely run for elective office on platforms related to crime and policing. The average American citizen probably had little knowledge of what police work entailed. Courts did not devote much energy toward scrutiny of the police. In all, policing remained closed to the eyes and ears of the public and their representatives (Walker 1980). For instance, during their landmark study of American policing in the early 1960s, a group of prominent legal scholars commissioned by the American Bar Foundation was surprised to learn about the wide-ranging discretion that police officers have when making such important decisions as whether to make an arrest, use force, detain a suspect, or conduct a search (Goldstein 1960; Walker 1980).

Several circumstances in the 1960s converged to expose American policing to the attention and scrutiny of external audiences. Widespread discontent about the military action in Vietnam, the civil rights movement, and other social forces led a generation of youth to rebel against the conventions of mainstream society (Barlow & Barlow 2000; Walker 1980). Police are the gatekeepers of mainstream society, and much of the civil unrest of this period brought the police face-to-face with citizens expressing various forms of protest, from peaceful civil disobedience to violent rebellion and rioting (Walker 1980).

Police use of force and mistreatment of minority citizens became a prominent theme during the 1960s. Research conducted during that period showed that many police officers held racist attitudes toward minorities (Bayley & Mendelsohn 1969; Reiss 1971: 147; Westley 1970: 99–104). Several of the riots that engulfed American cities occurred in the aftermath of police actions such as shootings, traffic stops, or raids occurring in minority neighborhoods (Walker 1980). The National Advisory Commission on Civil Disorders (1968) found that "deep hostility between police and ghetto communities" was a primary determinant of the urban riots that it studied. Stark (1972) chose the term "police riots" to describe many of these confrontations between police and citizens.

The growth of television news meant that many of these encounters between police and citizens were now broadcast to millions of homes on the evening news (Walker 1980). Classic news stories of the era captured images of police officers using excessive force against citizens. Shocking images of the police beating citizens emerged out of civil rights marches in Birmingham and Selma, Alabama, outside of the 1968 Democratic National Convention in Chicago, and in numerous other cities (Barlow & Barlow 2000; Greene 2000; Walker 1980). For the first time, Americans were exposed to massive coverage of the police beating those who looked very much like their children, their brothers, their sisters, and their friends.

The police also began to face significant challenges from the courts. The U. S. Supreme Court, under Chief Justice Earl Warren, began to closely scrutinize the activities of the police. In several "landmark" cases, the Court restricted the powers of the police to conduct searches, obtain confessions, or prevent detainees from consulting with an attorney. While civil libertarians praised this "due process revolution," others complained loudly that these new rules interfered with the ability of the police to fight crime (see Cassell & Fowles 1998; Leo 1996).

Finally, rising crime rates during the 1960s also began to cast doubts on the effectiveness of the police. Between 1958 and 1969, the number of serious crimes recorded by police in American cities more than tripled.[1] Taking into account changes in population, total crime rates nearly tripled, increasing from 13.3 to 30.5 per thousand population. Percentage increases in total crime rates were outpaced by increases in violent crime rates, which more than tripled, rising from approximately 1.5 to 4.8 violent crimes per thousand population. Thus, while Americans were questioning the fairness and equity of the police, rising crime rates led them also to doubt the effectiveness of the police at preventing and responding to crime (Hindelang 1974: 105–107).

All of these factors combined to produce an epidemic crisis of legitimacy for the American police. From 1968 to 1971, three national commissions recommended sweeping reforms: the National Advisory Commission on Civil Disorders, the National Advisory Commission on Criminal Justice Standards and Goals, and the President's Commission on Law Enforcement and the Administration of Justice. For instance, the President's Commission (1967) recommended that police agencies establish community relations units and citizen advisory committees, improve training on community relations, expand the recruitment of minorities, increase training and education opportunities, adopt policies limiting the use of firearms by officers, and dozens of other suggestions designed to improve the relationships between police and communities. While it is difficult to pinpoint exactly the birth of the community policing movement, most police scholars start with the crises of the 1960s and the resulting recommendations made by these prominent national commissions. Implicit in many of those recommendations was the need for communication reform in police organizations, both internally and externally.

The crisis of confidence in police as an institution was neither restricted to the American police, nor to the 1960s. Nearly every nation in the world, regardless of form of government, size, or location, has experienced an important crisis in the relationship between police and citizens, often as a result of police action, and often resulting in collective violence. For example, on April 13 1981, tensions between the police and minorities in Brixton, one of London's most impoverished and ethnically diverse neighborhoods, reached a climax that resulted in widespread rioting, looting, and vandalism. Dozens of police, citizens, and firefighters were injured in the ensuing melee. A Commission established to study the incident blamed a pattern of aggressive policing and poor police community relations for setting off the riots. Sir Kenneth Newman, Commissioner of the London Metropolitan Police, turned to the principles of community policing to prevent such occurrences from happening again (Sparrow, Moore & Kennedy 1990). Bayley (1985) has noted that across nations and throughout history, collective violence is often the spark that ignites the flame of police reform.

The next decade saw a number of further developments that laid the groundwork for the emergence of community policing. Evaluation research cast doubt on the three core strategies of policing: random preventive patrol, retrospective criminal investigations, and rapid response to calls for service from citizens (Bayley 1994). Collectively, these evaluations led numerous police leaders, scholars, and reformers to question the basic strategies of policing. A police research industry was born, with doctoral programs producing researchers specializing in the study of the police, and the creation of influential think tanks like the Police Foundation and the Police Executive Research Forum. Police agencies began to experiment with numerous reforms. Some of the most prominent reforms during the 1970s included college education programs for police officers, an increased emphasis on hiring females and minorities, efforts to improve the relationships between police and communities, and new strategies designed to improve the ability of the police to solve community problems.

Early evaluations of these efforts were less than promising. For instance, several communities instituted "team policing" strategies in which police officers were assigned expanded responsibility for improving conditions in certain impoverished and socially disorganized areas with a high volume of criminal activity. Community policing is a direct descendant of team policing, with some important differences that we will explore shortly (Walker 1993). Although the programs varied by city, they all shared three features: a team assigned to a specific geographic area, improved communication and cooperation among the members of a team, and improved communication between the team and the community (Sherman, Milton & Kelly 1973). Research showed that these efforts failed to meet their goals for three reasons: (1) mid-managers sabotaged the efforts because they were threatened by the autonomy of the teams; (2) other patrol officers refused to cooperate because they were jealous of the team's "elite" status within the organization; and (3) dispatch technology was insufficient to allow team officers to remain within their assigned areas (Sherman, Milton & Kelly 1973).

In addition, many agencies created community relations units to improve relationships between police and communities. The work of these units was largely symbolic and decoupled from the day-to-day encounters between police and citizens on the streets (Ahern 1972; Bordua & Tifft 1971; Geary 1975). Most commentators concluded that these units were ineffective at improving relationships between police and communities. According to Moore (1992), officers in the units were ridiculed by other officers for not doing 'real' police work. Assigning community relations to specialized units isolated it functionally, thus relieving others of the responsibility for improving community relations. Finally, the units were often unable to effectively communicate or disseminate the information they collected from the community to others inside the agency (Moore 1992). Although team policing and community relations units were not successful, they continued to lay the foundation for the community policing movement.

Throughout the 1970s, police agencies and researchers continued to institute reforms designed to improve the legitimacy and effectiveness of the police. By the end of the 1970s, two influential articles appeared that gave direction to the fledgling community policing movement. In 1979, Herman Goldstein sketched the foundation for a new theory of police effectiveness which he called Problem-Oriented Policing. Goldstein recommended that police agencies should stop treating "incidents" as their primary unit of work. Since incidents are often symptoms of one or more underlying problems, Goldstein argued, police should work in collaboration with citizens to identify and solve problems rather than simply responding to incidents. In 1982, James Q. Wilson and George Kelling (1982) published their influential article, "Broken Windows" in *Atlantic Monthly*. They claimed that the police have become so narrowly focused on serious crime that they tend to view other important community problems, such as disorder, as outside the scope of their responsibilities. Wilson and Kelling used broken windows as a metaphor for neighborhood disorder, arguing that unchecked disorder is an open invitation to further disorder and more serious crime. With the community policing movement still in its relative infancy, these two articles served an important role at a time when scholars and practitioners were struggling to redefine the proper role of police in a democratic society. While there were clear differences between the two reform strategies, both shared some important similarities: first, police need to expand their mandate beyond crime to include disorder and other persistent community problems; second, in responding to these problems, police need to be proactive rather than simply reactive. Both combined with other forces (such as organizational change reforms in the public and private sectors) to stimulate the birth of the community policing movement. Police departments were experimenting with these and other strategies for improving relationships with communities and reducing disorder, crime, and fear. Something was clearly afoot in policing.

Police departments continued to experiment with community policing strategies throughout the 1980s, and their work began to occupy a larger place in police-related scholarship. In 1983, Robert Trojanowicz established the National Center for Community Policing at Michigan State University. The Center provided training and technical assistance to police agencies around the world. In 1986, Skolnick and Bayley released *The New Blue Line*, which highlighted community policing efforts in six American cities. In Greene and Mastrofski's 1988 book, *Community Policing: Rhetoric or Reality*, several authors addressed the extent to which police agencies were truly embracing its substance, or merely latching on to its "feel-good" appeal. Shortly thereafter, Goldstein expanded his earlier thoughts in his popular 1990 book, *Problem Oriented Policing*. By the end of the 1980s, community policing had gained ground rapidly.

By the early 1990s, community policing was becoming a household term. It occupied a major role in President Clinton's election platform and the enactment of the 1994 Crime Act. At the dawn of a new millenium, the community policing movement rages on. Thousands of police agencies throughout the United States now claim to practice it (Maguire, et al. 1997; Wycoff 1994). While researchers are still attempting to determine the validity of these claims, the majority of changes appear to fall within three domains: improved relationships and partnerships with communities, the adoption of proactive problem-solving techniques, and the institution of various internal changes in police organizations, which Bayley (1994) refers to as organizational adaptation. Community partnerships, problem-solving, and organizational adaptation are the major components of community policing. The first two of these components are externally focused change efforts which concentrate on the relationship between police and external entities. The third component, organizational adaptation, is inwardly focused, concentrating on changes internal to the organization, such as structure, policy, or culture (Zhao 1996).

While communication reform is not the sine qua non of community policing, it is, nonetheless, inherent in both its internally and externally focused domains of change. Police organizations attempt to forge or improve community partnerships largely through communications efforts. These take many forms, from asking patrol officers to "stop and talk" to residents and business owners, to the installment of substations and community outposts. Community meetings, citizen advisory councils, and massive ad campaigns are all efforts to improve partnerships between police and communities. The core of problem-solving is also communication between police and citizens. Goldstein (1990), the pioneer of problem-oriented policing, views this as one of the central features of problem-solving: allowing citizens to nominate the problems to be solved and participate in the design of the solutions. Finally, improved communication is inherent in nearly every organizational adaptation strategy, from the adoption of total quality management to the flattening of organizational hierarchies. Much of the communication reform inherent in this sphere of community policing involves internal organizational communications such as those between officers, or between officers and supervisors. Reformers argue that these improved channels of communication will result in more efficient and effective service delivery, allowing line officers the opportunity to provide more customized services to their communities.

This chapter examines the role of communication reform in the community policing movement. Just as the community policing movement can be characterized by externally and internally focused change, organizational communications also have external and internal dimensions. Therefore, we examine external and internal communications separately. External communications are those between representatives of the police organization and its various external constituents, from citizens and business owners to other city agencies. In the External Communication Reform section that follows, we examine the communication reforms occurring within the externally focused elements of community policing.[2] Internal communications are those falling largely within the domain of community policing which we describe as organizational adaptation (Bayley 1994). They involve all of the various attempts that police managers employ to improve communications within the organization: between officers, civilian employees, supervisors, mid-level managers, and administrators.

External communication reform

Police organizations, like other public service bureaucracies, engage in a great deal of boundary spanning behavior. Line level police officers are among a class of workers that Lipsky (1980) describes as street-level bureaucrats. A notable characteristic of such workers is that they spend a great deal of their time engaging in communications and other transactions with clients or constituents outside the organization. Thus police officers span the boundary between the organization and its environment. While the nature of this boundary spanning behavior differs according the individual worker's hierarchical position in the organization, most police officials must engage in behaviors at the boundary. For instance, although the work of police chiefs involves the expression of leadership within the organization, much of their work consists of symbolic gestures to those in the external environment (Mastrofski 2001). These communications occur at multiple levels with varying degrees of complexity and formality, from individual level communications between a police officer and a citizen, to complex symbolic impression management efforts undertaken by public relations offices within the organization.

External communications are expected to play a central role in community policing. We thus focus attention on how organizations manage the transfer of information with their environments (Sutcliffe 2001). Despite the lack of attention from organizational theories to the transmission of information between organizations and their environments (Sutcliffe 2001), a predominant theoretical framework for understanding organizational communications can be found in public relations, a field concerned largely with the outward flow of information and with relationships between organizations and their publics.[3]

Like many other young disciplines, public relations has struggled to define itself and to establish guiding theories. According to Grunig and Hunt (1984:7), public relations can be understood as "the management of communication between an organization and its publics." It is concerned with management "that establishes and maintains mutually beneficial relationships between an organization and the publics on whom its success or failure depends" (Cutlip, Center and Broom 1994:6). This relational perspective of public relations focuses attention on the importance of establishing and maintaining relationships between organizations and their publics rather than simply manipulating public opinion (Bruning & Ledingham 1999). According to Ledingham and Bruning (1998), desirable relationships between organizations and their publics demonstrate mutual respect and provide benefits to all parties involved.

Furthermore, a primary purpose of public relations is to enable communication, acceptance, and cooperation between organizations and their publics; factors essential to the organization's survival (Bruning & Ledingham 1999). Many police personnel serve in a boundary-spanning role in which they interact frequently with the public. As liaisons between the organization and external groups, they are implicit agents of public relations (Grunig & Hunt 1984). Therefore, public relations theory provides a useful perspective for viewing both the way police communicate with citizens and the purposes and effects of that communication.

Public relations models

In 1984, Grunig and Hunt delineated four models of public relations that serve as a framework for understanding external organizational communications and for guiding public relations research. The models are useful for describing and explaining how public relations is practiced. Furthermore, they are normative in that they predict effective public relations (Grunig & Grunig 1992; Langworthy 1986). They are formed by cross classifying the direction (one-way vs. two-way) and the degree of symmetry (symmetric vs. asymmetric) in the communication (see Table 2.1).

Table 2.1 Public relations models

One-Way Asymmetric	Two-Way Asymmetric
One-Way Symmetric	Two-Way Symmetric

One-way communication disseminates information like a monologue, from sender to receiver, while two-way communication involves information exchange, more like a dialogue. A defining element of two-way communication is the opportunity it presents for mutual change to occur. One-way communication, on the other hand, allows an organization to control and dominate a public. Grunig and Hunt (1984:23) explain that feedback is not synonymous with two-way communication because feedback can be used by a source "to control a receiver's behavior." Research is another feature that distinguishes two-way communication from one-way communication; research plays a greater role in two-way communication (Grunig & Hunt 1984). As part of two-way communication, research can be used to accomplish a variety of goals: to determine what publics will embrace, to gauge how publics have reacted to messages that the organization has sent, and to understand how the organization and its environment perceive and affect one another. This latter type of research can ultimately be used to formulate policies and practices that improve the organization and help it to better serve its publics.

The symmetry of communication is important because it concerns the degree to which the organization adapts to or cooperates with its environment (Grunig 1984). The goal of asymmetrical communication is to change the environment while leaving the organization unchanged. The purpose of symmetrical communication, on the other hand is to modify the relationship between the organization and its environment. With symmetric communication publics can change organizations and organizations can change publics. This form of external communication can build and enhance relationships because it entails "creating a sense of openness, trust, and understanding between the organization and the key public, as well as a willingness to negotiate, collaborate, and mediate solutions to issues of concern to both the organization and critical publics" (Bruning & Ledingham 1999: 158). The process of symmetric communication appears to be in congruence with the goals of community policing.

Two-way symmetric communication is often prescribed as the most effective model of external communication because both the organization and its publics benefit. The purpose of this model is to establish mutual understandings between an organization and its environment. Communication takes the form of a dialogue with the possibility that both the organization and its publics will change. Successful communication in this model does not necessarily require mutual change because the communication process constitutes an end in itself (Kent & Taylor 1998). Using dialogue, the organization can enhance its legitimacy and autonomy through interactions with its publics, including those that pose both threats and opportunities to the organization (Sutcliffe 2001). The language used by public relations theorists to describe two-way symmetric communication and the rhetoric used by community policing reformers is strikingly similar. The public relations process of mutual recognition and dialogue is a central component of community policing. For instance, according to Skolnick and Bayley (1986: 212), "police–community reciprocity means that police must genuinely feel, and genuinely communicate a feeling, that the public they are serving has something to contribute to the enterprise of policing."

Community policing is based on the premise that the community[4] will be interested in forming a relationship with its police. Similarly, the two-way symmetric model of communication assumes that members of the public, or interest groups to which they belong, have the ability and motivation to engage in dialogue with an organization. Police officers are sometimes frustrated when they are unable to solicit the input and participation of citizens in crime prevention and other community policing activities. These groups of citizens are referred to as "inactive publics." Hallahan (2000) argues that public relations theory has tended to ignore groups who, despite their importance to the organization, possess a low degree of knowledge about or involvement in organizations and their services. These inactive publics might lack the motivation, ability, or opportunity to engage in activities that affect the organization. Hallahan (2000) claims that members of the public who possess this knowledge, ability, and motivation are the most likely to engage in collaborative relationships with an organization.

Recognizing that publics vary in terms of their motivation and ability forces organizations to tailor their communications according to the nature of the public with whom they are attempting to maintain or build relationships. Furthermore, understanding that an organization practices a limited range of communication strategies might explain why attempts to establish external relationships with publics sometimes fail. Organizations must identify and locate inactive publics in order to establish positive relationships, for the sake of the relationship itself, not necessarily because they will succeed in activating inactive members. The burden to engage in this communication process often falls on the organization (Hallahan 2000).[5]

Grunig and Grunig (1992) conclude that most organizations do not practice the model that would best serve them; in addition, organizations sometimes mix the communication models that they practice (see also Grunig 1984). Symmetrical communications are risky because they expose an organization to the turbulence of the external environment. As organization theorists have known for decades, a classic organizational response to a turbulent environment is to seal off its technical core, where the majority of the work is done. Given the nature of their work, police organizations operate within a particularly risky environment, therefore making it difficult for those within the organization who wish to move toward the development of two-way symmetric communications.

An institutional environment might impose pressure on an organization to justify its practices, which may affect external communication strategies

(Sutcliffe 2001). For instance, some police organizations implement community policing based on a heartfelt concern with technical efficiency and effectiveness. Others may face external pressure to adopt community policing, either because doing so will provide needed resources, or because it will confer legitimacy on the organization for "doing the right things" (Maguire & Mastrofski 2001). Structures, programs, and policies have symbolic value, and managing those symbols to send a message or convey meaning to those inside or outside the organization is a potent form of symbolic communication (Meyer 1979; Sutcliffe 2001). Agencies interested in the technical value of community policing would probably select a different model of external communications than those interested in capitalizing on its institutional value for conferring legitimacy. The former might adopt the two-way symmetric approach, while the latter might select one of the other methods in which the communication is either one-way, asymmetric, or both.

The parallels between two-way symmetric communications and community policing are substantial. Building strong and mutually beneficial relationships with community members and community groups is a core element of community policing. Two-way symmetric communication is expected to facilitate the practice of community policing where police organizations and publics, both active and inactive, engage in meaningful dialogue and change. Nevertheless, the practical challenges associated with such communications in policing will have to be carefully considered in order for those efforts to be successful. We now examine existing research on the external communication practices of police organizations and offer an analysis of a variety of forms of external communication prominent in community policing.

External communication by the police

Much of the academic writing on community policing offers a pessimistic appraisal of its impact on external communication by the police. According to Manning (1992:135), external communication by police is intended to persuade publics "of the legitimate authority, credibility, and power of the police organization." Although police organizations have always struggled to effectively manage their public image, they continue to experience crises of legitimacy and political authority (Maguire & Uchida 2000; Manning 1992). In Manning's view, police agencies actively use public relations to build and maintain better public images rather than to engage in mutually beneficial dialogue with their constituents. One perspective views community policing as a form of communication that serves to enhance the legitimacy and power of the police. For instance, Klockars (1988:240) views community policing as "the latest in a fairly long tradition of circumlocutions whose purpose is to conceal, mystify, and legitimate police distribution of non-negotiable coercive force." Hunter and Barker (1993) look at community policing as "BS and buzzwords." Lyons (1999:185) concludes that community policing simply rearranges and enhances "the power of the police to punish individuals and communities." Barlow and Barlow (1999:667) view community policing as "image-management policing." Bayley (1994:100) cautions that "police must not be allowed to make performance a 'con game' of appearance management." Numerous other policing scholars have voiced similar sentiments. The types of external police communication that Manning (1992) describes, including community policing, are not characteristic of two-way symmetric communication. Information flows from the police organization, the source, to the relevant publics, the receiver, with the purpose of changing the publics rather than facilitating mutual change for mutual benefit. Community policing, according to Manning (1992, 1997), is a presentational strategy; a communication device that seeks to reinforce the dominant position of police over their various publics.

Manning (1992) describes three primary types of external police communication: crisis communication, routine communication, and strategic communication. Crisis communication results from an immediate, spontaneous situation that is threatening to the police organization. Crisis communication draws community support for the police because the crisis symbolizes a threat to the entire community. Routine external communications consist of the ordinary, ongoing communications that occur between police and individual members of the public as officers engage in routine functions such as responding to calls for service or conducting patrols. Because various publics are handled one member at a time, there is little widespread awareness of the routine communication that occurs between the police and the public. Routine communications provide the opportunity to build quality relations with the public. Strategic external communication relies on publicity and the media to build a consensus of external support for the police. With strategic communication, the police present information to their publics about programs and policies through press releases, press conferences, and public announcements that reach aggregate groups as opposed to individuals one at a time. Furthermore, Manning asserts that police initiate and control such programs and policies that preserve police autonomy.

The symbolic nature of police external communication plays a central role in Manning's analysis. It is important to recognize the symbolic nature of external police communication because through external communication, the police "dramatize the appearance of control of crime and maintenance of social order" (Manning 1992: 139). The police use slogans, symbols, and encoded messages to create and maintain favorable police images (Manning 1992, 1997). This results partially from the inability of the police to meet the expectations and demands placed upon them by both themselves and society. While the police are expected and claim to control crime and maintain order in society, many observers believe they lack the resources and ability to affect the underlying forces responsible for crime and disorder. In response to this crisis, the police must maintain the appearance of control in order to retain and build public legitimacy. Police actively use publicity efforts to enhance their public image (Manning 1992, 1997).

According to Manning (1992), community policing is a prominent theme in American policing that allows police to maintain control over their environment. Community policing, as "a long-term management approach to organizational communication", has the purpose of controlling publics through a reduction in the social distance between the police and the public (Manning 1992: 155). As the police become a part of local community life and create the sense that the police and the community share a mutual fate, the police strengthen their position within the community. Furthermore, because the rhetoric of community policing is an appeal for communities to provide support and legitimacy, community policing has the ability to maintain or augment police authority and power (Manning 1992) rather than defuse power to the community itself. Manning's (1992) analysis suggests that external communications occurring under the banner of community policing are neither two-way nor symmetric.

Research on the validity of this perspective is mixed. Lyons's (1999) and Reed's (1999) recent analyses of community policing in Seattle both find evidence to support the critique voiced by Manning and other scholars. Skogan and Hartnett's (1997: 133–34) research in Chicago is less damning; in a little less than a third of the beat meetings they observed, citizens and police demonstrated a "balanced and cooperative" relationship or "acted as partners." Kessler's (1999) quantitative analysis found that a community policing effort in Houston reduced citizen complaints against police. Evidence from a recent national evaluation suggests that "true" community partnerships are rare (Koper, Roehl, Roth and Ryan 1998), though the modest progress made so far represents an important breakthrough in police–community relations. Overall, research is insufficient to draw sweeping conclusions about the extent to which community policing has produced a shift in the balance of power between police and communities.

External communication through the news media

The media play a critical role in communication between police organizations and their publics. Furthermore, Manning (1992) asserts that police organizations sell the community policing message through the media. Citizens form their impressions of community policing from what is presented in the media. The public image of community policing is critical; it forms the basis for how community policing will be judged and whether it will ultimately persist (Mastrofski & Ritti 1999). Yet, the police exercise some influence over their image by controlling the way they are presented in the news media (Chermak 1995). The way the police are portrayed in the media affects their legitimacy and authority (Manning 1992). Therefore, the media is a powerful and useful external communication tool for the police (Ericson, Baranek & Chan 1989; Skolnick & McCoy 1985). When the police influence media content they exert a degree of control over the messages that the public receives about crime and policing.

Guffey (1992) portrays the relationship between the media and the police as symbiotic. The police need the media in order to promote their activities and image in the community, and the media rely on the police for information about stories that are interesting to readers. Ericson, Baranek and Chan (1989) recognize that a degree of mutual dependency exists between the police and news media. They explain that research conducted from a journalism perspective perpetuates the view that the police — news media relationship is an asymmetrical one that favors police. Yet the conception of a symbiotic police — news media relationship runs the risk of over-simplifying the level of control that police have over official information about crime and police activities and the stake that the police have in shaping communications through the media.

Research suggests that the relationship between the police and the media is asymmetrical because police tend to dominate their interactions with the media and maintain a degree of control over what gets presented in the news media (Chermak 1995; Ericson, Baranek & Chan 1989; Skolnick & McCoy 1985). Reporters tend to depend on police sources for information about crime and police practices. Media personnel are constrained because compromising their relationship with the police, through critical accounts of police organizations and police behavior for instance, might limit their access to information about crime and law enforcement stories. Ericson, Baranek, and Chan (1989) found that when police culture values conflicted with the values of reporters who worked closely with the police, police values tended to dominate. Chermak (1995) conducted ethnographic research in a large Midwestern newspaper organization and analyzed the content of over 2,000 newspaper stories and over 600 television stories. He found that newspapers increase their access to police information by establishing beats within police organizations. While this arrangement is useful for the news media, it also allows police to promote particular stories for consideration.

Police affect the information that is presented in the media because they play a role in the news selection and production processes. Police affect the news selection process because they regulate the pool of stories from which the news media chose by controlling the flow of information to the news media (Chermak 1995). For instance, police can effectively kill news stories or reduce their impact by not releasing information. In addition to affecting the news selection process, the police also affect the news production process (Chermak 1995; Ericson, Baranek & Chan 1989). The news production process involves framing and writing the actual news stories. Police can shape the information that is available to the news media so that news stories are presented in ways that promote and legitimize police organizations. Chermak (1995:33) concludes that "police frame crime stories in a way that strengthens their position as a crime fighting institution." Nevertheless, Ericson, Baranek and Chan (1989) discovered that the media maintain a great deal of control over the news editing process. Furthermore, although research has successfully highlighted the control that police exercise over their portrayal in the media, many police complain that news organizations consistently portray them in a negative light (Ellis 2001).

Mastrofski and Ritti (1999) analyzed over 6,000 newspaper stories that discussed community policing from 1993 to 1997. They found that most stories (87%) contained factual news rather than editorial or analytical content. In the absence of independent analysis, the way that the media portrays community policing is likely to be a close reflection of what the police want to communicate. Indeed, Manning (1992) argues that the media seldom obtain information independent of the police that might contradict the police perspective. Mastrofski and Ritti (1999) found that news sources touted the effectiveness of community policing in 45 percent of the stories, presented differing points of view about community policing in about 13 percent of stories, and presented community policing in a completely positive light in the majority of stories.

Mastrofski and Ritti (1999:3) hypothesize that one possible outcome of insufficient debate about the merits of community policing is that "the public image of community policing will become even more unified and accepted without debate." It seems that police are able to easily send messages to their publics about community policing through a seemingly independent and credible source: the news media. This can, in turn, serve police organizational goals. By communicating to publics through the media, the police can maintain control of their environments as well as the programs and policies that will be implemented in local communities. At the same time, the police can enhance their legitimacy.

Through the media, police organizations engage in what Manning (1992) terms strategic communication. Such communication does not seem to be aimed at creating opportunities for dialogue and exchange, but rather at creating a positive perception of police practices within publics. The public relations literature explains that while one-way, asymmetric communication might meet important organizational needs, it is not well-suited to managing collaborative relationships between organizations and their publics.

Summary of external communication reform

Many of the strategies that have been adopted or reinvented as part of community policing can be viewed as a form of communication with external audiences. An analysis of these various strategic communications can shed light on the nature and direction of these communication efforts. Implicit in the reform movement is the assumption that two-way symmetrical communications increase the chances police and various publics will build and maintain meaningful, productive relationships. Community policing activities that involve external communication reform include, for instance, building community sub-stations, establishing citizen police academies, encouraging community members to help set police priorities, surveying the consumers of police services, and organizing citizen patrols. The use of these strategies provides the opportunity for direct communication with publics and also communicates symbolic messages to publics. Police use of these sorts of strategies can be viewed and analyzed from a communications perspective. Such an analysis would provide an understanding of the degree to which the strategies involve dialogue between the police and publics and the degree to which police *and* publics change as a result of the communication. Furthermore, this type of analysis will shed light on the degree to which the parties affect the decisions that have implications for the police and the public.

Internal communication reform

Community policing entails a variety of changes within police organizations (Greene, Bergman & McLaughlin 1994). Many of these changes, particularly with regard to structure and culture, are intended to improve internal communications. The dynamics of communication patterns within organizations are complex, and a rigorous analysis of them could easily fill several volumes. Therefore, our discussion of the relationship between community policing and internal communication reform is necessarily abridged. We begin by examining the formal aspects of internal organizational communication, including such important topics as organizational structures, rules, policies, procedures, and other formal elements of the organization that shape, constrain, enable, and otherwise influence communications. We will then examine the informal elements of communication within organizations, including such topics as culture, myths, traditions, symbols, and other informal elements that play an important role in organizational life.

Formal aspects of internal communication

The defining characteristic of organizations is that they are *organized*. They may not be well-organized, and they may even be thoroughly dysfunctional. Although there are numerous definitions (Hall 1999), organizations are comprised of a coordinated and formal set of linkages among actors working to achieve a goal or set of goals within an identifiable boundary. An organization is therefore defined, in part, by the formal relationships between its members. Examining the formal aspects of internal communications is vital. In this section, we begin with a focus on these formal aspects, paying particular attention first to structures and then to rules, policies, and procedures.

Organizational structure. The structure of an organization represents a framework within which communication takes place. An organization's structure has numerous dimensions, among them vertical, functional, spatial, and temporal. These dimensions interact to structure the internal communications of an organization. While the content and meaning of communication is not necessarily determined by the structure of an organization, these dimensions do play a role in formalizing, constraining, and otherwise structuring the pathways and processes through which information flows throughout an organization (Johnson 1993).

One popular framework for analyzing the structures of communication within organizations is to distinguish between horizontal communications, in which messages flow laterally, and vertical communications, in which messages flow both up and down the organization's hierarchy. Another popular approach views communication through the lens of network theory, tracing the way that messages (such as news, rumors, policies, etc...) make their way from person to person within the organization (Johnson 1993; Nohria & Eccles 1992). We believe that both approaches are applicable here, but that neither alone is well suited for examining communication structures within police organizations.

Police organizations divide their work and their workers according to the four primary dimensions we stated earlier: vertical, functional, spatial, and temporal.[6] Organizational structure provides a set of conduits and barriers that affect the patterns of communication: messages flow up and down the hierarchy, across functional and spatial boundaries, and over time. Taken together, these four dimensions have a profound effect on patterns of communication within a police organization. Community policing reformers propose to alter each structural form, both to improve communication patterns, and to achieve other desirable ends. We now explore each dimension in further detail.

Hierarchical or vertical divisions. Police organizations have been described for decades as command-and-control bureaucracies with rigid hierarchies (Reiss & Bordua 1967). While hierarchy is a useful tool for managing workers in industries where front line workers are little more than automatons, police officers are street-level bureaucrats endowed with the discretion to make important decisions about the lives of their clients (Lipsky 1980). Critics have argued that the police hierarchy is a dysfunctional structural form for police because it promotes rigidity and formality in an industry where flexibility and the ability to craft customized solutions to unique problems is a valuable skill (Angell 1971; Guyot 1979; Redlinger 1994; Wadman 1998; also see Cordner 1995). Community policing reformers claim that tall, rigid hierarchies also impede the effective flow of information throughout the organization. As information flows up and down, it is redefined, slotted, categorized, and otherwise modified; communications in police organizations typically do not make the journey from sender to receiver unaltered.

Police officers are the organization's greatest asset. They are like an army of information soldiers; taken together they contain vast pools of untapped information about the organization and its clients. Community policing reformers have argued that tapping into this gold mine of information is crucial to becoming a more responsive organization capable of self-learning (Alarid 1999; Geller 1997). Yet research has demonstrated that: (1) police organizations frequently do not even try to tap into the knowledge of their front-line workers, (2) even when these workers attempt to make their information known, it frequently does not make it very far up the hierarchy, and (3) as we know about communication in organizations more generally, the information is condensed further and further as it climbs the hierarchy (Geller & Swanger 1995). Information flows more quickly down the hierarchy than up it (Hall 1999: 173; Johnson 1993). For these reasons and more, community policing reformers have urged police executives to reduce the depth of their hierarchies (Cordner 1995; Redlinger 1994; Reiter 1999). Recent research demonstrates that while some police organizations have begun to eliminate middle-management ranks, most have not succeeded in reducing the depths of their hierarchies in the community policing era (Hassell, Peyton, Zhao & Maguire 1999). Furthermore, there is still no evidence to suggest that reducing the depth of the hierarchy will produce the intended benefits, most notably improved vertical communications.

Functional divisions. Police organizations are typically divided into a series of primary, secondary, and tertiary functional divisions. At the primary level, most are divided into patrol, investigations, and support services (Wadman 1998). Each of these divisions is typically broken down into smaller functional units. For instance, patrol is often broken down into a series of secondary divisions with responsibility for a particular time period (like the midnight shift), function (specialized patrol squad), or area (precinct or other spatial division). Each of these secondary divisions is often further divided into a number of specialty areas, with workers assigned to each. Although some police organizations have experimented with matrix-style organizational structures in which officers report to multiple supervisors, these arrangements are rare (Sabo & Kuykendall 1978). In general, officers are typically assigned to a specific organizational niche. These niches represent breeding grounds for intensive communications among those within the niche, but communications with those located outside the niche are often problematic. One of the greatest lessons in the last three decades of policing is that isolating functions within special units produces a myriad of communication-related problems. This problem was integral to the demise of community policing's predecessors — community relations units and team policing.

Community policing reformers argue that police organizations should become less specialized. They envision officers as "uniformed generalists" prepared to respond to a wide array of problem types, rather than the more common practice of referring clients to specialized niches within the organization. This need for officers to take ownership over the problems on their beats is central to the community policing reform movement. Yet, efforts to de-specialize face a number of predictable problems. Specialized units are a structural form that serve as a powerful signal to those both inside and outside the organization that the agency takes that particular problem seriously. For example, Katz (2001) has described the symbolic value of police gang units, even in those communities without a serious gang problem. To disband such units would send a signal that the agency no longer takes the problem seriously (Mastrofski 1998). For this reason, and perhaps others, community policing reformers have been unsuccessful in their efforts to convince police agencies to de-specialize. In fact, evidence suggests that police agencies may actually have grown even more specialized throughout the 1990s (Maguire 1997).

Spatial divisions. According to Gregory and Urry (1985: 3), spatial structure is "now seen not merely as an arena in which social life unfolds, but rather as a medium through which social relations are produced and reproduced." Spatial considerations represent one of the most important concerns in the community policing movement. Early in the history of police organizations, policing was organized according by neighborhood with Precinct Captains running local police stations like mini-chiefs. Citizens had their own beat cops and reported offenses or sought assistance at their own police precinct station. With the advent of the telephone, two-way radio, and patrol car, police organizations centralized administrative control, shut down many precinct stations, and asked citizens to call a centralized location (the 911 center) for help (Reiss 1992). Community policing beckons us to recall a bygone era when the kindly neighborhood beat cop lent a helping hand and maintained neighborhood order. Police historians have cautioned us that the good old days weren't all that good, with problems of corruption, brutality, and unequal treatment of citizens reaching back into the early history of policing (Strecher 1991; Walker 1984). Nevertheless, reformers have still pressed for police organizations to decentralize, organizing their service delivery around social or natural community boundaries rather than arbitrary boundaries that are often drawn through, rather than around, cohesive neighborhoods or communities.

Within the patrol division of nearly every major police department in the country is a secondary division which assigns a mid-level manager (usually a Lieutenant or a Captain) responsibility for either a time-period (often known as a "Platoon") or a geographic area. Community policing advocates call for reliance on spatial rather than temporal divisions. There is also a movement toward assigning investigative generalists to certain areas to handle a variety of offense types, rather than citywide jurisdiction for a single offense type (Cosgrove 1997). The major reasons for this shift are to produce administrative accountability for conditions within an area, but also to produce improved communications between officers, investigators, other personnel, and citizens within an area. Evidence suggests that spatial differentiation is increasing slowly as police agencies begin to build new precinct houses, mini-stations, and storefront police facilities. Whether these changes are producing the intended benefits for internal communication is unknown. Compstat, an independent but related innovation, involves holding district commanders accountable for criminal activity in their areas of responsibility. Doing so requires these commanders to have information at their fingertips about the conditions in their neighborhoods. Anecdotal evidence on the ability of Compstat to improve communication within geographic units is positive (Bratton 1998).

Temporal divisions. Police organizations are typically open 24 hours per day, 365 days per year. A common rule of thumb is that after factoring in holidays, sick days, shift rotations, and other contingencies, it takes between 5 and 10 officers to ensure that one officer is on patrol every shift of the year (Bayley 1994). Just as assigning officers to a particular functional niche or spatial division constrains and structures their patterns of communication, so too does assigning officers to work a particular shift. Students of police culture know that there are profound differences in the way policing is done during the day and midnight shifts. During the day shift, for instance, administrators and managers are milling about, the streets and sidewalks are being used frequently, and the actions of the police are more visible. During the midnight shift, the streets belong to the police and much of their work remains invisible to the public. While shift-work cannot reasonably be eliminated, assigning commanders responsibility for places rather than times shifts accountability for all that occurs within a certain district to a single individual. Presumably, this shift in accountability produces increased levels of communication between employees working different shifts within the same district. Whether that assumption is true remains untested to our knowledge.

Summary of organizational structure

Just as the skeleton serves as the framework within which the body's major organs operate, the structural dimensions of a police organization have a profound effect on patterns of communication. The formal structure of an organization does not determine the nature of its communications, but it does constrain, direct, or provide the context within which communication occurs (Johnson 1993). Just as the human body is more complex than its skeleton alone, there is much more to internal communications than the structures in which they occur. If changing the organizational structure of police agencies is supposed to produce changes in communication patterns, then community policing reformers are likely to be disappointed. Researchers have demonstrated that changes in structure are occurring glacially if at all. For instance, Maguire (1997) found that community policing had not significantly altered the structures of American police agencies. A recent study of Florida police agencies found that the "organizational impacts of community policing have been minimal" (Gianakis & Davis 1998:496). Similarly, Wadman (1998:68) concluded that "no substantive changes have been made in the organization of America's police departments to facilitate the implementation of community policing." That portion of communication reform that relies on changes in organizational structure does not appear to be occurring in the United States. Evidence from other nations is sparse.

Rules, policies, standards, and procedures

In addition to formal structures, organizations also function by establishing formal written rules, policies, standards, and procedures (Hall, Haas & Johnson 1967). Organizations vary in their levels of formalization, with some relying heavily on informal methods of coordination and control, and others resembling the classic Weberian bureaucratic form. Formalization is typically measured by counting or evaluating the depth of rules, policies, and procedures within an organization. Formalization serves to structure who can talk to whom, when, under what conditions, and in which format. In this sense, it is actually designed to inhibit communication. For instance, in some organizations, the police chief may have an open door policy for officers to voice grievances or recommend new ideas, whereas in others, upward communications may be heavily regulated by policies prescribing how such communications must take place in writing through the chain-of-command. Similar policies may regulate or prescribe how communications must occur vertically, functionally, and spatially.

Community policing advocates often argue that formalization stifles creativity and encourages generic "stock" responses to the complex social problems that the police face each day (Mastrofski 1998). Although police have generally become more formalized during the twentieth century (Reiss 1992), community policing reformers have sought to reverse this trend. Nevertheless, research fails to find evidence for decreases in formalization. If recent trends in accreditation and risk-management continue, police agencies may become even more formalized (Maguire 1997; Worrall, 2001). If this is the case, the flexible organizational atmosphere envisioned by community policing reformers, and the communication reforms such an atmosphere is intended to produce, are unlikely to thrive.

Informal communications

While the formal aspects of organizations are important for understanding patterns of communication, students of organizations have learned the importance of informal structures. In this section, we explore the role of culture in shaping communication in police organizations. Much of this analysis relies on Peter Manning's studies of police organizations in the United States and Britain, though due to space limitations we are unable to explore his work in depth.

Culture plays an important role in the lives of the police. The existence of a police subculture has been discussed by observers of the police for decades (Crank 1998). This culture is characterized by such features as bravery, adventure, and a code of silence which views the police as a "thin blue line" protecting the rest of society from chaos or anarchy. In addition to this occupational culture, police are also exposed to unique organizational cultures. Furthermore, depending on other factors such as race, gender, rank, assignment, and special interests, police officers may also belong to other subcultures within their occupation and their organization. Even though police officers work within the framework of an organizational structure, and are subjected to formal rules, policies, standards, and procedures, their immersion in various subcultures also has an effect on their patterns of communication.

There are as many definitions of culture as there are analysts to dream them up. According to Barnett (1988: 107–110), culture represents the interplay of several elements, including language, values, behaviors, stories, and legends. Members of a certain group, whether it is a profession, an organization, a gender, a race, or a special interest, may be culturally similar to other members of the group, using common language or jargon, sharing similar values, behaving in similar ways, and relying on the same pool of stories and legends to structure their behaviors and outlooks. Culture and communication are inextricably linked in a circular relationship. Cultures are created through communication, yet culture also has a profound effect on communication patterns, setting informal boundaries for the nature and duration of communications. Therefore, culture is both constituted and constitutive.[7]

One of the primary aims of community policing is to reorient the traditional culture of police away from an excessive focus on crime control toward a broader mandate that includes service to the community. Changing police culture has become one of the principal goals of community policing reformers. While the community policing reform literature is full of prescriptions about the need to change organizational culture, empirical studies of such changes are rare. Zhao, He and Lovrich (1998) argued that individual values and culture are linked, with each affecting the other. Their research showed that the value orientations of American police officers have remained stable over the past two decades. In a later study, Zhao and his colleagues (1999) surveyed police officers from an agency with a national reputation for community policing. They found that from 1993 to 1996, officers' value orientations changed significantly; values reflecting individual happiness, comfort, and security increased over the three-year period, while ratings for more social or collective values decreased. The social value experiencing the greatest decrease in importance among the officers was "equality." These findings were stable across all levels of education and experience. Zhao and his colleagues (1999) concluded that the value changes in their sample of officers were antithetical to the basic shifts in culture expected under community policing.

Research on police officers' attitudes might also be useful for drawing inferences about recent changes in organizational and occupational culture. For instance, studies examining attitudes about community policing have found a lack of understanding and/or acceptance among police officers (Kratcoski & Noonan 1995; Lurigio & Skogan 1994; Sadd & Grinc 1994). Greene and Decker (1989) found that a classroom program in Philadelphia designed to improve relations between police officers and residents actually resulted in poorer officer attitudes toward the community. Wood's (1998) study of community policing in Albuquerque finds that changes in organizational culture are difficult to achieve in the face of the traditional police culture. Despite these frequent negative findings, some research has found that police agencies can change officers' attitudes. For instance, a longitudinal study in Joliet, Illinois found that while "the absence of change was the norm rather than the exception," many officers showed favorable changes in attitudes toward and knowledge of community policing (Rosenbaum, Yeh & Wilkinson 1994:349). Other studies have also found evidence of positive changes in police officers' attitudes (McElroy, Cosgrove & Sadd 1993; Wycoff & Skogan 1994). Overall, these studies of police attitudes and values generally suggest that the culture of a police organization can change, but such shifts are not likely to occur often or quickly. Whether attempts to modify police or organizational cultures have succeeded in producing improved internal communications is also unknown.

Summary of internal communication reform

Reformers have urged police organizations to adopt a number of reforms intended to improve internal communications. Some of these involve changes in formal aspects of the organization, such as structures, rules, policies, and procedures. Others involve changes in the informal aspects of the organization, such as values, attitudes, and organizational and occupational cultures. Although we have separated the formal and informal aspects of organizations, they are inextricably linked. As Crank (1998:27) notes, "police culture is embedded in and bounded by organizational structure." Furthermore, the emergence of communications technologies has further blurred the lines between the formal and informal aspects of the organization. Information technologies make it easier to bypass layers in the hierarchy or communicate across functional, spatial, or temporal barriers (Rogers 1988). Research evidence on both communications technologies and community policing is not sufficiently developed at this point to enable us to draw sweeping conclusions about their impacts on internal communication in police organizations.

Epilogue

Communication reform is both implicit and explicit in much of the community policing reform rhetoric. Community policing is viewed as a solution to a number of problems in the internal and external environments of police organizations. Externally, the development of community partnerships and the use of collaborative problem-solving techniques is intended to produce safer, less fearful, and more satisfied communities. Internally, the adoption of various organizational change strategies is designed to produce less bureaucratic and more responsive police organizations. Across both the external and internal dimensions of community policing is a vision that improved communications will produce various benefits. Weaving together concepts and theories from public relations, organization theory, and policing, we have provided a framework useful for viewing the role of communication reform in community policing. This framework raises a number of questions about the relationship between community policing and communications. Research evidence is not well-developed at this point to answer many of these questions with confidence.

How can researchers begin to address some of the unanswered questions about the role of internal and external communications in community policing? The primary means is to treat communications themselves as units of analysis in social scientific research. Manning's (1988) research on how calls to the police are processed is one example of treating the content of communications as a unit of analysis. The same kinds of work could be applied to community policing research. To learn more about patterns of external communications, research could examine the nature and content of communications flowing from police to community and community to police. This would provide insights about both the symmetry and direction of communications, a crucial element of both the public relations models we explored earlier and the community policing movement more generally. To learn more about patterns of internal communications, research could examine the flow of information within a police agency, from informal messages such as rumors, myths and legends, to more formal communications like the modes through which new policies or procedures diffuse throughout the organization. Furthermore, the information age is fundamentally altering the way that organizational members communicate with one another, yet very little is known about how technology has affected communication patterns within police agencies. All of these are crucial questions for learning more about the linkages between community policing and communication reform.

Community policing has been described as a revolution in the way police deliver services to their communities. As this chapter goes to press, a variety of scandals continue to haunt the police. The Mayor of Los Angeles recently suggested that "the city set aside 25 years worth of tobacco settlement money — as much as $300 million — to pay for lawsuits anticipated from the city's latest police corruption scandal" in the Rampart Division (Los Angeles Times 2000). In the Washington, DC Metropolitan Police Department, nearly a quarter of the four million e-mails sent by officers to one another in a single year "contained obscenity or hate filled language" (Law Enforcement News 2001). In Cincinnati, the shooting of an unarmed black man by a white police officer prompted three days of riots resulting in "more than 800 arrests and hundreds of thousands of dollars of damage" (Washington Post 2001). While these are dramatic incidents, they illustrate that much remains to be done in developing a healthy relationship between police and communities. Communication reform, both internal and external, will continue to play a key role in this endeavor.

Notes

1. Serious crime includes the "index" crimes recorded by the FBI: murder, rape, robbery, aggravated assault, larceny, burglary, and motor vehicle theft. The first four offenses constitute violent crimes, while the latter three constitute property crimes. These data were drawn from the 172 American cities with a population of at least 75,000 in 1960 (Federal Bureau of Investigation 1997). This sample was chosen because it was the only comprehensive source available in public archives for crime data from that period.

2. Several forces have also led local police agencies to expand their external relationships with researchers, think tanks, state and federal justice agencies and other police organizations located outside their immediate jurisdictions. It is now common for police agencies, especially those deemed as innovative, to host visitors from numerous external groups (Weiss 1997). There are resources to be won for those agencies demonstrating the best reputations in community policing circles, from professional awards to federal, state, and private grants (Maguire & Mastrofski 2001). While these are all examples of external communication reform, our interest here is in exploring communications within the immediate jurisdiction of the police agency; the area which Scott (1992) describes as an areal organizational field. Thus, our coverage of external communication reform excludes these emerging relationships between local police agencies and other entities located outside their immediate jurisdiction.

3. Organizational theorists use the singular term "environment" to refer to everything outside its boundaries impacted by or having an impact on the organization. Public relations theorists use the plural term "publics" to refer to the various constituencies served by an organization. We use these terms interchangeably in this chapter, often for stylistic rather than substantive reasons. Nonetheless, we recognize the substantive difference between them, most notably that an organization's environment is heterogeneous, consisting of numerous publics, in addition to various other elements.

4. Just as public relations theorists use the plural term "publics" rather than the singular term "public" to describe an organization's multiple, heterogeneous constituencies, some critics have noted that community policing reformers mistakenly view the police as serving a single or homogeneous community (Correia 2000; Lyons 1999; Reed 1999).

5. Although this is nearly always true in community policing, there are some exceptions. For instance, the Omaha, Nebraska Coalition of Citizen Patrols is an independent, grass-roots organization providing volunteer neighborhood patrols (Gartin 1996).
6. There are other dimensions we do not consider here. For instance, one that is closely related to functional differentiation is occupational differentiation, in which workers are divided according to occupational specialty (Langworthy 1986; Maguire forthcoming).
7. We have heard this phrase in the past, but were unable to locate a source for it.

References

Ahern, J. F. 1972. *Police in Trouble.* New York: Hawthorn Books.
Alarid, L. F. 1999. "Law enforcement departments as learning organizations: Argyris's theory as a framework for implementing community policing". *Police Quarterly* 2: 321–337.
Angell, J. 1971. "Toward an alternative to the classic police organizational arrangements: A democratic model". *Criminology* 9:185–206.
Barlow, D. E. and M. H. Barlow. 2000. *Police in a Multicultural Society: An American Story.* Prospect Heights, IL: Waveland.
Barnett, G. A. 1988. "Communication and organizational culture". In *Handbook of Organizational Communication,* G. M. Goldhaber and G. A. Barnett (eds), 101–131. Norwood, NJ: Ablex.
Bayley, D. H. 1994. *Police for the Future.* New York: Oxford University Press.
Bayley, D. H. and Mendelsohn, H. 1969. *Minorities and the Police: Confrontation in America.* New York: The Free Press.
Bayley, D. H. 1985. *Patterns of Policing: A Comparative International Analysis.* New Brunswick, NJ: Rutgers.
Bordua, D. J. and Tifft, L. L. 1971. "Citizen interviews, organizational feedback, and police community relations decisions". *Law and Society Review* November: 155–182.
Bratton, W. 1998. *Turnaround: How America's top cop reversed the crime epidemic.* New York: Random House.
Bruning, S. D. and Ledingham, J. A. 1999. "Relationships between organization and publics: Development of a multi-dimensional organization-public relationship scale". *Public Relations Review* 25: 157–166.
Cassell, P. G. and Fowles, R. 1998. "Handcuffing the cops? A thirty-year perspective on Miranda's harmful effects on law enforcement". *Stanford Law Review* 50: 1055.
Chermak, S. 1995. "Image control: How police affect the presentation of crime news". *American Journal of Police* 14: 21–43.
Cordner, G. W. 1995. "Community policing: Elements and effects". *Police Forum* 5: 1–8.
Correia, M. 2000. "The conceptual ambiguity of community in community policing: Filtering the muddy waters". *Policing* 23: 218–232.
Cosgrove, C. 1997. "Investigations in the community policing context". Paper presented at the Community Policing: What Works? Conference, Arlington, VA: November 8–10.
Crank, J. P. 1998. *Understanding Police Culture.* Cincinnati, OH: Anderson.

Cutlip, S. M., Center, A. H. and Broom, G. M. 1994. *Effective Public Relations*, 7th Edition. Upper Saddle River, NJ: Prentice Hall.

Ellis, A. 2001. "If the news media won't cover your positive stories, try this". *The Police Chief* LXVIII: 16–21.

Ericson, R. V., Baranek, P. M. and Chan, J. B. L. 1989. *Negotiating Control: A study of news sources*. Toronto: University of Toronto Press.

Federal Bureau of Investigation. 1997. *Uniform Crime Reports, 1958–1969, and County and City Data Books, 1962, 1967, 1972*: Merged Data [Computer file]. ICPSR edition, Ann Arbor, MI: Inter-university Consortium for Political and Social Research [producer and distributor].

Gartin, P. 1996. *The Omaha Coalition of Citizen Patrols: A Case Study and Impact Assessment of the Integration of an Independent, Grass Roots Citizens' Organization into a City's Community Policing Approach to Crime Control*. Unpublished proposal submitted to the National Institute of Justice, University of Nebraska at Omaha.

Geary, D. P. 1975. "The impact of police–community relations on the police system". In *Community Relations and the Administration of Justice*, D. P. Geary (ed.), New York: Wiley.

Geller, W. 1997. "Suppose we were really serious about police departments becoming learning organizations?" *National Institute of Justice Journal*, December: 2–8.

Geller, W. A. and Swanger, G. 1995. *Managing Innovation in Policing: The untapped potential of the middle manager*. Washington, DC: Police Executive Research Forum.

Gianakis, G. A. and Davis, G. J. III. 1998. "Reinventing or repackaging public services? The case of community-oriented policing. *Public Administration Review* 58: 485–98.

Goldstein, H. 1979. "Improving policing: A problem-oriented approach". *Crime and Delinquency* 25: 236–58.

Goldstein, H. 1990. *Problem-Oriented Policing*. New York: McGraw-Hill.

Goldstein, J. 1960. "Police discretion not to invoke the criminal process: Low visibility decisions in the administration of justice". *Yale Law Journal* 69: 543–94.

Greene, J. R. 2000. "Community policing in America: Changing the nature, structure, and function of the police". In *Criminal Justice 2000, Volume Three: Policies, Processes, and Decisions of the Criminal Justice System*, J. Horney, R. Peterson, D. MacKenzie, J. Martin and D. Rosenbaum (eds), 299–370. Washington, DC: National Institute of Justice.

Greene, J. R., Bergman, W. and Mclaughlin, E. 1994. "Implementing community policing: Cultural and structural change in police organizations". In *The Challenge of Community Policing*, D. P. Rosenbaum (ed.), 92–110. Thousand Oaks, CA: Sage.

Greene, J. R. and Decker, S. H. 1989. "Police and Community Perceptions of the Community Role in Policing: The Philadelphia Experience". *The Howard Journal* 28: 105–123.

Greene, J. R. and Mastrofski, S. D. (eds). 1988. *Community Policing: Rhetoric or Reality*. New York: Praeger.

Gregory, D. and Urry, J. 1985. "Introduction". In *Social Relations and Spatial Structures*, D. Gregory and J. Urry (eds), Hong Kong: McMillan.

Grunig, J. E. 1984. "Organizations, environments, and models of public relations". *Public Relations Research and Education* 1: 6–29.

Grunig, J. E. and Hunt, T. 1984. *Managing Public Relations*. New York: Holt, Rinehart and Winston.

Grunig, J. E. and Grunig, L. A. 1992. "Models of public relations and communication". Pp. 285–327 in *Excellence in Public Relations and Communication Management*, J. E. Grunig (ed.), 285–327. Hillsdale, NJ: Lawrence Erlbaum Associates, Publishers.
Guffey, J. E. 1992. "The police and the media: Proposals for managing conflict productively". *American Journal of Police* 11: 33–51.
Guyot, D. 1979. "Bending granite: Attempts to change the rank structure of American police departments". *Journal of Police Science and Administration* 7: 253–84.
Hall, R. H. 1999. *Organizations*. Upper Saddle River, NJ: Prentice Hall.
Hall, R. H., Haas, J. E., and Johnson, N. J. 1967. "Organizational size, complexity, and formalization". *American Sociological Review* 32: 903–12.
Hallahan, K. 2000. "Inactive publics in public relations". *Public Relations Review* 26: 499–515.
Hassell, K., Peyton, J., Zhao, J. and Maguire, E. R. 1999. "Structural change in large municipal police organizations: Evidence from a national study". Presentation delivered at the annual meeting of the Academy of Criminal Justice Sciences, Orlando, Florida (March 12).
Hindelang, M. J. 1974. "Public opinion regarding crime, criminal justice, and related topics". *Journal of Research in Crime and Delinquency* July: 101–116.
Hunter, R. D. and Barker, T. 1993. "BS and buzzwords: The new police operational style". *American Journal of Police* 12: 157–168.
Johnson, J. D. 1993. *Organizational Communication Structure*. Norwood, NJ: Ablex.
Katz, C. M. 2001. "The creation of police gang units." *Criminology* 39: 37–74
Kent, M. L. and Taylor, M. 1998. "Building dialogic relationships through the World Wide Web". *Public Relations Review* 24: 321–329.
Kessler, D. A. 1999. "The effects of community policing on complaints against officers". *Journal of Quantitative Criminology*, September.
Klockars, C. 1988. "The rhetoric of community policing." In *Community Policing: Rhetoric or Reality*, J. Greene and S. Mastrofski (eds), 239–258. New York: Praeger.
Koper, C. S., Roehl, J. Roth, J. and Ryan, J. 1998. "Return on investment: A national evaluation of the COPS program". Paper presented at the National Conference on Community Policing, Alexandria, VA: November 9.
Kratcoski, P. C. and Noonan, S. B. 1995. "An Assessment of Police Officers Acceptance of Community Policing". In *Issues in Community Policing*, P. C. Kratcoski and D. Dukes (eds), 169–186. Cincinnati, OH: Anderson.
Langworthy, R. H. 1986. *The Structure of Police Organizations*. New York: Praeger.
Law Enforcement News. 2001. "You've got hate mail!" March 31.
Ledingham, J. A. and Bruning, S. D. 1998. "Relationship management in public relations: Dimensions of an organization-public relationship". *Public Relations Review* 24: 55–60.
Leo, R. A. 1996. "The impact of Miranda revisited". *Journal of Criminal Law and Criminology* 86: 621.
Lipsky, M. 1980. *Street-level Bureaucracy: Dilemmas of the Individual in Public Services*. New York: Russell Sage Foundation.
Los Angeles Times. 2000. "L. A. mayor suggests tobacco money to pay off lawsuits over corruption". February 17.
Lurigio, A. J. and Skogan, W. G. 1994. "Winning the hearts and minds of police officers: An assessment of staff perceptions of community policing in Chicago". *Crime and Delinquency* 40: 315–330.

Lyons, W. 1999. *The Politics of Community Policing: Rearranging the Power to Punish.* Ann Arbor: University of Michigan.

McElroy, J.E., Cosgrove, C. and Sadd, S. 1993. *Community Policing: The CPOP in New York.* Newbury Park, CA: Sage Publications.

Maguire, E.R. 1997. "Structural change in large municipal police organizations during the community policing era." *Justice Quarterly* 14: 701–730.

Maguire, E.R. Forthcoming. *Organizational Structure in Large Police Agencies: Context, Complexity and Control.* Albany, NY: SUNY Press.

Maguire, E.R., Kuhns, J.B., Uchida, C.D. and Cox, S.M. 1997. "Patterns of community policing in non-urban America." *Journal of Research in Crime and Delinquency* 34: 368–394.

Maguire, E.R. and Mastrofski, S.D. 2000. "Patterns of community policing in the United States". *Police Quarterly* 3: 4–45.

Maguire, E.R. and Uchida, C.D. 2000. "Measurement and explanation in the comparative study of American police organizations." In *Criminal Justice 2000, Volume 4: Measurement and Analysis of Crime and Justice*, D. Duffee (ed.), 491–457. Washington, DC: National Institute of Justice.

Manning, P.K. 1988. *Symbolic Communication: Signifying calls and the police response.* Cambridge, MA: MIT Press.

Manning, P.K. 1992. *Organizational Communication.* New York: Aldine de Gruyter.

Mastrofski, S.D. 1998. "Community policing and police organization structure." In *How to Recognize Good Policing: Problems and issues*, J.P. Brodeur (ed.), 161–189. Newbury Park, CA: Sage.

Mastrofski, S.D. 2001. "The Romance of police leadership." In *Theoretical Advances in Criminology*, E. Waring, D. Weisburd and L. Sherman (eds), 153–196. New Brunswick: Transaction Books.

Mastrofski, S.D. and Ritti, R.R. 1999. *Patterns of Community Policing: A View from Newspapers in the United States* [COPS Working Paper #2]. Washington, DC: Community Oriented Policing Services.

Meyer, M.W. 1979. "Organizational structure as signaling". *Pacific Sociological Review* 22: 481–500.

Moore, M.H. 1992. "Problem solving and community policing". In *Modern Policing*, M. Tonry and N. Morris (eds), 99–159. Chicago: University of Chicago Press.

National Advisory Commission on Civil Disorders. 1968. *Report of the National Advisory Commission on Civil Disorders.* New York: Bantam Books.

Nohria, N. and Eccles, R.G. 1992. *Networks and Organizations: Structure, Form, and Action.* Boston: Harvard Business School.

President's Commission on Law Enforcement and Administration of Justice. 1967. *The Challenge of Crime in a Free Society.* Washington, DC: U.S. Government Printing Office.

Redlinger, L. 1994. "Community policing and changes in the organizational structure". *Journal of Contemporary Criminal Justice* 10: 36–58.

Reed, W.E. 1999. *The Politics of Community Policing: The Case of Seattle.* New York: Garland.

Reiss, A.J. Jr. 1971. *The Police and the Public.* New Haven: Yale University Press.

Reiss, A.J. Jr. 1992. "Police organization in the twentieth century". In *Modern Policing*, M. Tonry and N. Morris (eds), 51–97. Chicago: University of Chicago.

Reiss, A. J. Jr. and Bordua, D. J. 1967. "Environment and organization: A perspective on the police." In *The Police: Six Sociological Essays*, D. J. Bordua (ed.), 25–55. New York: Wiley.

Reiter, M. S. 1999. "Empowerment policing". *FBI Law Enforcement Bulletin* 68: 7–11.

Rogers, E. M. 1988. "Information technologies: How organizations are changing". In *Handbook of Organizational Communication*, G. M. Goldhaber and G. A. Barnett (eds), 437–453. Norwood, NJ: Ablex.

Rosenbaum, D. P., Yeh, S., and Wilkinson, D. L. 1994. "Impact of Community Policing on Police Personnel: A Quasi-Experimental Test". *Crime and Delinquency*, 40: 331–353.

Sabo, L. O. and Kuykendall, J. L. 1978. "Matrix organization — Applications to a police organization". *The Police Chief* 45: 70–72.

Sadd, S. and Grinc, R. 1994. "Innovative Neighborhood Oriented Policing: An Evaluation of Community Policing Programs in Eight Cities." In *The Challenge of Community Policing: Testing the promises*, D. P. Rosenbaum (ed.), 27–52. Thousand Oaks, CA: Sage Publications.

Scott, W. R. 1992. *Organizations: Rational, Natural, and Open Systems*, 3rd Edition. Englewood Cliffs, NJ: Prentice Hall.

Sherman, L. W., Milton, C. H. and Kelly, T. V. 1973. *Team Policing: Seven case studies*. Washington, DC: Police Foundation.

Skogan, W. G. and Hartnett, S. M. 1997. *Community Policing, Chicago Style*. New York: Oxford.

Skolnick, J. H. and Bayley, D. H. 1986. *The New Blue Line: Police Innovation in Six American Cities*. New York: The Free Press.

Skolnick, J. H. and McCoy, C. 1985. "Police accountability and the media". In *Police Leadership in America*, W. A. Geller (ed.), 102–135. New York: American Bar Foundation.

Sparrow, M. K., Moore, M. H., and Kennedy, D. M. 1990. *Beyond 911: A New Era for Policing*. New York: Basic Books.

Stark, R. 1972. *Police Riots: Collective violence and law enforcement*. Belmont, CA: Wadsworth.

Strecher, V. 1991. "Revising the histories and futures of policing". Reprinted in *The Police and Society: Touchstone Readings* (1995), V. Kappeler (ed.), 66–80. Prospects Heights, IL: Waveland.

Sutcliffe, K. M. 2001. "Organizational environments and organizational information processing". In *The New Handbook of Organizational Communication: Advances in Theory, Research, and Methods*, F. M. Jablin and L. L. Putman (eds), 197–230. Thousand Oaks, CA: Sage.

Wadman, R. C. 1998. *Organizing for the Prevention of Crime*. Doctoral dissertation, Idaho State University (May).

Walker, S. 1980. *Popular Justice*. New York: Oxford University Press.

Walker, S. 1984. "Broken windows and fractured history: The use and misuse of history in recent police patrol analysis". *Justice Quarterly* 1: 75–90.

Walker, S. 1993. "Does anyone remember team policing? Lessons of the team policing experience for community policing". *American Journal of Police* 12: 33–55.

Washington Post. 2001. "Findings near on Cincinnati shooting". May 7: A02.

Weiss, A. 1997. "The communication of innovation in American policing". *Policing: An International Journal of Police Strategies and Management* 20: 292–310.

Westley, W. A. 1970. *Violence and the Police: A sociological study of law, custom, and morality*. Boston: Massachusetts Institute of Technology.

Wilson, J. Q. and Kelling, G. L. 1982. "Broken windows". *The Atlantic Monthly* March: 29–38.

Wood, R. L. 1998. "Creating a Culture of Community Policing: Police Cultures and Organizational Independence". Paper presented at the National Conference on Community Policing, Alexandria, VA: November 9.

Worrall, J. L. 2001. *Civil Lawsuits, Citizen Complaints, and Policing Innovations.* New York: LFB Scholarly Publishing.

Wycoff, M. A. 1994. *Community Policing Strategies.* Final report submitted to the National Institute of Justice. Washington, DC: NIJ.

Wycoff, M. A. and Skogan, W. G. 1994. "The Effect of a Community Policing Management Style on Officers' Attitudes." *Crime and Delinquency,* 40: 371–383.

Zhao, J. 1996. *Why Police Organizations Change: A Study of Community Oriented Policing.* Washington, DC: Police Executive Research Forum.

Zhao, J., He, N. and Lovrich, N. 1998. "Individual value preferences among American police officers: The Rokeach theory of human values revisited". *Policing: An International Journal of Police Strategies and Management* 21: 22–37.

Zhao, J., He, N. and Lovrich, N. 1999. "Value change among police officers at a time of organizational change: A follow-up study using Rokeach values". *Policing: An International Journal of Police Strategies and Management* 22: 152–170.

CHAPTER 3

Attitudes, culture and emotion in police talk

Keith Tuffin
Massey University, New Zealand

This chapter begins with some questions about modern police work. Broadly speaking, these questions come from the psychology of policing, and are concerned with fundamental aspects of how the police manage their work. More specifically, these questions focus on gaining an intimate and detailed inside view of a variety of issues relevant to policing. These issues include the unique pressures which have to be managed when dealing with members of the public, attitudes police hold with respect to certain groups in society, the emotional reactions associated with dealing with trauma or danger, and the internal workings of police culture. Each of these issues represents an important aspect of working in law enforcement, and as such are likely to impact on the daily interactions between officers as they conduct the important business for which they are responsible. This chapter aims to introduce readers to the discursive study of these issues.

Let us consider some of these questions more directly. How do police deal with the tension of having to maintain credibility in the eyes of the public, while also having the task of policing that same public? What do police officers think about having gay cops as partners on the job? How important is the reputation of the police force in the eyes of the public? In the often dangerous and traumatic work which the police must routinely deal with, how do cops deal with their personal reactions to these events? What emotions are associated with this type of work and how are these managed by officers? How powerful an influence is the culture of the police? To what extent does the internal workings of police culture hinder or assist officers in the daily conduct of their duties?

These questions are relevant to the day-to-day work which individual officers undertake, and in this regard have very practical consequences. However, they are also important to researchers who are interested in studying the workings of the police in greater detail. It is the second of these two concerns which is the focus of this chapter. Indeed, these questions and others like them have been the driving force behind research which I have become involved with in recent years. Readers should be aware that this chapter reports on research which has examined attitudes, culture and emotion within the police, not all of the above questions have been directly answered. While many of these questions are addressed, it is important to note that from a research perspective, psychologists, social scientists, and students of communication will be interested to find out how these questions, and others like them, may be addressed.

This chapter attempts to provide some of the background as to how these kinds of research questions can arise and, more importantly, how they can be addressed through the adoption of a radical new approach to doing research within the social and communication sciences. This approach may be conceptualized as a method in the sense of providing a way of doing research, but it must also be considered as a unique epistemological orientation. A further aim, therefore, is to delineate the epistemology and the methodology involved. In this regard, we are working with both the theory and practice of conducting a particular style of research. While this contribution adopts a clear research focus, it is important to remember the broader agendas which apply to any research. Conducting research with the police is something which, at best, will increase our understanding of the unique occupational and psychological demands and stresses with which the police work. Ultimately, these understandings may usefully be applied in ways which assist in the management of the pressures with which the police routinely work. This level of application is beyond the scope of this chapter which, more modestly, sets out to introduce both researchers and practitioners to a research method which involves the collection and analysis of language use.

A new research method for studying law enforcement

Discursive psychology (Edwards & Potter 1992) provides an alternative approach to research for those scholars who are interested in the detailed study of particular settings, particular groups of people, and particular cultures. Arguably, the police qualify on all three of these criteria, especially if we consider cultures to include occupational subgroups. This introduction will outline some features of a discursive approach in terms of the philosophical underpinnings, and the methods involved. The above aims will be augmented with illustrations drawn from recent discursive studies which have been conducted with data obtained through interviews with the police. Those readers who have little interest in philosophical and methodological issues might like to move straight to the section titled "Attitudes to Gay Cops" where the kinds of questions raised earlier become the focus of attention. These questions are examined in a way which highlights the active and constructive properties of language and shows how this perspective can work to increase our understanding of these unique aspects of police work.

Social constructionist philosophy

At its simplest level, discursive psychology seeks to find out about human activities by simply asking people, thereby placing a premium on the value of everyday, ordinary language use. The availability and sheer pervasiveness of everyday talk has perhaps contributed to assumptions about its taken-for-granted status. As Wooffitt (1993) notes, it is perhaps this assumption which has prevented talk and text from being treated as one of the central topics of social scientific research. The approach presented in this chapter seeks to address this situation by focussing on common language use in police settings.

Where discursive psychology differs from other approaches which focus on language use is in the way in which language is theorized. Discursive psychologists are intensely interested in language and adopt a social constructionist epistemology in their theorization about language. This interest in language has been stimulated by the work of the linguistic philosophers Wittgenstein (1953) and Austin (1962) who regard language as constitutive rather than representational. The constitutive view assumes language to be active, constructive, and inextricably involved in a huge range of social achievements. Social constructionists (e.g., Gergen 1985) assume that language is actively involved in the construction of our experiences, our subjectivities and our realities. This action orientation becomes a basic philosophical tenet for discursive psychologists, with the examination of how language works as an underlying rationale for discursive research (Harré & Gillett 1994). This assumption directly challenges the assumption of linguistic neutrality, and fundamentally alters the way in which language is thought to work. The representational view of language assumes passivity and neutrality. Representationalists regard language as merely describing the reality which it claims to portray. This view suggests that language operates in a way which is able to capture the absolute truth and transport this neutrally to an audience (Reddy 1979). This abstract and rather disconnected view of language overlooks both the subtlety and power of language.

While the single most salient aspect of social constructionism is its commitment to the study of language in its own right, it also provides an intellectual challenge to contemporary understandings of social and psychological life (Burr 1995). The constructionist challenge (Gergen 1985; Gill 1995) encourages epistemological scepticism which questions the often taken-for-granted assumption that the nature of reality may be simply revealed by observation. In questioning the representational view of language, constructionists take issue with both the underlying linguistic philosophy and the perceptual metaphor around which the approach is framed.

The dominance of this perceptual metaphor has been criticized by social constructionists who argue for the privileging of linguistic and rhetorical metaphors as the basis of an alternative epistemology. Billig (1985), for example, has suggested that the popularity of perceptual metaphors stems from the widespread adoption of biological models within the social and communication sciences, and psychology in particular. These models which emphasize the commonality among organisms assume the pervasiveness of perceptual abilities to have explanatory power. Billig's argument is that when we examine specific human characteristics (he uses the example of prejudice) we should focus on those processes which are uniquely human for explanations. This means replacing perceptual models of cognition with linguistic and metaphorical models. Wetherell (1995) extends this line of argument in suggesting that we begin to examine the social and linguistic aspects of particular phenomena as these may provide advantages over what has previously been considered the psychological.

Discursive methods

In advocating such a radical epistemological reorientation, discursive psychologists have been critical of existing methods which seek to establish decontextualized causal relationships. The search for such knowledge often takes place in artificial settings (laboratories) utilizing interventionist (experimental) manipulations. Experimental and laboratory based methods typify this approach within psychology, with the seminal texts in discursive psychology (Edwards & Potter 1992; Potter & Wetherell 1987) arguing for a contextualized approach to the study of naturally-occurring data. At the heart of this approach is an ethnomethodologically inspired respect for, and interest in, everyday language use. For the discursive psychologist, this interest in the everyday use of language is combined with a view of language as performing particular social actions. In short, language is regarded as a form of social practice which is worthy of study in its own right.

The assumption that language is active and thereby pivotal to a broad range of social achievements seems even more convincing when we consider the relentless involvement of language in social transactions. Consider, for example, activities which a police officer may be expected to do — questioning a suspect, taking a witness' statement, responding to a directive from a superior officer, providing courtroom evidence — all of these acts involve either talk or text and thereby occur in and through language. This alone should argue for the importance of the detailed study of police language use.

Recent interest in the workings and functions of language has spawned a renewed interest in the study of everyday talk. Within the social sciences, ethnomethodologists, conversation analysts, interactional sociolinguists, and discursive psychologists are involved in vigorous debates concerning theory, method, and practice. The commonality within these disciplines is an interest in the detail of ordinary language use. Scholars working within these traditions also share an understanding of the importance of recording talk-in-interaction and providing transcriptions of the talk which then form the data for subsequent analysis. The need for detailed transcription is obviated when written material is analysed, as in the case of court transcripts, letters, diaries and newspapers.

These various approaches have been applied to a number of policing related areas. The following provides an indication of this growing volume of research which studies language use in contexts relevant to law enforcement. Discursive studies in the area of police interviewing (Auburn, Drake & Willig 1995; Auburn, Lea & Drake 1999; McConville, Sanders & Leng 1991; Watson 1983, 1990) have provided detailed analyses of interrogative techniques. In particular, Auburn, Drake and Willig (1995) forward the notion of the preferred version of events as one which is carefully attended to by participants. This institutionally facilitated version assumes its importance as it is likely to advance the core business of policing and justice. Courtroom dynamics, processes and organizations have received considerable attention from conversation analytic studies (Atkinson & Drew 1979; Drew 1985, 1992) and ethnomethodological work (Pollner 1987; Pomerantz 1987). For example, Drew (1992) looked at cross-examination as courtroom talk in interaction. The purpose of such questioning is clearly to identify inconsistencies which, in turn, may work to discredit the witness, or reduce the plausibility of the witness' account. Drew's analysis highlights how competing versions of events are carefully and purposefully managed by lawyers and witnesses who orient to differing outcomes in the presentation and challenge of courtroom testimony. Finally, the conversation analytic work of Whalen and Zimmerman (1990) deserves mention. This study examined telephone interactions when callers sought police assistance. This analysis looked at the 'practical epistemology' which callers were required to negotiate in order to counter suspicions regarding the genuineness of the reported trouble.

The above studies provide a sample of the areas where language based methods have been applied to police-related work. The focus of this chapter is discursive research, and the remainder of the chapter will be devoted to the presentation of three discursive studies which have examined attitudes, culture, and emotion in the police. In terms of specifics of method readers are referred to the work of Potter and Wetherell 1987, Tuffin and Howard (2002), and Wooffitt 1993.

Attitudes to gay cops

In a study of attitudes toward homosexuality (Praat & Tuffin 1996), male police were interviewed about a range of relevant issues. A number of points are important to clarify before outlining the contextualized nature of this project. Firstly, this study was conceptualized as a discursive study of attitudes. Unlike most attitudinal studies, this approach does not assume that attitudes are unitary, stable, quantifiable entities. Rather, it is assumed that people will make a wide range of variable and sometimes conflicting comments. In fact, it is just this variability in accounts and explanations which is of greatest interest, and thus becomes a significant focus of analytic attention. In this way, ordinary talk and text is regarded as being organized as a matter of social practice (Potter 1996). The broad discursive aim becomes the fine grained analysis of those social practices.

Secondly, there exists a history of disquiet about the usefulness of the notion of attitudes (La Piere 1934). In a searching review of the attitude literature, Wicker (1969) concluded that expressed attitudes have little predictive power. In other words, people are likely to say one thing and then act in a manner which is the exact opposite of what would have been predicted by the expressed attitude. This variability argues strongly against the notion that attitudes are enduring, stable entities which are amenable to reliable measurement. Attitude critiques (Kline 1988; Potter & Wetherell 1987) have also made the point that attitudes (and, indeed, any evaluative or judgemental statement) are contextually sensitive. In this regard, context informs understanding and should therefore be taken into account if we wish to further understand the action orientation of talk.

One significant contextual feature of the Praat and Tuffin (1996) study was the unique socio-historical background which was important to both the rationale for conducting the study and the way in which the results were interpreted. This work was conducted in New Zealand where the Homosexual Law Reform Act (1986) had recently passed into law. This legislation legalized homosexual activity between consenting males over the age of 16. A further piece of legislation provided an additional legal overlay to the context in which this study was conducted. In 1993 the Human Rights Act was amended, such that discrimination on the grounds of sexual orientation became illegal. This anti-discrimination legislation applied to selection procedures (among other things), which meant that aspiring applicants to the police and the military forces could no longer be excluded on the grounds of sexual orientation.

The combination of these two pieces of legislation meant that within eight years the law had changed from outlawing homosexuality to outlawing employment discrimination *against* homosexuals. This created an ironic situation, whereby police officers could face the prospect of working along side the same people who were regarded as criminals prior to the 1986 law change. It was this mixture of social, historical and political context which gave rise to the kind of questions which were to the forefront of our thinking when we set out to interview officers about this intriguing situation. What *did* cops say about the possibility of working with gay cops as partners? What did they anticipate would be the public reaction to having gay cops on the force?

Of the discourses to emerge from the study by Praat and Tuffin (1996), one deserves some reiteration as it bears on the question of how context informs understanding and ultimately how the results of such research are interpreted. The term 'discourse' is used here simply as a way of organizing talk, about talk. Such talk may be thought of as utilizing particular linguistic resources — which are commonly available and commonly used. This commonality allows them to be identified and talked about, which is what the studies referred to in this chapter have done. Potter and Wetherell (1987) use an alternative term, 'interpretative repertoires', which they describe as ideological themes. All officers who were interviewed spoke about the problems which gay recruits would face on entering the police.

Interestingly, while prepared to detail numerous reservations, the officers were also quick to distance themselves from harboring any personal dislike or prejudice against homosexuals. The reservations could be broadly categorized into two key areas: internal pressures from within the police force itself and, secondly, the predicted negative reaction from the public which would impact on the reputation of the police force. Both of these pressures were constructed in such a way as to be significant factors over which participants were themselves powerless. Thus, the source of unfavorable reactions to having gay cops on the force was constructed as being outside the control of individual officers. In this way, officers exempted themselves from being the enforcers of prejudice by claiming to be the victims of wider forces. This particular accounting procedure closely resembles the 'reasoning' uncovered by Gill (1993) in interviews with radio managers. This study showed how the managers were able to justify the injustice of employing mostly male announcers, by casting themselves as innocent victims of public preferences. They personally had no bias against women announcers, but were warranted in their actions by the need to satisfy public demand.

Police culture

The pressures operating within the culture of the police force became the basis for a more detailed discursive analysis (Frewin and Tuffin 1998). A significant contextual feature of this work was the backdrop provided by discourses of homosexuality for the study of the wider police culture. In asking about how gay cops might manage on the job, some insight was gained into how the police culture works with regard to tolerance of difference and the acceptance of change. Of particular interest were the ways in which external warrants were maintained internally, and were thereby able to illustrate how the production of discourses within police culture affect all officers. This work highlighted three discourses (police status, conformity, and internal pressure) which collectively contribute to social practices which are supportive of the status quo and contribute to a climate of conformity.

The *police status* discourse was organized around suggestions that the relative standing and reputation of the police was based on and, therefore, demanded respect for standards. The reputation of the police was constructed as essential to the operation of the police and was, accordingly, regarded as precious and requiring protection. Indeed, the reputation of the police was never assumed. Rather it was something which was seen as requiring active protection and maintenance. This was achieved through a strict and rigid adherence to a broad range of standards. In linking these standards to the vigilant maintenance of police reputation, any significant change to standards was seen as a potential threat to the standing of the police force in society. Admitting gay cops to the force was regarded as just such a change — which was talked about as a direct threat to the otherwise good reputation of the police. The analysis presented by Frewin and Tuffin (1998) illustrates several standards (visual appearance, masculinity, accessibility) which are based around participants' understandings of public acceptability. In turn, these public considerations are regarded as critical to the efficacy of police work. This argument draws on the importance of the relationship between the public and the police, such that police work is dependent on public trust and cooperation. In turn, the imperative of maintaining the reputation of the police is used as a means of justifying the exclusion of 'undesirable' recruits into the force.

The *conformity* discourse overlaps with the police status discourse — to the extent that there is talk of fitting in with existing standards. Frewin and Tuffin (1998) suggest that, ironically, conformity may be understood as a standard in its own right. The standard of conformity was uniformly talked about in terms of 'fitting in'. The imperative of conformity is warranted by the strict adherence to the standards upon which the reputation of the force rests. In the data, talk of conformity often emerged through discussions about the notion of discipline. Notably, discipline was constructed as residing within the individual, and also provided by immediate peers. As such, conformity was not an explicit requirement of the police culture itself. However, considerable extremes were imposed in the name of conformity. In particular, participants spoke of the concealment of non-conforming views and the public agreement with standards with which they privately disagreed. Public disagreement was likely to result in sanctions which became evident as part of the internal pressure discourse.

The *internal pressure* discourse deals with the pressures which are imposed on those who fail to fit in (nonconformists). Frewin and Tuffin (1998) note that this discourse is internally warranted and includes the social practices of ostracism, peer monitoring, threats to immediate safety on the job, and threats to long-term career prospects. These practices operate to suppress challenges to existing police standards and culture. The following extract is part of the data collected for the Praat and Tuffin (1996) study and illustrates a life threatening form of internal pressure.

(1) 1   It could come from anywhere, yeah
     2   it could be done on a supervisory role
     3   it could be done from your peers
     4   they could just make life so unpleasant
     5   like they wouldn't talk to you, or
     6   they don't respond to your call
     7   your out there ...
     8   you stop a vehicle
     9   you go to an incident and
    10   you get hit
    11   you get attacked
    12   you call for a backup, and ...

Bringing such data to a brief chapter like this has the advantage of providing a more solid grounding for the analytic conclusions. The data is intended to be illustrative of both the internal pressure discourse and, more generally, of aspects of conducting discursive analysis. This data is relevant to a consideration of the question of how a police officer could fail to respond immediately to a fellow officer's direct call for assistance.

The discursive aspects of the police culture which enable this inversion of urgency are to the forefront of concern in this analysis. Consistent with the broad aims of discursive research (Harré & Gillett 1994; Potter 1996), the analysis focussed on the related concerns of identifying the descriptive resources which are used to build our understanding of police culture, and studied the way in which accounts are organized. Such analysis requires interpretive skill which is exercised through the way in which the analyst attempts to make sense of the data. Such analytic readings invite the participation and involvement of readers. Indeed the above extract has been included for this very reason — to highlight the interpretive nature of analysis and to show how analysis may proceed from data to conclusions. While space limits the extent to which these aims may be satisfactorily achieved here, hopefully readers will be provided with a flavor of how this style of research is conducted. Before examining the data we should be aware that this is a textual analysis, and it is important to remain agnostic about whether such a description relates to events which have actually happened. Such concerns lie beyond the current analytic interest.

The extract deals with a description of the kind of pressure which could be brought to bear on a nonconforming cop. In particular, a cop who declared his gay sexual orientation would be regarded as significantly breaching acceptable standards and could expect to be exposed to the discourse of internal pressure.

Lines 1 to 3 detail the potential origin of internal pressure as coming from all levels within the organization. The inclusiveness and vagueness ('anywhere') of line 1 is contrasted with the specific identification of both supervisors and peers as potential sources of internal pressure. An interesting feature of this contrast is the use of both vagueness and detail. While systematic vagueness often functions to provide a barrier against rebuttal (Edwards & Potter 1992), in this case the vagueness can be read as a contrast to the two specific categories mentioned. Further, it would seem to raise the inference that such internal pressures are likely to come from any source — even though the speaker moves to detail two groups from which this would be likely. Clearly, seniority within the police force is no barrier to the application of internal pressure. The organization of these first three lines utilize the rhetorical features of a three part list. The list points to the origin of internal pressure as coming from a range of potential sources (anywhere, supervisors, and peers). Such lists were originally discussed in terms of their rhetorical effectiveness for political speeches (Atkinson 1984) and have since become an almost standard analytic tool. Edwards and Potter (1992) highlight, for example, how such three-partedness serves the useful rhetorical function of conveying an implication of completeness and representativeness. In the present case, the inclusiveness of 'anywhere' suggests that internal pressure is pervasive within the culture. While such pressure could come from either supervisors or fellow officers, the speaker does not discount the possibility of internal pressure coming from both these sources.

Line 4 specifies the degree to which this pressure could adversely affect one's life. The assumption here is that this refers to professional or working life which, in turn, would have a negative impact on life more generally. What is bluntly acknowledged is the power others (specified in the first three lines) have to disrupt and upset. This is not simply a matter of life being made uncomfortable, but involves a qualified degree of unpleasantness ('so unpleasant'). This degree of pressure is both extreme and intolerable, as the remaining lines of the extract make clear.

In lines 5 and 6 the illustrative actions which could be taken to contribute to this unpleasantness are spelt out. Line 5 deals with the kind of ostracism whereby basic communication is withheld and silent non-responsiveness is imposed. Similarly, line 6 addresses the possibility of further non-responsiveness, albeit of a more sinister form. Line 7 sets the scene for the possibility of further inaction with the hypothetical police officer ('you') being positioned on duty, presumably on the street. The threatened failure to respond to 'your call' is placed in the context of conducting routine everyday duties such as stopping a vehicle or attending an incident (lines 8 and 9) which prove to have extraordinary consequences when the officer involved (lines 10 and 11) is shot or comes under attack. The call for assistance (line 12) remains unanswered. What makes this non-responsiveness even more pointed is the contrast whereby requests would normally be responded to with the utmost urgency. As the speaker later indicates, such requests from fellow officers are usually treated as "make or break stuff, you get there as quick as you can".

This account clearly specifies the possibility of internal pressure in the form of sanctions which could include non-communication from colleagues and, more alarmingly, non-responsiveness in the face of a call for assistance on the part of a fellow officer who has been attacked. The clear consequence of this would be a dangerous increase in the level of threat to which officers could be exposed. Given the inherent dangers involved in police work, this additional threat would make police work simply untenable. This could well be the desired effect for those who participate in actions, and inactions, which the internal pressure discourse gives rise to.

A final point regarding the above analysis, which has examined the basic descriptive resources and rhetorical organization of a single account, is that this account does not stand alone. Indeed other versions of the internal pressure discourse were available in the data. The purpose of focussing attention on a single account is to show how the culture involved becomes enabled by talk about internal pressures. This account and others like it were all too common in the data, indicating a level of common understanding about how such pressures are brought to bear on those members of the police culture, whose commitment and conformity to the standards of the culture make them dangerously vulnerable.

Unspeakable emotion

The third example comes from a study of police emotion talk (Howard, Tuffin & Stephens 2000). A founding assumption of this study is the stress of police work (Beehr, Johnson & Nieva 1995), which routinely requires police officers to deal with dangerous, unpleasant, and horrific situations (Stratton 1981). These situations may include dealing with the aftermath of violent deaths, being subject to a life-threatening personal attack, and working with those who may be violent and unpredictable. These kinds of situations could be expected to provoke emotional responses (de Sousa 1987) and this study aimed to explore this emotionality discursively. Previous work in the social construction of emotions (Edwards 1997; Harré 1986; Stenner 1993) has contested the interiority of emotions by studying the ways they are negotiated through specific conversational interactions.

Twelve officers from the New Zealand police were interviewed about topics dealing with trauma from a personal, professional and organizational perspective (Stephens 1996). In terms of emotion talk, a simple content analysis suggested that fear was a commonly talked about emotion, with mention of grief, anger, and frustration also being prevalent. The analysis presented by Howard et al. (2000) contains a number of strands which touch on issues of dramatic data variability, the use of humor in dealing with reactions to trauma, the unspeakability of emotion, and finally tensions surrounding emotional disclosure. Space dictates that this discussion be limited, hence only the final of these strands will be presented.

The most striking feature of the interview data was variability in emotion accounts. Officers indicated their preparedness to discuss emotions following an incident while, contrastively, also stating that they would remain silent about such matters. Howard et al. (2000) suggest that this variability might be explained in terms of contextual contingency. That is to say that a closer analysis revealed that when talking about general cases, the discourse of *desirable disclosure* prevailed. General cases were ones where officers talked about what might happen in general, but avoided personal inclusion. The discourse of desirable disclosure draws on the long standing Western tradition of regarding emotions as natural human responses whose expression is important for psychological well-being (Georges 1995). In psychology, this discourse forms an essential part of several key schools of psychotherapy which incorporate this notion into their practices. The prevalence of this view was also apparent in the talk of police officers who presented as culturally competent by discussing the desirability of ventilating emotion following unsettling incidents. Officers claimed that the organization had moved with the times and that such emotion talk would be readily accepted now. This acceptance was contrasted with former traditions in the police whereby such talk would certainly not have been part of the accepted culture.

In glaring contrast to this discourse, a discourse of *unspeakable emotion* was also common. When officers were asked to talk about the specifics of their personal emotional responses and how they dealt with these, they indicated that such discussions mostly did not occur! Howard et al. (2000) argue that a tension exists between these two discourses with officers presenting as culturally competent, while also admitting to the unspeakability of emotion. This tension gives rise to the question of why emotion talk should be silenced within the culture of the modern police force.

In addressing this question, Howard et al. (2000) present an analysis suggesting that the discourse of desirable disclosure is constructed as a threat to the professionalism of the police. This is explained in terms of emotion being variably constructed. Firstly, the desirable disclosure discourse frames emotions as a natural human response, which is most usefully dealt with by full expression. Secondly, emotion is constructed as the antithesis of reason and emotional articulation is therefore regarded as a potentially dangerous activity. Emotional expression was often linked with irrational uncontrolled actions, which was contrasted with the standards required of officers. These performance standards demand that officers are firm, decisive, rational, and controlled. The earlier work of Frewin and Tuffin (1996) made it clear that such standards are regarded as absolutes, with cultural expectations that officers show unequivocal conformity to the required standards.

The dangerousness of emotional disclosure, does not suppress such talk totally. Officers did talk about emotion but, as the Howard et al. (2000) analysis shows, those with whom this talk is shared are carefully chosen. In deciding whom to talk to, issues of maturity, gender, and trustworthiness were all mentioned as being important considerations. With respect to the question of location for such talk, matters of privacy were talked about as being important. The fact that officers indicate that emotion talk does occur, does not counter the general argument that such talk is widely regarded as risky and dangerous. Indeed, the caution with which officers talked about how they manage such talk, highlights the potential danger with which such talk is regarded. While a discourse of unspeakability does operate, officers were quick to point out that this was often breached — but only under carefully chosen circumstances in terms of who was involved in the talk, and with a clear concern that such talk remain private.

Epilogue

This chapter has introduced readers to some features of discursive psychology in the context of the psychology of policing. The general approach has been outlined and the core philosophical assumptions which guide this type of work have been stated. These assumptions all argue for the view that our use of language is designed not to simply describe and represent the world, but to achieve specific tasks in the world. A discursive approach to research regards language as not detached from the world, but inextricably involved in the very construction of that world. Three studies have been presented as illustrations of how discursive work may contribute to our understanding of aspects of police work. These three related discursive studies have considered police attitudes to gay officers, the strong internal pressures which operate within the culture of the police, and finally issues surrounding emotion talk following traumatic incidents on the job.

The studies of police work which have been presented here are pertinent to, and in some cases directly answer, some of the research questions raised at the beginning of this chapter. However, it is also the case that there are many other questions which remain to be addressed. These unanswered questions form part of the future research agenda which may be taken up by those interested in following the path which discursive psychology offers.

One of the aims of this chapter has been to show that questions of attitude, culture and emotion can usefully be explored through studying the language practices which construct these matters in a contextualized and occasioned manner. In a broad sense, it is hoped that the studies presented here serve to illustrate the point that not only does language matter, but that when it comes to the study of human activities (and policing in particular), it does so in profoundly important ways.

References

Atkinson, J.M. 1984. *Our Masters' Voices: The language and body language of politics*. London: Methuen.
Atkinson, A.M. and Drew, P. 1979. *Order in Court: The Organization of Verbal Interaction in Judicial Settings*. London: Macmillan.
Auburn, T., Drake, S. and Willig, C. 1995. " 'You punched him, didn't you?': Versions of violence in accusatory interviews". *Discourse and Society* 6: 353–386.
Auburn, T., Lea, S. and Drake, S. 1999. "' It's your opportunity to be truthful': Disbelief, mundane reasoning and the investigation of crime". In *Applied Discourse Analysis: Social and Psychological Interventions*, C. Willig (ed.), 44–65. Buckingham: Open University Press.
Austin, J.L. 1962. *How To Do Things With Words*. Oxford: Clarendon Press.
Beehr, T.A., Johnson, L.B. and Nieva, R. 1995. "Occupational stress: Coping of police and their spouses". *Journal of Organizational Behavior* 16: 3–25.

Billig, M. 1985. "Prejudice, categorization and particularization: From a perceptual to a rhetorical approach". *European Journal of Social Psychology* 15: 79–103.
Burr, V. 1995. *An Introduction to Social Constructionism*. London: Routledge,
de Sousa, R. 1987. *The Rationality of Emotion*. Cambridge, MA: The MIT Press.
Drew, P. 1985 "Analysing the use of language in courtroom interaction". In *Handbook of Discourse Analysis, Vol. 3*, T. A. Van Dijk (ed.), 133–147. London: Academic Press.
Drew, P. 1992. "Contested evidence in courtroom cross-examination: the case of a trial for rape". In *Talk at Work: Interaction in institutional settings*, P. Drew and J. Heritage (eds), 470–520. Cambridge: Cambridge University Press.
Edwards, D. 1997. *Discourse and Cognition*. London: Sage.
Edwards, D. and Potter, J. 1992. *Discursive Psychology*. London: Sage.
Frewin, K. and Tuffin, K. 1998. "Police status, conformity and internal pressure: A discursive analysis of police culture". *Discourse and Society* 9: 173–185.
Georges, E. 1995. "A cultural and historical perspective on confession". In *Emotion, Disclosure and Health*, J. W. Pennebaker (ed.), 11–24. Washington, DC: American Psychological Association.
Gergen, K. J. 1985. "The social constructionist movement in modern psychology". *American Psychologist* 40: 266–275.
Gill, R. 1993. "Justifying injustice: Broadcasters' accounts of inequality in radio". In *Discourse Analytic Research: Repertoires and Readings of Texts in Action*, E. Burman and I. Parker (eds), 75–93. London: Routledge.
Gill, R. 1995. "Relativism, reflexivity and politics: Interrogating discourse analysis from a feminist perspective". In *Feminism and Discourse*, S. Wilkinson and C. Kitzinger (eds), 165–188. London: Sage.
Harré, R. 1986. "An outline of the social constructionist point of view". In *The Social Construction of Emotions*, R. Harré (ed.), 2–14. Oxford: Basil Blackwell.
Harré, R. and Gillett, G. 1994. *The Discursive Mind*. London: Sage.
Homosexual Law Reform Act. 1986. Wellington: New Zealand Government Printer.
Howard, C., Tuffin, K. and Stephens, C. 2000. "Unspeakable emotion: A discursive analysis of police talk about reactions to trauma". *Journal of Language and Social Psychology* 19: 295–314.
Human Rights Act. 1993. Wellington: New Zealand Government Printer.
Kline, P. 1988. *Psychology Exposed, or, the Emperors New Clothes*. London: Routledge.
La Piere, R. T. 1934. "Attitudes vs actions". *Social Forces* 13: 230–237.
McConville, M., Sanders, A. and Leng, R. 1991. *The Case for the Prosecution: Police Suspects and the Construction of Criminality*. London: Routledge.
Pollner, M. 1987. *Mundane Reason: Reality in Everyday and Sociological Discourse*. Cambridge: Cambridge University Press.
Pomerantz, A. M. 1987. "Descriptions in legal settings". In *Talk and Social Organization*, G. Button and J. R. E. Lee (eds), 226–243. Clevedon, Avon: Multilingual Matters.
Potter, J. 1996. *Representing Reality*. London: Sage.
Potter, J. and Wetherell, M. 1987. *Discourse and Social Psychology: Beyond attitudes and behavior*. London: Sage.
Praat, A. and Tuffin, K. 1996. "Police discourses of homosexual men in New Zealand". *Journal of Homosexuality* 31: 57–73.

Reddy, M.J. 1993. "The conduit metaphor: A case of frame conflict in our language about language". In *Metaphor and Thought* (2nd ed.), A. Ortony (ed.), 164–201. Cambridge: Cambridge University Press.

Stenner, P. 1993. "Discoursing jealousy". In *Discourse Analytic Research: Repertoires and readings of texts in action*, E.Burman and I. Parker (eds.), 114–134. London: Routledge.

Stephens, C. 1996. "The impact of trauma on health and the moderating effects of social support: A study with the New Zealand Police". Unpublished doctoral dissertation, Massey University, New Zealand.

Stratton, J.G. 1981. "Pressures in law enforcement marriages: Some considerations". In *Stress and Police Personnel*, L.Territo and H.J.Vetter (eds), 233–241. Boston: Allyn and Bacon.

Tuffin, K. and Howard, C. 2002. "Demystifying discourse analysis: Theory, method and practice". In *How To Analyse Talk in Institutional Settings: A Casebook of Methods*, A. McHoul and M. Rapley (eds), 199–208. London: Continuum International.

Watson, D.R. 1983. "The presentation of victim and motive in discourse: The case of police interrogations and interviews". *Victimology: An International Journal* 8: 31–52.

Watson, D.R. 1990. "Some features of the elicitation of confessions in murder interrogations". In *Interactional Competence*, G. Psathas (ed.), 263–295. Maryland: University Press of America.

Wetherell, M. 1995. "Romantic discourse and feminist analysis: Interrogating investment, power and desire". In *Feminism and Discourse*, S. Wilkinson and C. Kitzinger (eds), 128–144. London: Sage.

Whalen, M.R. and Zimmerman, D.H. 1990. "Describing trouble: Practical epistemology in citizen calls to the police". *Language in Society* 19: 465–92.

Wicker, A.W. 1969. "Attitudes versus actions: The relationship of overt and behavioral responses to attitude objects". *Journal of Social Issues* 25: 41–78.

Wittgenstein, L. 1953. *Philosophical Investigations* (G.E.M. Anscombe, Trans.). Oxford: Basil Blackwell.

Wooffitt, R. 1993. "Analysing accounts". In *Researching Social Life*, N.Gilbert (ed.), 287–305. London: Sage.

CHAPTER 4

The impact of contemporary communication and information technologies on police organizations

Andrew J. Flanagin
University of California, Santa Barbara, USA

Police in the United States have long embraced the use of communication and information technologies in the conduct of their work. As early as 1877, police organizations employed the telegraph to bridge distances and improve their core communication processes (Manning 1992). Today, computer-assisted dispatching, mobile data computers and terminals, and information-based data repositories are among the tools used to improve enforcement effectiveness, organizational efficiency, and officer safety. Although positive effects are certainly not guaranteed (Brynjolfsson 1993; O'Mahoney & Barley 1999; Sproull & Kiesler 1991), contemporary organizations are experiencing considerable benefits from modern communication and information technologies and are undergoing consequential and fundamental changes in form and function. However, compared to workers in other organizations, police may not be experiencing the same degree of benefit from these tools. The structure of police organizations, the nature of police work, and the demands of effective information processing combine to pose considerable barriers that inhibit police officers' ability to benefit fully from modern communication and information technologies.

These issues are explored first by examining the potential benefits of modern communication and information technologies in contemporary organizations. Communication and information technologies are considered in terms of their intra- and interorganizational impacts, as well as their influence as a basis for organizing. Next, the nature of police organizations and police work is considered by focusing on information, intelligence, and operational strategies.[1] Based on this assessment, the use (and lack of use) of modern communication and information technologies in police organizations is examined by considering police knowledge, skill, and the nature of successful information processing. Finally, and in spite of the considerable obstacles to the effective use of these tools, strategies are suggested whereby police organizations may make better use of modern communication and information technologies.

Benefits of modern communication and information technologies for contemporary organizations

Technological advances have profoundly increased the capabilities of contemporary organizations. Compared to more traditional means, electronic communication and information technologies can carry more information faster, at a lower cost, to more people while also offering increased data communality, processing, and powerful recombinant capabilities (Beniger 1996; Fulk & DeSanctis 1995). Furthermore, the use of advanced electronic technologies in organizations is widespread and commonplace, due to the development of a dependable technical infrastructure, decreasing technology costs and, in many cases, the achievement of a critical mass of users (Gurbaxani 1990; Markus 1990). The use of these technologies has resulted in substantial changes to intraorganizational relations, interorganizational relationships, and contemporary organizational forms.

Intraorganizational relationships

Research on technologies such as electronic mail (Fulk 1993; Markus 1994; Rice 1992; Schmitz & Fulk 1991), videoconferencing (Finn, Sellen & Wilbur 1997), group support systems (Benbasat & Lim 1993; Seibold, Heller & Contractor 1994), and corporate intranets (Hills 1997), illustrates the capacity of electronic technologies to alter intraorganizational relations and to extend organizational scope and reach. Electronic communication and information technologies have been credited with extending the number and variety of people involved in organizational decisions (Huber 1990; Sproull & Kiesler 1991), diminishing temporal and physical interaction constraints (Eveland & Bikson 1988; Kaye & Byrne 1986), and increasing horizontal and vertical communication in the organization (Hinds & Kiesler 1995). Pinsonneault and Kraemer (1990) reported that technological advancements have affected group processes in organizations by increasing consensus reaching, increasing confidence in group decisions, increasing members' satisfaction with group process and group decisions, and decreasing decision time. Within organizations, electronic technologies affect the potential for, and the dynamics of, interpersonal relationships. By virtue of increased connectivity and communality among individuals (Fulk, Flanagin, Kalman, Monge & Ryan 1996), electronic technologies alter organizational dynamics that were, a generation ago, based primarily on proximate, hierarchical relations, where both the flow and control of information were relatively predictable. In view of new technologies, communication with others is faster and easier and information is more widely distributed and more readily available to a broad range of organizational members.

Moreover, as these tools become more prevalent, organizations are relying on increasingly dispersed groups of workers in order to accomplish organizational goals (DeSanctis & Poole 1997; Fulk & Collins-Jarvis 2001). Accordingly, the study of electronic communication tools designed to help group members collaborate has become an important area of study in recent years (Dennis, George, Jessup, Nunamaker & Vogel 1988; Huber 1990; Scott 1999) and its continued examination is perhaps more important now than ever before (Jelassi & Beauclair 1987).

Interorganizational relationships

Connectivity *among* organizations has also become increasingly important as economic, technological, and social factors enable and encourage organizational linkages. There are several advantages for organizations that work together in networks to achieve their goals. Network relations aid organizations in gaining knowledge and learning (Powell, Koput & Smith-Doerr 1996), provide a competitive advantage (Jarillo 1988), and buffer organizations from failure (Miner, Amburgey & Stearns 1990). In addition, interorganizational links serve to increase network centrality and influence (Boje & Whetten 1981) and provide firms with greater stability and flexibility than pure market relations by providing access to complementary resources and knowledge (Tödtling 1992).

Organizations, for example, are experiencing economic benefits from closer coordination of their activities. Tools such as "just in time" or electronic data interchange (EDI) technologies enable firms to link together in the value chain, thus reducing coordination costs and increasing profits (Davidow & Malone 1992; Ferioli & Migliarese 1996). In addition, as linkages among organizations become more prevalent, organizational interconnectivity propagates based on competitive advantages (Jarillo 1988; Porter 1985), institutional pressures (Abrahamson & Rosenkopf 1993; DiMaggio & Powell 1983; Flanagin 2000), and specific organizational benefits (Chesbrough & Teece 1996; Joyce, McGee & Slocum 1997; Mowshowitz 1994). Of course, appropriate organizational structure depends on the tasks being performed (Ahuja & Carley 1999), the type of innovations incorporated or produced (Chesbrough & Teece 1996), and managers' skills (Joyce et al. 1997).

New forms of organizing

Organizational *forms* are also changing as a result of advances in communication and information technologies. By facilitating coordination tasks once performed by middle managers, electronic technologies result in the "flattening" of the organizational hierarchy. New methods of horizontal coordination decrease lag times in the shipment of goods and the need for physical proximity among individuals, while increasing the importance of well-coordinated communication and information flow between organizations. This increased connectivity has prompted a return to market relations among organizations (as opposed to vertical integration), where organizations are tightly coupled in the value chain (Malone & Rockart 1991; Malone, Yates & Benjamin 1987).

So profound are the effects of electronic technologies that researchers posit the emergence of the "virtual" (Davidow & Malone 1992) or "network" forms of organization (Miles & Snow 1986; Nohria & Berkley 1994; Nohria & Eccles 1992; Powell 1990), that exist irrespective of the physical proximity of organizational members. Organizations are increasingly turning to network forms that link multiple organizations to one another and stress complementarity, relational communication, interdependence, and high trust over more contractual or formal relations (Miles & Snow 1984, 1986; Powell 1990). These organizational forms are based on "permeable and continuously changing interfaces between company, supplier, and customers" (Davidow & Malone 1992: 5–6) that rely on advanced technologies for their sustenance.

The nature of police organizations and police work

Although contemporary communication and information technologies deliver substantial intra- and interorganizational benefits, even altering the form of modern organizations in the process, the nature of police organizations and police work mediate these benefits. Police organizations are a form of traditional rational bureaucracy, with a clear system of super- and subordination and activities that are dictated in fixed ways as duties. Authority is based on the position of the office held and personnel are concentrated at the foundation of a flat hierarchy, as patrol officers and in communication/dispatch centers. In this manner, "the social organization of policing amplifies the asymmetrical nature of information flow in which information...concentrates at the 'bottom' of the organization" (Manning 1992:388).

Rather than controlling their external environments, police organizations largely react to them in the conduct of event-driven tasks (see, however, Chapter 2). Because these environments can be extremely unpredictable, and the consequences of being unprepared can be substantial, police organizations hold considerable slack resources in reserve in the form of personnel and other assets. In the realization of the goals of protecting and serving members of the public, "the core technology of the police is situated decision making with the potential for application of violence (Bittner 1990)" (Manning 1992:354).

Although there are clear rules and regulations that guide police behavior (see Chapter 3), because "police-relevant events are sporadic and uncertain in appearance, duration, extent, and potential" police often rely on the use of "*situational rationality* that takes into account the particular times and places of events, rather than a set of firm rules, regulations, or laws" (Manning 1992:357). Thus, police work takes place in an environment distinguished by decentralized decision-making, problem-oriented management, and the exercise of discretionary powers. Consequently, police knowledge is believed to be highly contextual and is based on officers' implicit understanding of the nature of events and situations.

Types of information

Manning (1992) identifies 3 types of information gathered by police: primary information, secondary information, and tertiary information. Primary information constitutes the vast majority of data encountered by police and consists of the raw information that is processed in the normal conduct of police work. Examples include information that patrol officers might record in a personal log and discuss with other officers. Secondary information is that information that has been processed within policing, such as the same log information already mentioned, once it is recorded in a police report and made available to officers in other divisions (such as detectives). Secondary information thus changes in both location and format. Tertiary information is "managerial" information that is processed more than once; for instance, between several units. Administrative authority often rests on the exercise of tertiary information.

Although crucial to the information processing and sharing functions of the police organization, primary information is often not widely shared among officers (apart, that is, from round-table discussions in briefings), due to the personalized practices of information storage. Because of this, "most of the information that exists in policing is primary data possessed by aggregated records or files or the information stored mentally by an officer" (Manning 1992:370). Secondary and tertiary information, by contrast, are most often codified and handled in a manner that enables reliable storage, retrieval, and recombination. As a consequence, secondary and tertiary information are best suited to take advantage of the substantial capabilities of advanced communication and information technologies.

Forms of police intelligence

Police intelligence, or the "systematized, classified, and analyzed information that has been encoded in police-relevant categories," can be prospective, applied, or retrospective (Manning 1992:365). Prospective intelligence, such as that used for criminal targeting, is gathered in advance of a crime or problem and is intended to help anticipate and control the phenomenon of interest. By contrast, applied intelligence is used to link known deeds that have already occurred with previously named suspects. Consequently, applied intelligence is often the basis of detective work. Retrospective intelligence, however, is sought out from past records as part of current investigations. Retrospective intelligence occurs in the normal conduct of police work and consists of such activities as checking for outstanding warrants for criminal suspects confronted in connection with events that are in progress. Recent training efforts in crime and intelligence analysis are aimed at further developing prospective and applied intelligence within police organizations. However, retrospective intelligence remains a primary area where advanced communication and information technologies may extend the capability of the police officer.

Operational strategies

Operational strategies describe the ways in which police cope with the various activities that warrant their attention. There are three main operational strategies (Manning 1992; Reiss 1971) that interact with the type of information and intelligence in order to produce the outcome goals of the police. *Proactive* strategies are used to create the conditions of crime in order to catch criminals. A prime example is a police "sting operation" designed to lure criminals into committing illegal acts in a highly controlled environment in which apprehension is more certain. Proactive policing strategies rely on prospective intelligence in order to predict events. In similar fashion, *preventive* strategies require substantial intelligence on past and potential behaviors and are used to alter, prevent, or intervene in criminal situations. Examples are community crime prevention programs. Although Manning (1992) notes that preventive strategies are not central to the specified aims of policing, which are focused on response and control over prevention, prevention is increasingly emphasized through such initiatives as community-oriented policing (Rosenbaum 1994; see Chapter 2). Finally, the vast majority of police work relies on *reactive* strategies that are invoked in response to specific events. Reactive strategies take advantage of both retrospective and applied intelligence and encourage the officer to act largely autonomously.

Overall, the nature of police work and police organizations, the types of information processed in the conduct of police work, the character of police intelligence, and the various operational strategies invoked by the police combine to form a specific environment to which advanced communication and information technologies may be applied. Although the capabilities of these tools are vast, and their effects on contemporary organizations can be substantial (as documented above), the specific environment of police work holds somewhat idiosyncratic possibilities for the effective and widespread use of these tools. The following section explores this in detail.

The use (and nonuse) of modern communication and information technologies in police organizations

Police in the United States have a long history of employing technologies to aid them in their work. According to Manning (1992), as early as 1877, police and fire departments in Albany, New York used the telegraph to connect remote officers. This was followed by the use of teletype by Pennsylvania State police in 1923, the use of one-way radio in Detroit in 1928, two-way radio in Boston in 1934, and the widespread use of the automobile in the 1930s. More recent innovations include centralized call collection and computer-assisted dispatching (CAD) and information-based data repositories among decentralized populations of police organizations (Flanagin, Monge & Fulk 2001; Monge, Fulk, Kalman, Flanagin, Parnassa & Rumsey 1998; Monge, Fulk, Parnassa, Flanagin, Rumsey & Kalman 1999). However, although police organizations have adopted a wide variety of technologies, there exist considerable barriers specific to police organizations that may inhibit the wholesale acceptance (and attendant benefits) of advanced communication and information technologies in particular.

Tacit versus explicit officer knowledge

Nonaka (1994) argues that, in order to prosper in uncertain environments, organizations must not only react to environmental forces by processing information efficiently, but must also create new knowledge so that they can solve recurring problems more effectively. In his view, organizational knowledge creation occurs through a continuous dialog between what he terms "tacit" and "explicit" knowledge. Ultimately, knowledge creation occurs as information is transferred between explicit and tacit knowledge across levels of the organization (i.e., individual to group to organizational).

Explicit or codified knowledge is "transmittable in formal, systematic language" whereas *tacit* knowledge "has a personal quality, which makes it hard to formalize and communicate. Tacit knowledge is deeply rooted in action, commitment, and involvement in a specific context" (Nonaka 1994: 16). Thus, although explicit knowledge can be codified and secured in formal records such as archives and databases, tacit knowledge resides in individuals' situational understanding and is accumulated through shared experience.

Knowledge creation, through the transfer between tacit and explicit knowledge, can take many forms. For instance, sharing explicit knowledge in organizations is relatively straightforward: because it can be readily codified and transported without difficulty, explicit knowledge is easily perpetuated in databases of information, procedure manuals, and handbooks. The transfer of explicit organizational knowledge from one person to another is thus a straightforward matter of information processing. By contrast, because the accumulation of tacit knowledge depends on situated individual experiences, its transfer is more complex. Tacit knowledge is acquired only through shared experience. Therefore, passing tacit knowledge from one organizational member to another requires socialization into the organization's culture and the practices of its members, a process that requires learning organizational norms and modifying one's own behavior accordingly (Jablin 1987).

The nature of police officers' skill

Tacit and explicit knowledge are critical in understanding the nature of organizational members' skill and the role this plays in police organizations' use of modern communication and information technologies. Stinchcombe (1990:21) defines skill as the "capacity to routinize most of the activity that comes to a given work role in an uncertain environment." In this view, skill is the knowledge of many routines, or sets of tasks used to solve specific problems, and the ability to select the proper routine under uncertain conditions. Highly skilled workers are adept at choosing from among many routines they have mastered, according to the demands of the situation, by means of "principles of decision" that guide their choice. Thus, skill consists of "the capacity to use the news about what uncertainty has come in, to decide what to do and then to do it … in a fast and effective way" (Stinchcombe 1990:32). Less skilled workers, by contrast, know fewer skills and/or have less need or ability to choose from among them. With completely *un*skilled work, all decisions are prespecified and the task is entirely routinized.

Highly skilled workers thus rely to a large extent on tacit knowledge whereas explicit knowledge is sufficient to accomplish most low skill work. The principles of decision are learned by situated experience, are accumulated over time, and are guided by fellow organizational members. As such, the principles of decision, and even the routines, of highly skilled workers are difficult to articulate and pass on, absent shared experience. Zuboff (1988) elaborates on the nature of this type of "action-centered" skill, noting that it requires high sentience, dependence on action and context, and high personalism.

Obstacles to the use of advanced communication and information technologies in police organizations

Although the positive influence of advanced communication and information technologies on contemporary organizations can be substantial, police organizations do not seem to benefit to the extent that other types of organizations do. In fact, there exist considerable obstacles in the adoption of these tools that might explain why their use has been limited in scope, as compared to other types of contemporary organizations. According to Manning (1992:350), "information technologies, the most important and influential kinds of technology, have been constrained by the traditional structure of policing and by the traditional role of the officer" and, as a consequence, "the computer revolution in policing...has yet to take place" (p. 390). Reasons for the relatively low return from these technologies in police organizations include (a) the conditions of information processing for the effective use of these tools and (b) the character of organizational knowledge and the nature of police officers' skill.

Barriers to implementation: Information characteristics for the effective use of technological support
There are several obstacles to obtaining the complete benefits from advanced technologies that stem from the requisite characteristics of information required for their most effective use. The effective use of advanced technologies for wide scale communication and information sharing requires that information be accurate, complete, and readily processable. Accuracy and comprehensiveness are obvious requirements for information used in police work. Whereas up-to-date and precise information may improve decision-making dramatically, inaccurate or incomplete information cannot be trusted and is of little value. Indeed, the largely reactive strategies invoked by patrol officers imply that data on criminal suspects and situations must be current, accurate, and easily accessible.

Furthermore, information must exist in a format that is suitable for efficient processing in order to be useful — more specifically, information that is to be shared widely through electronic means must be readily stored, easily searched, and simply interpreted. In order to accomplish this in view of the rich primary data encountered by officers in the conduct of their work, information is necessarily streamlined, by reducing the amount of raw information to be processed and by increasing the capacity to process information (a process Weber referred to as "rationalization"). Although computer technologies are proficient at increasing the human capability to process large amounts of information (Beniger 1990), data reduction prior to input is unavoidable in order to handle the copious amounts of primary information encountered in the field.[2]

Data reduction occurs by use of set formats (e.g., standard report forms) and standard codes that are invoked to reduce a wide range of potentially diverse information to a manageable number of categories that can be interpreted easily. Each of these methods, however, necessarily neglects information detail. Whereas explicit knowledge meets the conditions of data reduction relatively well, tacit knowledge, which constitutes the basis for the majority of patrol officers' information, does not. Although the goal of effective data reduction, however tenuous, is to maintain information fidelity while also retaining information richness and depth, often "what is entered into computer records is a severely edited version of the primary reality encountered on the street by officers" (Manning 1992:372). As a consequence, the situated rationality endemic to the patrol officer's work is often lost with the application of electronic communication and information technologies. Furthermore, because primary information is the *basis* for both secondary and tertiary information, the loss of primary information tends to endure as the information is forwarded to others.

Barriers to implementation: Police knowledge and skill
As already discussed, police labor is highly skilled and is formed from tacit knowledge that relies heavily on officers' use of situational rationality. For the most part, police work is reactive, with strategies invoked in response to specific events. Furthermore, reactive strategies take advantage primarily of retrospective intelligence by seeking links between ongoing events and past data. Thus, successful police work hinges on a relatively esoteric situational understanding and the ability to quickly and accurately arrive at an appropriate decision. As Nonaka (1994) points out, the tacit knowledge required to be successful under such conditions is difficult to transfer from person to person, except by active and continued socialization.

Therefore, police work is not conducive to the type of distillation and categorization required of most advanced communication and information technologies (as described in the previous section). In fact, the application of situational rationality in the field is best learned *in the field*, and is only tangentially supported by the use of electronic technologies. In effect, such tools are used most effectively to *augment* officers' decision making and to provide additional data that might inform them, and not to routinize or automate their work (as is the case in most other types of organizations). Thus, widely used technologies, such as the two-way radio and mobile data terminals that are linked to databases of information (e.g., Department of Motor Vehicles information), inform officers' actions but do not determine them.

This highlights the unique nature of police work and the attendant problems of applying technologies to policing in the field. From an information processing standpoint, vast amounts of primary data "in raw and unintegrated form, are organized and stored in chunked and coded units in individual officers' memories. When (or because) data are full and rich, they are not entered into the computer in many cases..." (Manning 1992:371–372). Overall, the use of communication and information technologies effectively in the field, in any manner that fundamentally alters the nature of highly skilled police work, is a complex issue not easily resolved by the application of technologies to complex human behaviors.

Consequently, the most effective use of technologies for the transfer of tacit knowledge from officer to officer takes place outside of the field, and not in "live" situations. For example, patrol car videotapes of traffic stops have been used not only to document officers' activities (in order to provide evidence to build legal cases against criminal suspects) but also for training new officers. Videotapes of traffic stops can serve as examples of both proper and improper field behaviors. Similarly, situation "simulators" that project fictitious scenarios (based on real events provided by experienced officers) enable junior officers to experience realistic conditions, without the considerable risk involved in the field. In both cases, the goal of these tools is to capture tacit knowledge and make it more explicit (in videotape form or within the scenarios provided by the simulator). In turn, by studying the events and practicing how to approach various situations, this explicit knowledge is again made tacit, and officers' skill levels are raised in a reduced risk, controlled environment.

Strategies for more effective use of modern communication and information technologies in police organizations

In spite of these considerable obstacles, a number of strategies exist that might help police organizations to enjoy greater benefits from the use of modern communication and information technologies. Although many of these strategies are currently in use in contemporary police organizations, their use is uneven, due to differences such as organizational size, the amount of funding available, the perceived need for the functions supported by these technologies, officers' technical training, the acceptance of these tools by administration, and a diversity of interests in using these technologies that can arise from several additional factors. Thus, several opportunities exist whereby police organizations may benefit, or benefit more completely, from the use of contemporary communication and information technologies.

First, one means by which to augment the retrospective intelligence of the patrol officer is to link together a greater number of the core databases of information that are germane to officers' work. For example, the use of Department of Motor Vehicles data, criminal records, and other databases currently available to the patrol officer serves to provide relevant and timely information at the point at which it is needed most. By linking an even *larger* number of nonredundant information sources together, this information base can be greatly expanded. Initiatives such as the National Crime Information Center (NCIC), a comprehensive information system first established in 1967, provide precisely this type of resource. Furthermore, with the recent introduction of the NCIC 2000, these capabilities have been vastly increased in many police organizations: NCIC 2000 serves 80,000 local, state, and federal law enforcement agencies in the U.S. through 17 databases that provide access to mug shots, stolen vehicles, articles, and guns records, wanted and missing persons information, gang data, and suspected terrorist profiles. In addition, it also provides investigative tools such as fingerprint matching and online ad hoc searches (U.S. Department of Justice 1999). In this manner, "as law enforcement enters the 21st century, NCIC 2000 provides capabilities to fight crime that law enforcement officers lacked" prior to the advent of these tools.

Second, the collection of primary information by the patrol officer is a key element of effective policing that can be enhanced by the use of technologies. With the use of instant or digital photographs and information solicited directly from individuals, officers are able to build databases of known gang members, for example. These databases, in turn, add to the retrospective information that officers rely upon and serve to provide valuable tools for the identification of gang members at subsequent points in time. Electronic tools thus enable officers to record and share primary information more effectively and reduce the substantial reliance on what Manning (1992:366) terms "officer's good memory, shrewd judgment, and patience". It is important to note, however, that the collection and use of personal information must always be tempered by legal and ethical guidelines of appropriate use and privacy protection.

Third, greater reach and contact can be achieved by making advanced communication technologies more readily available to officers. For example, the use of mobile data terminals (MDTs) and mobile data computers in patrol cars serves to put officers in better contact with dispatchers, one another, and directly with data sources. Similarly, cellular phones may serve to augment officer communication, and can be used to verify assignments and to discuss tasks with fellow officers (Manning 1996). The potential of these tools also increases the chances of the formation of advice networks among officers and encourages wider information sharing in the field. Furthermore, this type of direct contact may become more important with the current shift from fewer multiple officer patrol units to a higher number of single officer patrols. However, as is always the case with technological implementation, technologies can be used in ways quite different than intended (Sproull & Kiesler 1991). Such is the case, for example, with the implementation of the cell phone among patrol officers, used for such diverse and unintended tasks as to order pizza and even for phone sex (see Manning 1996).

Fourth, there are a number of ways in which to facilitate the transfer of tacit knowledge among officers, and to disseminate the type of information that constitutes the situated decision-making that is the core of officers' work. For instance, following the lead of corporate information systems, police organizations might benefit from the establishment of "best practices" or "expert systems" databases. Such data repositories hold information, often in the form of scenarios or descriptive accounts, provided by experienced organizational members. Organizational members draw upon this information when they encounter situations with which they are unfamiliar or that may be atypical. In such cases, the information contained in these systems is often valuable in providing a course of action, based on previous strategies that have proven useful. The establishment of such databases of information might be especially useful in capturing and retaining information from organizational members who are no longer with the organization and for use in officer training. Of course, a key issue with such systems is incentives for encouraging the input of information from officers, as addressed later.

Fifth, and relatedly, computer-mediated communication has successfully been employed to minimize status differences among communication partners. For instance, gender differences have been reduced when users take advantage of *anonymous* computer-mediated communication (e.g., online text-based communication, such as "chat" features and electronic mail). Gopal, Mirana, Robichaux and Bostrom (1997), for example, found that females preferred communicating in computer-mediated environments because of the anonymity afforded by the technology. In addition, Flanagin, Tiyaamornwong, O'Connor and Seibold (2002) found that males and females differed in their experiences using computer-mediated communication (CMC). Their findings suggest that whereas men may have favored face-to-face communication, in order to maintain the advantages they experience in that environment, women may have preferred the anonymous environment of CMC, possibly in order to recapture some of the equality lost in face-to-face encounters. Accordingly, Dubrovsky, Kiesler and Sethna (1991) found that females who were typically uncomfortable with or discouraged from participating in groups were more at ease when participating in CMC environments than in a face-to-face atmosphere. Although these studies explored sex differences in particular, these findings suggest that there is a potential to equalize status more generally with the use of anonymous communication supported by communication technologies.

For police, this suggests that communication and idea sharing via anonymous means might serve to reduce status differentials.[3] Doing so might, in turn, promote a more open exchange of ideas and tacit knowledge that is more readily shared. Practical applications may include such things as the use of anonymous "listservs" or electronic bulletin boards whereby officers would be able to share opinions and experiences without fear of reprimand or appearing ignorant. Especially important might be the benefits of anonymous communication and data seeking among less senior officers, who may have legitimate reasons to "save face" among their colleagues. Furthermore, truly anonymous communication might also serve to make public some of the more private moments that officers encounter in efforts to seek opinions on procedure and advice about how to perform their duties. However, the successful implementation and use of these tools relies on high *trust* — of fellow officers, of the integrity of the technical system, and of the police administration (Bok 1989; Cummings & Bromily 1996; Jarvenpaa & Leidner 1999; Lewis & Weigert 1985; Monge et al. 1998). As Manning (1992:384) points out, "Police in lower-level segments are in danger of losing discretion and autonomy as on-line monitoring of their activities becomes more common and technological devices permit increased review of their actions and choices." Thus, in order to be successful, officers must be certain that communication assumed to be anonymous remains anonymous, under all conditions.

Sixth, and finally, the necessity to encourage *collective action* among several organizational members is at the core of the success of many of these ideas. The creation of some communication and information resources, such as a database of "best practices" information or an effective communication system wherein ideas are openly shared, depends on the collective action or participation among many organizational members. Particularly when each member holds unique information, everyone's contribution is important because "when information resources are *distributed*, participation in the information system by each member is a necessary condition for the success of the communal endeavor" (Fulk et al. 1996:73). This suggests that personal motivations for contributing, and individual perceptions of the resource, are both important in the realization of these communication and information goals.

However, there exist two key obstacles in the successful provision of these "public goods": "free riding", which occurs when participants enjoy benefits without helping to contribute to or maintain the public good (Connolly & Thorn 1990; Hardin 1968; Olson 1965; Sweeney 1973), and disincentives to contribute that occur for some public goods because early contributors must invest in the absence of contributions by others, and thus receive little in terms of direct, immediate benefits from their contributions. In such cases, each participant is rewarded for waiting until others contribute, thus serving as a disincentive for early contributors.

One means by which to reduce free riding among users, and to motivate the contribution of resources in the absence of a fully provided good, is to implement *incentives* for information sharing among officers. For example, direct incentives for contributing information or communicating about certain aspects of one's job (e.g., monetary or other compensation), disincentives for noncontribution (e.g., punishment or loss of resources), or aid (e.g., secretarial or other support) in the input of ideas are strategies that might help to provide collective goals. However, the key is to maintain a balance between incentives and disincentives in order that the problem does not shift from the nonprovision of valuable information to the overprovision of useless information (Fulk et al. 1996; Monge et al. 1998). Thus, stimulating collective action within police organizations is a crucial, yet difficult, task.

Epilogue

Modern communication and information technologies have fundamentally altered connections between people within and among contemporary organizations. In many instances, this transformation has facilitated dramatic improvements in organizational efficiency and individual effectiveness. However, although police have adopted a wide variety of these tools, there exist considerable barriers specific to police organizations that may inhibit the wholesale acceptance (and attendant benefits) of advanced communication and information technologies.

Although police organizations in the United States continue to take advantage of technologies to improve their operation, structural factors and information processing concerns inhibit the degree to which police officers stand to benefit from modern communication and information tools. Due to the focus and structure of police organizations, where the majority of workers (patrol officers and communication personnel) are located at the bottom of a relatively flat hierarchy, "information is most used in reactive strategies where a suspect is known, a crime is known to have been committed, and a prior record exists on the suspect. The most important information is retrospective intelligence...[and]...computer-based information is most relevant and used in doing routine 'housekeeping tasks'" (Manning 1992:383). Consequently, the most important application of computer technologies occurs in personnel and organizational administration and in the relatively specific areas of police work where proactive and preventive strategies can take advantage of prospective and applied intelligence. By contrast, patrol officers will rarely take advantage of the majority of these communication, information, and analytical tools. As a result, the greatest potential benefit of modern communication and information technologies, as realized in other types of contemporary organizations, may go untapped within police organizations.

Nonetheless, there exist several possibilities for the more effective use of these tools in street level policing, including strategies to link core information and officers in the field, greater collection of primary information, greater reach and contact among officers, means of facilitating the transfer of tacit knowledge, computer-mediated communication used to minimize status differences, and means by which to encourage collective action among police. Overall, although substantial obstacles exist, it would seem that taking better advantage of modern communication and information technologies in police organizations remains an important, and attainable, goal.

Notes

1. Throughout this chapter, local level police organizations (as opposed to Sheriffs' Departments or other agencies) within the United States are the focus of attention. As a result, the work of the patrol officer is emphasized, due to the high proportion of patrol officers relative to other roles in most local level police organizations (Manning 1996). Furthermore, advanced communication and information technologies are considered, as opposed to other types of technologies, because of the substantial documented benefits of these tools in contemporary organizations.

2. Although the problem of data reduction in order to enable searchability is substantial, there are marked advantages to technologies that are able to record the true richness of officers' experience (e.g., high quality video data recorders that are feasible for use in the field). Consequently, such tools provide important alternatives to relying on officers' fallible memories. For instance, video evidence from a crime scene can be used to review details that may have been overlooked at the time of the initial investigation. Overall, although accuracy and comprehensiveness are potential strengths of these tools, the difficulties in ease of processing suggest that they may be appropriate for only certain types of police work.

3. In fact, anonymous telephone numbers and web sites are in use in many police organizations today.

References

Abrahamson, E. and Rosenkopf, L. 1993. "Institutional and competitive bandwagons: Using mathematical modeling as a tool to explore innovation diffusion". *Academy of Management Review* 18: 487–517.

Ahuja, M.K. and Carley, K.M. 1999. "Network structure in virtual organizations". *Organization Science* 10: 741–757.

Benbasat, I. and Lim, L. 1993. "The effects of group, task, context, and technology variables on the usefulness of group support systems: A meta-analysis of experimental studies". *Small Group Research* 24: 430–462.

Beniger, J.R. 1990. "Conceptualizing information technology as organization, and vice-versa". In *Organizations and Communication Technology*, J. Fulk and C. Steinfeld (eds), 29–43. Newbury Park, CA: Sage.

Beniger, J.R. 1996. "Who shall control cyberspace?" In *Communication and Cyberspace: Social Interaction in an Electronic Environment*, L. Strate, R. Jacobson and S.B. Gibson (eds), 49–58. Cresskill, NJ: Hampton Press.

Bittner, E. 1990. *Aspects of police work*. Boston: Northeastern University Press.

Boje, D.M. and Whetten, D.A. 1981. "Strategies and constraints affecting centrality and attributions of influence in interorganizational networks". *Administrative Science Quarterly* 26: 378–395.

Bok, S. 1989. *Secrets: On Concealment and Revelation*. New York: Vintage.

Brynjolfsson, E. 1993. "The productivity paradox of information technology: Review and assessment". *Communications of the ACM* 36: 67–77.

Chesbrough, H.W. and Teece, D.J. 1996 "When is virtual virtuous? Organizing for innovation". *Harvard Business Review* 74: 65–71.

Connolly, T. and Thorn, B.K. 1990. "Discretionary databases: Theory, data, and implications". In *Organizations and Communication Technology*, J. Fulk and C. Steinfeld (eds), 219–233. Newbury Park, CA: Sage.

Cummings, L.L. and Bromiley, P. 1996. "The organizational trust inventory (OTI)". In *Trust in Organizations: Frontiers of Theory and Research*, R.M. Kramer and T. Tyler (eds), 302–330. Thousand Oaks, CA: Sage.

Davidow, W.H. and Malone, M.S. 1992. *The Virtual Corporation*. New York: Harper Collins.

Dennis, A.R., George, J.F., Jessup, L.M., Nunamaker, J.F. and Vogel, D.R. 1988. "Information technology to support electronic meetings". *MIS Quarterly* 12: 591–624.

DeSanctis, G. and Poole, M.S. 1997. "Transitions in teamwork in new organizational forms". *Advances in Group Processes* 14: 157–176.

DiMaggio, P.J. and Powell, W.W. 1983. "The iron cage revisited: Institutional isomorphism and collective rationality in organizational fields". *American Sociological Review* 48: 147–160.

Dubrovsky, V.J., Kiesler, S. and Sethna, B.N. 1991. "The equalization phenomenon: Status effects in computer-mediated and face-to-face decision-making groups". *Human Computer Interaction* 6: 119–146.

Eveland, J.D. and Bikson, T.K. 1988. "Work group structures and computer support: A field experiment". *Transactions on Office Information Systems* 6: 354–379.

Ferioli, C. and Migliarese, P. 1996. "Supporting organizational relations through information technology in innovative organizational forms". *European Journal of Information Systems* 5: 196–207.
Finn, K. E., Sellen, A. J. and Wilbur, S. B. (eds) 1997. *Video-Mediated Communication.* Mahwah, NJ: Lawrence Erlbaum.
Flanagin, A. J. 2000. "Social pressures on organizational website adoption". *Human Communication Research* 26: 618–646.
Flanagin, A. J., Monge, P. R. and Fulk, J. 2001. "The value of formative investment in organizational federations". *Human Communication Research* 27: 69–93.
Flanagin, A. J., Tiyaamornwong, V., O'Connor, J. and Seibold, D. (2002). "Computer-mediated group work: The interaction of member sex and anonymity". *Communication Research* 29, 66–93.
Fulk, J. (1993). "Social construction of communication technology". *Academy of Management Journal* 36: 921–950.
Fulk, J. and Collins-Jarvis, L. 2001. "Wired meetings: Technological mediation of organizational gatherings". In *The New Handbook of Organizational Communication*, F. M. Jablin and L. L. Putnam (eds), 624–663. Thousand Oaks, CA: Sage.
Fulk, J. and DeSanctis, G. 1995. "Electronic communication and changing organizational forms". *Organization Science* 6: 337–349.
Fulk, J., Flanagin, A. J., Kalman, M., Monge, P. R. and Ryan, T. 1996. "Connective and communal public goods in interactive communication systems". *Communication Theory* 6: 60–87.
Gopal, A., Mirana, S. M., Robichaux, B. P. and Bostrom, R. P. 1997. "Leveraging diversity with information technology: Gender, attitude, and intervening influences in the use of group support systems". *Small Group Research* 28: 29–71.
Gurbaxani, V. 1990. "Diffusion in computing networks: The case of BITNET". *Communications of the ACM* 33: 65–75.
Hardin, G. 1968. "The tragedy of the commons". *Science* 162: 1243–1248.
Hills, M. 1997. *Intranet Business Strategies.* New York: John Wiley and Sons.
Hinds, P. & Kiesler, S. 1995. "Communication across boundaries: Work, structure, and use of communication technologies in a large organization". *Organization Science* 6: 373–393.
Huber, G. P. 1990. "A theory of the effects of advanced information technologies on organizational design, intelligence, and decision-making". In *Organizations and Communication Technology*, J. Fulk and C. W. Steinfield (eds), 237–274. Newbury Park, CA: Sage.
Jablin, F. M. 1987. "Organizational entry, assimilation, and exit." In *Handbook of Organizational Communication*, F. M. Jablin, L. L. Putnam, K. H. Roberts and L. W. Porter (eds), 679–740. Newbury Park, CA: Sage.
Jarillo, J. C. 1988. "On strategic networks". *Strategic Management Journal* 9: 31–41.
Jarvenpaa, S. L. and Leidner, D. E. 1999. "Communication and trust in global virtual teams". *Organization Science* 10: 791–815.
Jelassi, M. T. and Beauclair, R. A. 1987. "An integrated framework for group decision support systems design". *Information & Management* 13: 143–153.
Joyce, W. F., McGee, V. E. and Slocum, J. W., Jr. 1997. "Designing lateral organizations: An analysis of the benefits, costs, and enablers of nonhierarchical organizational forms". *Decision Sciences* 28: 1–25.

Kaye, A. R. and Byrne, K. E. 1986. "Insights on the implementation of a computer-based message system". *Information and Management* 10: 277–284.
Lewis, J. D. and Weigert, A. 1985. "Trust as a social reality". *Social Forces* 63: 967–985.
Malone, T. W. and Rockart, J. F. 1991. "Computers, networks, and the corporation". *Scientific American* September: 128–136.
Malone, T. W., Yates, J. and Benjamin, R. I. 1987. "Electronic markets and electronic hierarchies". *Communications of the ACM* 30: 484–496.
Manning, P. K. 1992. "Information technologies and the police". In *Modern Policing 15*, M. Tonry and N. Morris (eds), 349–398, Chicago: The University of Chicago Press.
Manning, P. K. 1996. "Information technology in the police context: The 'sailor' phone". *Information Systems Research* 7: 52–62.
Markus, M. L. 1990. "Toward a critical mass theory of interactive media". In *Organizations and Communication Technology*, J. Fulk and C. W. Steinfield (eds), 194–218. Newbury Park, CA: Sage.
Markus, M. L. 1994. "Electronic mail as the medium of managerial choice". *Organization Science* 5: 502–527.
Miles, R. E. and Snow, C. C. 1984. "Fit, failure, and the hall of fame". *California Management Review* 26: 10–28.
Miles, R. E. and Snow, C. C. 1986. "Organizations: New concepts for new forms". *California Management Review* 28: 62–73.
Miner, A. S., Amburgey, T. L. and Stearns, T. M. 1990. "Interorganizational linkages and population dynamics: Buffering and transformational shields". *Administrative Science Quarterly* 35: 689–713.
Monge, P. R., Fulk, J., Kalman, M., Flanagin, A. J., Parnassa, C. and Rumsey, S. 1998. "Production of collective action in alliance-based interorganizational communication and information systems". *Organization Science* 9: 411–433.
Monge, P. R., Fulk, J., Parnassa, C., Flanagin, A. J., Rumsey, S. and Kalman, M. 1999. "Cooperative interagency approaches to the illegal drug problem". *International Journal of Police Science and Management* 2: 229–241.
Mowshowitz, A. 1994. "Virtual organization: A vision of management in the information age". *Information Society* 10: 267–288.
Nohria, N. and Berkley, J. D. 1994. "The virtual organization: Bureaucracy, technology, and the implosion of control". In *The Post-Bureaucratic Organization: New Perspectives on Organizational Change*, C. Heckscher and A. Donnellon (eds), 108–128. Thousand Oaks, CA: Sage.
Nohria, N. and Eccles, R. (eds) 1992. *Networks and Organizations: Structure, Form and Action.* Boston: Harvard Business School Press.
Nonaka, I. 1994. "A dynamic theory of organizational knowledge creation". *Organization Science* 5: 14–37.
Olson, M. 1965. *The Logic of Collective Action.* Cambridge, MA: Harvard University Press.
O'Mahoney, S. and Barley, S. R. 1999. "Do digital telecommunications affect work and organization? The state of our knowledge". In *Research in Organizational Behavior, Volume 21*, B. Staw and L. L. Cummings (eds), 125–161. Greenwich, CT: JAI Press.

Pinsonneault, A. and Kraemer, K. L. 1990. "The effects of electronic meetings on group processes and outcomes: An assessment of the empirical research". *European Journal of Operational Research* 46: 143–161.

Porter, M. 1985. *Competitive Advantage: Creating and Sustaining Superior Performance.* New York: The Free Press.

Powell, W. W. 1990. "Neither market nor hierarchy: Network forms of organization". *Research in Organizational Behavior* 12: 295–336.

Powell, W. W., Koput, K. W. and Smith-Doerr, L. 1996. "Interorganizational collaboration and the locus of innovation: Networks of learning in biotechnology". *Administrative Science Quarterly* 41: 116–145.

Reiss, A. J. Jr. 1971. *The Police and the Public.* New Haven, CT: Yale University Press.

Rice, R. E. 1992. "Task analyzability, use of new media, and effectiveness: A multi-site exploration of media richness". *Organization Science* 3: 475–500.

Rosenbaum, D. P. (ed.). 1994. *The Challenge of Community Policing: Testing the Promises.* Thousand Oaks, CA: Sage.

Schmitz, J. and Fulk, J. 1991. "Organizational colleagues, media richness, and electronic mail: A test of the social influence model of technology use". *Communication Research* 18: 487–523.

Scott, C. 1999. "Communication technology and group communication". In *The Handbook of Group Communication Theory and Research*, L. R. Frey, D. S. Gouran and M. S. Poole (eds), 432–472. Thousand Oaks, CA: Sage.

Seibold, D. R., Heller, M. A. and Contractor, N. S. 1994. "Group decision support systems (GDSS): Review, taxonomy, and research agenda". In *New Approaches to Organizational Communication*, B. Kovacic (ed.), 143–167. Albany, NY: State University of New York Press.

Sproull, L. and Kiesler, S. 1991. *Connections: New ways of Working in the Networked Organization.* Cambridge, MA: The MIT Press.

Stinchcombe, A. L. 1990. *Information and Organizations.* Berkeley, CA: University of California Press.

Sweeney, J. W. 1973. "An experimental investigation of the free-rider problem". *Social Science Research* 2: 277–292.

Tödtling, F. 1992. "Technological change at the regional level: The role of location, firm structure, and strategy". *Environment and Planning* 24: 1565–1584.

U. S. Department of Justice 1999. "U. S. Department of Justice, Federal Bureau of Investigation". Retrieved June 15, 2001, from the World Wide Web http://www.fbi.gov/pressrel/pressrel99/ncic2000.htm

Zuboff, S. 1988. *In the Age of the Smart Machine.* New York: Basic Books.

CHAPTER 5

Fictional cops
Who are they, and what are they teaching us?

Jan J. M. Van den Bulck
Katholieke Universiteit Leuven, Belgium

Police fiction produced and aired in the United States can be seen all over the world. *N. Y. P. D.-Blue, Miami Vice, Hill Street Blues* or *Kojak*, to name but a few old and new shows, have been or are being broadcast in many countries. While those shows are fictitious and most viewers appear to be aware of this, there is a lot of academic concern about the potential effects they might have on the viewer. Some fear that the amount of fictional mayhem will turn some viewers into criminals themselves. Others fear that the antics of fictional cops are telling viewers something about the real world, thus distorting their image of law enforcement. Clearly, if crime fiction influences criminal and aggressive behavior and the expectations and image people have of law enforcement, the issue of its effects is relevant even to the law enforcement community.

This chapter attempts to summarize the available literature on the effects of police fiction. It starts by looking at the demography of law enforcement fiction: how are police officers presented? How are perpetrators and victims portrayed? How fairly are different races treated? Second, immediate and direct effects of television fiction are looked at. Many critics worry about the imitation of violent media exemplars and increased aggression in the viewer, but there are other concerns that are often overlooked. Many viewers, who identify more readily with victims than with criminals, may become fearful rather than aggressive. Finally, the evidence is reviewed regarding long term and cumulative effects. It is argued that viewers' perception of, and attitudes about, the world are affected by decades of exposure to fictional crime and violence.

Who are they? The demographics of law enforcement fiction

Levels of violence on television have always been quite high. In the 1950s, early studies of television content found that a large proportion of the characters presented in fiction were either criminals or law enforcement officers (Head 1954; Smythe 1954,). Head (1954) estimated that 17% of occupations on television were police-related. While there have always been genres in which an emphasis on crime and law enforcement was the main theme ("crime drama" or "police series"), law enforcement roles are omnipresent even in other genres. Dominick (1973) estimated that 60% of all fiction programs, including comedy shows, showed at least one crime. Similarly, recent findings from a three-year sample of television programs (collected as part of the "National Television Violence Study" project in the United States) showed that 61% of programs analyzed contained some form of violence, averaging 6.8 violent acts per hour (Smith, Wilson, Kunkel, Linz, Potter, Colvin & Donnerstein 1998). Like medical doctors and lawyers, law enforcement officers feature prominently in most fiction genres, including soap operas (Greenberg, Neuendorf, Buerkel-Rothfuss & Henderson 1982). In this respect, crime drama or police series are special only in that the main character or characters are crime or law enforcement-related, and crime or law enforcement is the main theme of each episode.

The demographics of television fiction crime show a seriously skewed picture. Reiner (1985: 148) remarked that, in general, both factual and fictional television show similar patterns of representation of crime, both of which he called "the precise opposite of the pattern of real offending and policing". Potter, Vaughan, Warren, Howley, Land and Hagemeyer (1995) showed that the distribution of fictional crimes differed from criminal justice statistics. Television fiction paid too much attention to serious (mainly violent) crime. Similarly, in an analysis of a sample of police and detective drama including shows from over three decades, still aired in 1997, Scharrer (2000) found that murder (30.7%), attempted murder (19.9%), assault (6.6%) and (armed) robbery (4.6) accounted for 61.8% of all crimes portrayed in the sample. A similar over-emphasis on violent crime was found earlier by Pandiani (1978). Apart from a skewed distribution of crimes, their nature is presented in a way that differs considerably from reality. Fabianic (1997) discussed the lack of adequate explanation offered in most cases where a homicide is portrayed, with (often far-fetched or strange) motives as the sole cause of the criminal act. Similarly, Potter et al. (1995) showed that, unlike in real life, television perpetrators usually do not know their victims.

While television news has been shown to overestimate the proportion of African American and Hispanic perpetrators (Dixon & Linz 2000; Oliver 1994), in fiction African American perpetrators in particular appear "to be represented in proportion (about 11%) to their numbers in (...) real life" (Potter et al. 1995:508). Possibly, however, this does not represent an attempt by the industry to show a correct and fair image of crime, even in its fictional representations, but rather an overemphasis on White characters altogether. As Potter et al. (1995) showed, African American perpetrators are over-represented in some categories such as 'social harm' (portraying the perpetrator as a threat to society) and underrepresented in less harmful categories such as 'deception' or 'property harm' (where no physical violence is concerned). A similar picture emerges from an analysis of victims which showed that Whites form the large majority of victims, which means that in television fiction African Americans are more likely to be initiators than victims of violence (Potter et al. 1995).

Less is known about the demography of law enforcement officers in TV drama, though it seems safe to assume that the majority of them are White, male and "in middle adulthood" (Reiner 1985:148). African American actors now feature widely as sergeants, supervisors or even captains or commissioners. Nevertheless, Pines (1995:74) argued that the range of roles they get to play is limited. When they play ordinary "cops" they tend to be portrayed as "noble figures whose mission is to clean up the criminalized black neighborhoods". Recent content analyses, nevertheless, noted that "in general, representations of minority characters involved with the justice system were on par with depictions of Whites with regards to the characteristics examined" (Tamborini, Mastro, Chory-Assad & He Huang 2000; see also Mastro & Greenberg 2000).

Generally, television fiction presents enforcing the law as an action-packed job which mainly means "crime fighting" (Culver 1978; Perlmutter 2000), with little or no attention given to counseling, paperwork or arbitrating. Another important TV demographic is the emphasis on police detectives, with patrol officers or uniformed police relegated to the background, guarding crime scenes (Perlmutter 2000; Reiner 1985). While private investigators or even private citizens are often portrayed as being more effective than the police in solving crimes, research nevertheless showed that law enforcers are mainly represented in a positive way (Lichter & Lichter 1983). Their jobs almost always involve violence to resolve the crimes they investigate (Reiner 1985), which they do thanks to their personal brilliance, not because of the combined effort of the members of a formal organization (Sparks 1992). The absence of organization is most obvious when fictional cops are portrayed breaking the law or ignoring procedures with apparent impunity (McNeely 1995). An often-recurring cliché states that crimes cannot be solved by "going by the book", or even that the "book" makes solving crimes impossible. Apart from the effect such would have on the admissibility of evidence in a real case (which often is not a problem on television because the perpetrator will end up being killed), breaking the rules is acceptable to the viewer because the viewer knows why it has to be done: s/he knows that a criminal or evidence is hidden inside when police illegally search a house (McNeely 1995). In real life, intuition without probable cause combined with an illegal procedure is probably more likely to lead to an irate and innocent private citizen suing a law enforcement department.

In the 1960s, Gerbner (1969) found that violence on television in general, and originating from law enforcement officers in particular, usually was not shown to have any consequences for the officer, nor did crimes often seem to lead to any kind of trial. The story seldom showed "postarrest procedures" (McNeely 1995:8). Smith et al.'s (1998) data showed that, in general, 82% of the "good characters" seemed to get away with violence without being punished. Of the "bad characters", 45% were not shown to be punished. Punished or not, one third of all violent interactions did not lead to physical injury to the target. A classic punch-up is often presented as a healthy and innocent way for men to settle their differences.

Behavioral and emotional effects of police fiction: The direct effects approach

Imitation and contagion

Various authors have made estimates of the amount of fictitious and real violence the average television viewer has to digest, all suggesting that even young people or adolescents will have watched literally tens of thousands of homicides and hundreds of thousands of violent acts (for an overview, see Weimann 2000:94). This obviously worries parents, policy-makers, and academics alike. Gould (1990) makes a distinction between *imitation*, which refers to media exemplars becoming actual models for future behaviors, and *contagion*, which refers to a facilitation of similar behaviors by media exemplars. In the former case, media examples of behaviors are expected to lead to behavior resembling the example, in the latter case the media example is expected only to remove inhibitions or to create new or increase existing tendencies. Even though most attention seems to be given to the question of imitation of crime or activation of aggressive tendencies, the potential effects of crime fiction are more complex and wide-ranging.

Imitation of television violence

Is there evidence of imitation?
Many authors have listed examples of people imitating crimes they saw in some kind of television or movie drama. Harris (1989) recounted the story of a 13 year old from Kansas City who is said to have killed himself re-enacting the "Russian Roulette"-scene from the movie "The Deer Hunter". Harris added that by 1984 thirty-one examples of similar deaths were known. Grossberg, Wartella and Whitney (1998) quoted examples of a rape which resembled a scene from a movie aired on TV and a series of attempted homicides in which a poisoned painkiller was used — imitating a real case which had received media attention. While some of the examples are very convincing (see also Berkowitz 1993), much of this evidence is anecdotal and often based on media reports. This means that it is difficult to establish whether the similarity between the media exemplar and the ensuing crime are real or a result of selective perception and interpretation either by the journalists reporting the crime or the academics interpreting it. More solid and often quoted analyses were produced by Phillips (1974, 1979, 1986; Phillips & Carstensen 1986) who claimed that well publicized suicides (including fictional portrayals in soap operas or other TV drama) resulted in an increase of the number of suicides. Phillips (1986) believed to have shown that homicides, too, increased after media attention for violence between human beings, though he did not look at fiction for that study. Phillips' work has been refuted by some (e.g., Kessler & Stipp 1984; Marks 1987; Mastroianni 1987; Wasserman 1984), but replicated by others (Ishii 1991). Reviewing the evidence, both Berkowitz (1993) and Signorielli (1993) concluded that Phillips' research and his responses to criticism were convincing enough to suggest that some behaviors are prompted by both real and fictitious examples in the media. That said, Berkowitz (1993) suggests that people imitating media behavior may have already had the intention or urge to perform such an act or a similar one. The media, in other words, might only offer a model or the "last drop" for what is already an accident waiting to happen.

Imitation and the intention to harm
An important distinction that is often ignored in this discussion is the matter of *intention*. There is a clear distinction between a child accidentally killing or maiming a friend after imitating behavior which seemed harmless (or without consequences) on television or the attempted murder of president Ronald Reagan by John Hinkley who, some think, tried to imitate what he had seen in the movie *Taxi Driver* (Harris 1999). This distinction raises an important issue. As indicated above, much violence in television fiction is shown to have no consequences. Sometimes a conscious attempt is even made to "clean" it to avoid showing children gruesome images. As a result, some children imitating karate-kicks or other aggressive behaviors portrayed as "fun" in popular series are not actually trying to hurt each other. It has been argued that much of this kind of behavior is intended to be harmless play — and negative consequences are unintended accidents (Snow 1974; see also Berkowitz 1993; Potter 1998). Others have called such behavior the "Evil Knievel Syndrome" (Daven, O'Conner & Briggs 1976): the imitation of dangerous behavior which is perceived as being without any danger because of the way it is generally portrayed in the media. If this theory holds, not all behaviors displayed by children should be labeled as "aggressive" by adults who have learned to identify karate-kicks or other imitations of television "fun" as acts of aggression.

Contagion: Does crime fiction cause aggression?
In 1963, Bandura, Ross and Ross (1963a, b), showed that children who had been exposed to violent television images subsequently behaved more aggressively towards a "Bobo-doll". Despite criticism about the validity of extrapolating the artificial settings of a laboratory to conclusions about a phenomenon in the natural setting of the real world (Harris 1999; Wicks 1992), Berkowitz (1993:207), in a book on aggression, believed that "a considerable body of experimental research indicates that violent movies can increase the likelihood of aggressive behavior to an extent that ranges from small to moderate". Furthermore, non-experimental research showed a similar relationship. One, often quoted and remarkable, study by Centerwall (1989a,b, 1993), using methods from epidemiology, showed that homicide rates increased in Canada and the United States after the introduction of television, more or less doubling in both cases. In comparison, no such increase took place in South Africa, until, there, too, television was introduced. In an impressive longitudinal study, using multiple controls, Huesmann (1986) showed that boys who prefer violent

television at age 8 are more likely to be convicted of a serious crime by the age of 30, regardless of their TV consumption at a later age.

Nonaggressive and noncriminal effects of violent fiction
Much research about the effects of crime fiction and much of the societal debate surrounding it seem to have been focused on questions of aggressiveness and imitation of crimes. Nevertheless, it is obvious that a large majority of television viewers does *not* respond to television drama with outbursts of serious aggression or imitations of violent crimes. It would be wrong to imply, however, that the absence of increased crime or aggression indicates an absence of direct behavioral or emotional effects. A large part of the audience probably does not readily identify with the usual perpetrators of non-punished violence (who, as noted above, belong to a fairly homogenous group). Instead, they might identify with the victims or become more aware of (not necessarily realistic) dangers surrounding them.

Cantor (e.g., 1994) in particular has done extensive research on the phenomenon of children's fright reactions to scary media content. Fright reactions appear to be widespread and persistent. Even years after viewing a scary scene some form of residual anxiety might still be present (Harrison & Cantor 1999). While watching a scary scene on television is not the same as witnessing a real event in real life, Cantor (1994) argued that the media depiction of a stimulus that would evoke fear in real life will, through *stimulus generalization*, evoke a similar, albeit less intense, response. It is common for many respondents to recall fright experiences vividly (Hoekstra, Harris & Helmick 1999), and some extreme examples exist of children needing medical attention and displaying the symptoms of post-traumatic stress disorder (Simons & Silveira 1994). Despite these reactions, there is also evidence of *desensitization* as a result of continuous exposure to real and fictitious media violence (Harris 1999). This means that viewers become accustomed to violence as a result of TV use and react less strongly when confronted with real violence.

While this might make some people more tolerant towards violence, there are also pro-social effects. Potter (1998) referred to the therapeutic use of desensitization as a tool to decrease fears. Finally, it has been argued that, for some people, television might be used for *mood repair* (Minnebo 2000; Zillmann & Wakshlag 1985). Frightened people might turn to television fiction as a way of coping with their fears. Television, after all, usually shows how the good guys win and order is restored. The mood repair hypothesis assumes that such TV use reassures anxious viewers.

Long-term cognitive and attitudinal effects

How can fiction teach about reality?

Perlmutter's (2000) personal observations of law enforcement officers showed that many officers worry that TV might be shaping what people think and expect of them. Nevertheless, ordinary viewers usually know that what they are watching is just fiction and that the deaths they witness are actually actors pretending to be killed. How, then, can television fiction have any long term effects on people's perception of and opinions about reality?

It is important to make a distinction between realism and reality. Television fiction does not offer what Potter (1988) called "literal reality", it does not show events and people in such a way as to suggest to the viewer that what is being shown is a registration of something that was really happening at the time it was recorded. Much television drama, however, contains a different, more symbolic kind of reality. While the actual story may be fiction, there is often a "lesson about life". Furthermore, in press interviews directors will mention how actors were forced to go on ride alongs or spend time with real law enforcement officers for the purpose of making their acting and the way the story is portrayed as "realistic" as possible. Often they even receive some kind of help from police departments or retired officers etc. (Bauer 1992). In other words, there are many indications to ordinary viewers that what they are watching resembles what would happen in reality. Even fiction which does not make any special attempt to appear realistic might contain lessons about reality. In fact, some authors believe that even cartoons can teach viewers important "truths" about real life (Funkhauser & Shaw 1990; Gerbner, Gross, Morgan & Signorielli 1980; Potter 1988; Snow 1983).

Another important factor is repetition. The fact that countless episodes of different series or films often depict law enforcement in a particular way carries a strong suggestion of realism. If a police officer is given a gold shield upon becoming a detective or if suspects are "read" a particular wording of the Miranda rights time and again, there is, in fact, little reason for the viewer to doubt that this is exactly what would happen in real life. Rosengren (1994), therefore, remarked that the biggest effects of television and the media are not the kind of short term, fairly immediate effect discussed in the previous sections, but rather what remains after decades of exposure to a steady stream of messages.

Viewers might be particularly vulnerable in the case of law enforcement, because there is little to counter impressions learned from the media. Perlmutter (2000) referred to the situation in the United States to remark that, in 1996, only about a fifth of all Americans aged twelve or older had ever had any kind of face-to-face contact with a law enforcement officer. Only a third of these (or 6.6% of the total) were victims of or witnesses to a crime, meaning that the large majority of these contacts were rather general and had little to do with police work or crime-fighting. One might state, therefore, as did McNeely (1995:9), that "in some ways, the most direct 'contact' that most persons have with the criminal justice system is through the 'television experience'."

Some authors have argued that the apparent realism of much law enforcement fiction, the repetition of similar cliches and the long-term exposure of most television viewers throughout their lifetime, particularly affects people's construction of an image of the real world. One of the most fruitful, but also heavily debated, theories in this field is the *cultivation hypothesis* of George Gerbner, which originated in the sixties. This theory dealt with the effects of the "mean world" of television fiction (for recent overviews see, for example, Signorielli & Morgan 1990, Signorielli 1993, and for a meta-analysis, Shanahan & Morgan 1999). One recent definition stated that "(...) television viewing cultivates assumptions about the facts of life that reflect the medium's most recurrent portrayals" (Morgan & Shanahan 1997:8) or "that watching a great deal of television will be associated with a tendency to hold specific and distinct conceptions of reality, conceptions that are congruent with the most consistent and pervasive images and values of the medium" (Shanahan & Morgan 1999:3). Generally, two types of cultivation effects seem to occur (e.g., Potter 1991b). *First-order cultivation* occurs when viewers deduct factual knowledge about the real world from watching television fiction. Typically, this refers to "the prevalence of things" (Shrum 1995), such as perceptions of the amount of violence and the frequency with which certain crimes occur or the number of men and women working as law enforcement officers. *Second-order cultivation* occurs when television affects attitudes and beliefs about the real world (Shrum 1995), such as "the extent to which heavy viewers see themselves as likely to be victims of violence, or are fearful for their own personal safety, or are mistrustful of others" (Shanahan & Morgan 1999:175). These concepts describe the long term effects of the demography of the TV world which was discussed above.

First-order cultivation effects of law enforcement fiction

There are amusing anecdotal examples of first-order effects of crime fiction in which viewers believed to have learned factual information about real life from watching television. Altheide (1985) remarked that many people visiting *Alcatraz*, the former island prison near San Francisco, believed that they already knew a lot about life in prison from watching popular movies — and felt the need to make this obvious to the tour guides. Gerbner and Gross (1976) mentioned a defense attorney who raised an objection in court which he had seen on the Perry Mason show but which, unfortunately, was not part of the California code.

Gunther (1971) believed that television fiction is an important source of factual information about criminal investigations and about the rights of arrested people (see also Carlson 1985; McNeely 1995). In a recent study, 90% of a group of European undergraduate students of media studies could quote at least some of the *Miranda Rights* when asked about an arrested person's rights in the United States, even though similar rights did not exist in their own country. None of the respondents had any previous experience with American law enforcement nor had any other source than television fiction for acquiring this knowledge. Nevertheless, a debriefing of the respondents showed that most were absolutely sure they knew how arrests and interrogations are conducted in the United States (Van den Bulck 1999). There is a lot of evidence that the demography of the television world is leaving clear traces in the minds of viewers (Van den Bulck 1996). Heavy viewers of television gave higher estimates of crime rates, overestimated the number of men with a job in law enforcement (as the demography of the television world is full of law enforcement officers), and had been influenced in their perceptions of police procedures and crime characteristics. Generally, heavy viewers also seem to see the world as a more dangerous place (Hawkins, Pingree & Adler 1987). Television fiction appears to have a significant impact on people's perception of crime, the police, and police work.

Second-order cultivation effects of law enforcement fiction

In the first cultivation studies, Gerbner introduced the idea of *risk ratios* (Gerbner & Gross 1976) that measured the likelihood of a particular category of television characters (e.g., old ladies and pregnant women) becoming a victim of crime. Regarding the potential effects of these images, some have argued that a distinction should be made between people's perceptions of their own risk and their fears of becoming a victim (Sparks & Ogles 1990; Van den Bulck 1996). There is some evidence of a relationship between television viewing and fear of crime or fear for one's personal safety (Morgan 1983), but there is a lot of discussion about the meaning of these findings. Some believed the relationship is an artifact (Potter 1988; Tamborini, Zillmann & Bryant 1984; Weaver & Wakshlag 1986) others presented surprising findings (Doob & Macdonald 1979) which can be interpreted as showing that only people with some kind of personal experience with crime will become more frightened as a result of watching television, possibly because they receive a "double dose" of influences (Gerbner et al. 1980).

Carlson (1983) found that heavy viewers of crime shows were less likely to support civil liberties (see also Van den Bulck 1996). The liberties used in the study reflect a number of television cliches ("police should be allowed to ignore the rules in some cases by searching a house without a warrant", "there are too many regulations restricting police work", etc.). Hawkins and Pingree (1981), Signorielli (1990) and, in Europe, Van den Bulck (1996) found that heavy viewers tend to see the world as a mean and dangerous place in which people cannot trust each other.

Challenges to the media effects hypothesis

Simkin et al. (1995) and Hawton et al. (1999) analyzed the effects of a single episode of the British Emergency Room series *Casualty*. The episode showed the effects of an overdose of the painkiller paracetamol (more generally known in the USA as acetaminophen). Instead of the expected and hoped for dissuading effect the researchers found a surprising **increase** in the number of suicide attempts in which an overdose of the painkiller was used. Even though some have suggested that the study showed some methodological inaccuracies (e.g., Davies et al. 1999; Pell & Murdoch 1999), it illustrates an important shortcoming of many studies of media effects. As McQuail (1994) has remarked, all too often media effects theories start from an underlying *transmission model* suggesting that the media "transport" certain perceptions and opinions directly into the heads of receivers. In reality, however, many cognitive processes intervene. As a result, the same media message will have a different meaning to different people. Beck (1994), therefore, introduced a distinction between *data* (those stimuli produced by the media and serving as "input" to a "cognitive system", i.e. a person) and *information* (the end-product of the personal and cognitive processing of the data by the media user). Researchers are often in danger of ascribing very personal meanings to data and passing them off as the only and most logical interpretation, which is what seems to have happened in the paracetamol-case.

Applied to media effects theories, Beck's ideas warrant the introduction of two new concepts: *data setting* and *boundary setting*. A *data setting* effect occurs when data in the media message offer little or no room for interpretation. This appears to occur when viewers believe they learn "facts" from fiction (e.g., the *Miranda Rights*). Either people believe that what they see is as it is in reality, in which case they learn the data, or they do not, in which case no effect occurs. The "data" in the program differ little from the "information" ending up in the head of the viewer. It becomes more complicated when the data offered by the program can be interpreted in several meaningful ways. Data in television fiction showing a "mean and dangerous world" may frighten, make aggressive, or simply entertain viewers. In this case, *boundary setting* effects may occur, because these data allow very different interpretations within broad or narrow boundaries. Few people will get the impression that television fiction is telling them the world is a safe place where people can trust one another and are seldom at risk, an interpretation clearly falling outside the "boundaries" of television fiction. Within the boundaries, however, big differences between viewers may occur.

The distinction between the data offered by television and the interpretation the viewer attaches to it seems to explain the remarkable findings regarding paracetamol poisoning. There was an obvious data setting effect: at least part of the viewers seemed to have learned that high doses of paracetamol are potentially deadly. In some viewers, however, this led to an imitation effect. The surprise of the researchers seemed to be the result of an unnecessary generalization of their own interpretation of the television data. Some viewers did get the message, but drew their own conclusions. These conclusions were not contrary to the message of the television program and were, therefore, well within the boundaries. The only conclusions not supported by the program would have been ideas suggesting that large doses of paracetamol are harmless or even healthy. Media fiction may therefore have effects much like those of the agenda setting effect of news, of which Cohen (1963:13) stated in the sixties that it "may not be successful much of the time in telling people what to think, but it is stunningly successful in telling (people) what to think **about**".

Consequences for law enforcement

Media images of crime and law enforcement not only influence the general public, they may even be changing the face of real life law enforcement. Several issues can be raised. First, research has shown that childrens' career aspirations are influenced by the images they get about certain professions on television (Wright, Huston, Truglio, Fitch, Smith & Piemyat 1995; Wroblewski & Huston 1987). Heavy viewers, particularly those who believe that much of the fiction they watch has a high degree of realism, are more likely to aspire to jobs shown on TV. The potential impact of such images is shown by Wallack and Bingle (1996) who found that the number of medical students enrolling in emergency medicine programs in a particular university doubled since the medical drama series *E.R.* was first aired. Second, members of the public might be deriving much of their expectations about behaviors of officers from media examples. If real officers do not live up to these expectations (if only because the reality of police work is often very different), this may lead to unfavorable impressions, disappointment, or even legal action (Radelet & Carter 1994). If people believe they know what police work is like and how officers should behave, they will be convinced that officers have not done their jobs properly or even wrongly if these officers do not behave the way their fictional colleagues do. Officers and the communication and legal specialists of their departments may have to take this into account when dealing with the public in certain situations. Gross and Jeffries-Fox (1978) even referred to one extreme instance in which a respondent said that police officers appeared to be more real on television than in reality! Expectations about behaviors and outcomes in the criminal justice system at large may be influenced as well (Gerbner & Gross 1976). A popular theme in much drama suggests a "litigation explosion" in which juries award extraordinary damages. Real jurors have been shown to justify their own low awards by referring to this "explosion", even though research suggests no such phenomenon exists (Hans & Dee 1991).

Finally, law enforcement officers themselves may be influenced by television fiction. At the simplest and least harmful sounding level, it has been shown that references to fictional police officers have found their way into the police vernacular (Pacanowsky & Anderson 1982). Police officers regularly refer to situations and characters from crime fiction when commenting on or describing situations they are faced with (see also Perlmutter 2000). Altheide and Snow (1979) and Snow (1983) quoted a number of examples of LAPD officers changing behaviors to look more like their fictional colleagues. Dees (1996) worried about the ethical ramifications of law enforcement officers imitating tactics shown on television drama and warned departments not to condone such behavior. There are also innocent examples of the worlds of real and fictitious policing meeting each other as in the case of British police officers inviting famous television actors to police dinners (Hurd 1981) or Horst Tappert, the German actor who, after playing the popular TV police detective "Derrick" for decades, was elected honorary commissioner by an organization of real police officers.

Epilogue

Media effects research often finds very small correlations between television consumption measures and variables used as indicators of the kind of effects discussed in this chapter (Cook, Kendzierski & Thomas 1983; Potter 1991a). Shanahan and Morgan (1999) found an overall effect size of approximately $r = .09$ in a meta-analysis of 5633 findings from several hundred studies of cultivation and television effects conducted in the past 20 years. Some authors argue, however, that even a small effect can be substantial from a societal and ethical perspective because television attracts such large audiences. Thus an effect on just .001% of an audience of 20 million people would mean that 200 people have been affected (Harris 1999; Signorielli 1993). Rosenthal (1986) followed a similar line of thought by referring to medical experiments where even a tiny difference in mortality or recovery between an experimental group and a control group receiving a placebo might lead to a termination of the experiment on the grounds that even small differences are an ethical problem when people's well-being is at stake.

Clearly, questions regarding the effects of television crime fiction are important, given the amount of time people all over the world are spending watching it. While there is much research on issues of fictional crime and violence and the effects these might have on fears, aggressive behaviors, perceptions and attitudes, researchers have not given much attention to law enforcement specifically. In fact, the need to study media violence in a broader context has given rise to a broader, but therefore vaguer, definition of the concept which, in recent studies, now also encompasses swearing and other kinds of symbolic violence. While these are necessary refinements for a study of television violence, they make it more difficult to isolate data dealing with law enforcement issues — as this chapter no doubt illustrates. The relative importance of law enforcement themes and personnel in television fiction and the societal relevance of studying the impact of such images seem to warrant a specific research agenda. After all, the issues are not the same. On the one hand, not all violence on television has a law enforcement theme. On the other hand, the effects of law enforcement fiction should not be limited to the consequences of violence and aggression.

Research focusing on the role and effects of portrayals of law enforcement in television fiction should address a number of issues. First, careful content analyses of portrayals of law enforcement officers and their behaviors ought to be conducted to establish what the "demography" of the fictitious law enforcement world is. While previous studies at best counted the number of officers as a proportion of the total television "population", more detailed data would be welcome. How are plain-clothes and uniformed officers portrayed? Which law enforcement departments are most prominent? Is the impression true that the LAPD, the NYPD, and the FBI are proportionally over-represented? More important still is the context in which officers and departments are portrayed. How are various groups represented and what is suggested about the relationships between them? How are local, small-town and county level departments portrayed compared to large city, state or federal agencies? Are there evolutions in these portrayals? Do developments in the real world affect portrayals of policing and, if so, is there a delay? Are drug policies or news about drug issues influencing the way in which the policing of narcotics is represented? What is suggested about the relative importance of each group and the relationships between them? Storylines in which local officers collide with federal officers seem to be common themes. Some seem to suggest that local police are incompetent or even corrupt. Other storylines appear to suggest that federal agencies lack morality and local knowledge and rely too much on technology and "textbook" approaches. Even tactics and procedures might be looked at.

One tactical issue that often recurs is the use of SWAT-teams. It seems that SWAT-teams are often represented as blundering, trigger happy idiots when they are deployed as a team, while individual officers with a SWAT-background are often shown to be superhuman heroes. With regard to procedures, it would be interesting to compare the practices of fictional cops with legal and constitutional requirements and the consequences this might have for convictions of criminals or disciplinary or legal action against officers. Race, gender, and age-issues seem to be particularly important at every level of comparison. While race has received at least some attention, the portrayal (and often absence) of female officers in a leading, independent role is undoubtedly equally relevant.

For researchers interested in exploring into these issues, the chapter of Reiner (1985) on themes of police fiction might be a fruitful starting point. Reiner shows that looking at the message and meaning of recurring storylines is insightful. Generally speaking, a detailed and adequate content analysis of fictional policing would probably require at least basic knowledge of police organization and procedure.

Second, once an adequate picture exists of the world of fictional policing, attempts can be made to look at the ways in which viewers are affected by what they see. A number of these effects have been discussed in the foregoing, but further content analyses would make even more complex analyses possible. First and second order cultivation effects in particular seem to be relevant. First order effects would include the knowledge viewers believe to distil from television fiction. The list of themes is endless: from people's perceptions of particular law enforcement departments and their procedures to questions of personal safety or "knowledge" of rights. Second order effects would include opinions and attitudes, for instance, regarding the funding of departments, the professionalism (or lack thereof) of certain (types) of departments, the acceptability of policy brutality, etc. An issue of particular importance may be the job aspirations of younger viewers (potential future police recruits). Minority members or women may specifically be affected by the way in which their own kind are portrayed.

Third, it is worth wondering whether television fiction has any effect on policy makers. While news is more likely to influence them, it is possible that those who make decisions about law enforcement are affected by police fiction, either because they are influenced just like any viewer might be influenced or because they are influenced by members of the public or by pressure groups that have been influenced.

Finally, as argued above, law enforcement departments may be affected by some of the messages of television fiction. Officers may start to behave differently or may experience changing behaviors and attitudes in members of the public they have to deal with. Department policy-makers may equally be affected.

Meanwhile, law enforcement organizations would do well to take heed and realize that when confronted with ordinary members of the public, they will often be dealing with people who's expectations, perceptions and beliefs about the nature of police work, the behaviors and attitudes to be expected from officers and the procedures that define adequate responses to their complaints and wishes, may be based partially on fictional images. Several continental European police officers have told the author anecdotes about suspects demanding to be "read their rights", a reference to the Miranda Rights from the American legal system. In many European judicial systems, which have their roots in Napoleontic law, such rights do not exist. Fictitious images are so strong and convincing that even people watching these images in a different country appear to develop the impression that what is in fact mainly a dramaturgical tool to help tell a good story is actually an education about what are perceived to be universal truths of law enforcement.

References

Altheide, D. 1985. *Media Power.* Beverly Hills: Sage.
Altheide, D. and Snow, R. P. 1979. *Media Logic.* Beverly Hills: Sage.
Bandura, A., Ross, D. and Ross, S. 1963a. "A comparative test of the status of envy, social power, and secondary reinforcement theories of identificatory learning". *Journal of Abnormal and Social Psychology* 67: 527–534.
Bandura, A., Ross, D. and Ross, S. 1963b. "Imitation of film-mediated aggressive models". *Journal of Abnormal and Social Psychology* 66: 3–11.
Bauer, L. 1992. *Authentizität, Mimesis, Fiktion: Fernsehunterhaltung und Integration von Realität am Beispiel des Kriminalsujets.* München: Schaudig, Bauer and Ledig.
Beck, K. 1994. *Medien und die Soziale Konstruktion von Zeit, Über die Vermittlung von Gesellschaftlicher Zeitordnung und Sozialem Zeitbewusstsein.* Opladen: Westdeutscher Verlag.
Berkowitz, L. 1993. *Aggression: Its Causes, consequences, and control.* New York: McGraw Hill.
Cantor, J. 1994. "Fright reactions to mass media". In *Media Effects: Advances in Theory and Research,* J. Bryant, and D. Zillmann (eds), 213–245. Hillsdale, NJ: Erlbaum.
Carlson, J. M. 1985. *Prime Time Law Enforcement: Crime show viewing and attitudes toward the criminal justice system.* New York: Praeger.
Centerwall, B. S. 1989a. "Exposure to television as a cause of violence". In *Public Communication and Behavior,* G. Comstock (ed.), 1–58. New York: Academic Press.
Centerwall, B. S. 1989b. "Exposure to television as a risk factor for violence". *American Journal of Epidemiology* 129: 643–652.
Centerwall, B. S. 1993. "Television and violent crime". *The Public Interest* 111: 56–71.
Cohen, B. 1963. *The Press and Foreign Policy.* Princeton: Princeton University Press.
Cook, T. D., Kendzierski, D. A. and Thomas, S. V. 1983. "The implicit assumptions of television research: an anlysis of the 1982 NIMH report on television and behaviors". *Public Opinion Quarterly* 47: 161–261.
Culver, J. H. 1978. "Television and the police". *Policy Studies Journal* 7: 500–505.
Daven, J., O'Conner, J. F. and Briggs, R. 1976. "Consequences of imitative behavior in children: Knievel, E. syndrome". *Pediatrics* 57: 418–419.
Davies, S. J. C., Atherton, M., Williams, T., Purkis, J., Combe, G., Brindley, A. J., McCarthy, G. and Denny, R. 1999. "Effects of drug overdose in television drama on presentations for self poisoning — study is impressive but raises methodological concerns". *British Medical Journal* 319: 1131–1132.

Dees, T. M. 1996. "Ethics and the Sipowicz factor". *Law Enforcement Technology* 23: 58–60.
Dixon, T. L. and Linz, D. 2000. "Overrepresentation and underrepresentation of African Americans and Latinos as lawbreakers on television news". *Journal of Communication* 50: 131–154.
Dominick, J.-R. 1973. "Crime and law enforcement on prime-time television". *Public Opinion Quarterly* 37: 241–250.
Doob, A. N. and Macdonald, G. E. 1979. "Television viewing and fear of victimization: is the relationship causal?" *Journal of Personality and Social Psychology* 37: 170–179.
Fabianic, D. 1997. "Television dramas and homicide causation". *Journal of Criminal Justice* 25: 195–203.
Funkhauser, G. R. and Shaw, E. F. 1990. "How synthetic experience shapes social reality". *Journal of Communication* 40: 75–87.
Gerbner, G. 1969. "Institutional pressures on mass communicators". In *The Sociology of Mass Media Communicators*, P. Halmos (ed.), 205–248. Keele: University of Keele.
Gerbner, G. and Gross, L. 1976. "Living with television: the violence profile". *Journal of Communication* 26: 173–199.
Gerbner, G., Gross, L., Morgan, M. and Signorielli, N. 1980. "The "mainstreaming" of America: Violence profile no. 11". *Journal of Communication* 30: 10–29.
Gould, M. S. 1990. "Suicide clusters and media exposure". In *Suicide over the Life Cycle: Risk factors, assessment, and treatment of suicidal patients*, S. J. Blumenthal and D. J. Kupfer (eds), 517–532. Washington, DC: American Psychiatric Press.
Greenberg, B. S., Neuendorf, K., Buerkel-Rothfuss, N. D. and Henderson, L. 1982. "The soaps: What's on and who cares?" *Journal of Broadcasting* 26: 519–536.
Gross, L. and Jeffries-Fox, S. 1978. "What do you want to be when you grow up, little girl?" In *Heath and Home: Images of Women in the Mass Media*, G. Tuchman, A. K. Daniels and J. Benet (eds), 240–265. New York: Oxford University Press.
Grossberg, L., Wartella, E. and Whitney, D. C. 1998. *MediaMaking: Mass Media in a Popular Culture*. Thousand Oaks: Sage.
Gunther, M. 1971. "You have the right to remain silent". *TV Guide* (December 18): 3–24.
Hans, V. P. and Dee, J. L. 1991. "Media coverage of law. Its impact on juries and the public". *American Behavioral Scientist* 35: 136–149.
Harris, R. J. 1989. *A Cognitive Psychology of Mass Communication*. Hillsdale: Erlbaum.
Harris, R. J. 1999. *A Cognitive Psychology of Mass Communication*. Hillsdale: Erlbaum.
Harrison, K. and Cantor, J. 1999. "Tales from the screen: enduring fright reactions to scary media". *Media Psychology* 1: 97–116.
Hawkins, R. P. and Pingree, S. 1981. "Uniform content and habitual viewing: Unnecessary assumptions in social reality effects". *Human Communication Research* 7: 291–301.
Hawkins, R. P., Pingree, S. and Adler, I. 1987. "Searching for cognitive processes in the cultivation effect: Adult and adolescent samples in the United States and Australia". *Human Communication Research* 13: 553–577.
Hawton, K., Simkin, S., Deeks, J. J., O'Connor, S., Keen, A., Altman, D. G., Philo, G. and Bulstrode, C. 1999. Effects of a drug overdose in a television drama on presentations to hospital for self poisoning: time series and questionnaire study. *British Medical Journal* 318: 972–977.

Head, S. 1954. "Content analysis of televised drama programs". *Quarterly of Film, Radio, and Television* 9: 175–194.
Hoekstra, S.J., Jackson Harris, R. and Helmick, A.L. 1999. "Autobiographical memories about the experience of seeing frightening movies in childhood". *Media Psychology* 1: 117–140.
Huesmann, L.R. 1986. "Psychological processes promoting the relation between exposure to media violence and aggressive behavior by the viewer". *Journal of Social Issues* 42: 125–139.
Hurd, G. 1981. "The television presentation of the police". In *Popular Television and Film*, T. Bennet, S. Boyd-Bowman, C. Mercer and J. Woollacott (eds), 53–70, London: British Film Institute, Open University Press.
Ishii, K. 1991. "Measuring mutual causation: Effects of suicide news on suicides in Japan". *Social Sience Research* 20: 188–195.
Jarvis, J. 1991. "Lawyers get out of their briefs and into our homes". *Rolling Stone* 605: 79–80.
Kessler, R.C. and Stipp, H. 1984. "The impact of fictional television suicide stories on U.S. fatalities". *American Journal of Sociology* 90: 151–167.
Lichter, L. and Lichter, R. 1983. *Prime Time Crime*. Washington, DC: Media Institute.
McNeely, C.L. 1995. "Perceptions of the criminal justice system: television imagery and public knowledge in the United States". *Journal of Criminal Justice and Popular Culture* 3: 1–20.
McQuail, D. (1994). *Mass Communication Theory: An Introduction*. London: Sage.
Marks, A. 1987. "Television and suicide: Comment". *New England Journal of Medicine* 316: 877.
Mastro, D.E. and Greenberg, B.S. 2000. "The portrayal of racial minorities on prime time television". *Journal of Broadcasting and Electronic Media* 44: 690–703.
Mastroianni, G.R. 1987. "Television and suicide: Comment". *New England Journal of Medicine* 316: 877.
Minnebo, J. 2000. "Fear of crime and television use: A uses and gratifications approach". *Communications* 25: 125–142.
Morgan, M. 1983. "Symbolic victimization and real-world fear". *Human Communication Research* 9: 146–157.
Morgan, M. and Shanahan, J. 1997. "Two decades of cultivation research: An appraisal and meta-analysis", In *Communication Yearbook* 20, B.R. Burleson and A.W. Kunkel (eds), 1–45. Thousand Oaks, CA: Sage.
Oliver, M.B. 1994. "Portrayals of crime, race, and aggression in "reality based" police shows: A content analysis". *Journal of Broadcasting and Electronic Media* 38: 179–192.
Pacanowsky, M.E. and Anderson, J.A. 1982. "Cop talk and media use". *Journal of Broadcasting* 26: 741–754.
Pandiani, J.A. 1978. "Crime time TV: If all we know is what we saw ..." *Contemporary Crises* 2: 437–458.
Pell, J. and Murdoch, R. 1999. "Effects of drug overdose in television drama on presentation for self poisoning — a causal association cannot yet be inferred". *British Medical Journal* 319: 1131–1131.
Perlmutter, D.D. 2000. *Policing the Media: Street Cops and Public Perceptions of Law Enforcement*. Thousand Oaks: Sage.
Phillips, D.P. 1974. "The influence of suggestion on suicide: substantive and theoretical implications". *American Sociological Review* 39: 340–354.
Phillips, D.P. 1979. "Suicide, motor vehicle fatalities, and the mass media: evidence toward a theory of suggestion". *American Journal of Sociology* 84: 1150–1174.

Phillips, D. P. 1986. "Natural experiments on the effects of mass media violence on fata aggression: Strengths and weaknesses of a new approach". In *Advances in Experimental Social Psychology* 19, L. Berkowitz (ed.), 207–250 Orlando, Fla: Academic Press.

Phillips, D. P. and Carstensen, L. L. 1986. "Clustering of teenage suicides after television news stories about suicide". *New England Journal of Medicine* 315: 685–689.

Pines, J. 1995. "Black cops and black villains in film and TV crime fiction". In *Crime and the Media, the Post-Modern Spectacle*, D. Kidd-Hewitt and R. Osborne (eds), 67–77. London: Pluto Press.

Potter, W. J. 1988. "Perceived reality in television effects research". *Journal of Broadcasting and Electronic Media* 32: 23–41.

Potter, W. J. 1998. *Media Literacy*. Thousand Oaks, CA; Sage.

Potter, W. J. 1991a. "The linearity assumption in cultivation research". *Human Communication Research* 17: 562–583.

Potter, W. J. 1991b. "The relationship between first- and second-order measures of cultivation". *Human Communication Research* 18: 92–113.

Potter, W. J., Vaughan, M. W., Warren, R., Howley, K., Land, A. and Hagemeyer, J. C. 1995. "How real is the portrayal of aggression in television entertainment programming?" *Journal of Broadcasting and Electronic Media* 39: 496–516.

Radelet, L. A. and Carter, D. L. 1994. *The Police and the Community*. New York: Macmillan.

Reiner, R. 1985. *The Politics of the Police*. Hemel Hempstead: Wheatsheaf.

Rosengren, K. E. 1994. "Culture, media and society: agency and structure, continuity and change". In *Media Effects and Beyond: Culture, Socialization and Lifestyles*, K. E. Rosengren (ed.), 3–28. London: Routledge.

Rosenthal, R. 1986. "Media violence, antisocial behavior and the social consequences of small effects". *Journal of Social Issues* 42: 141–154.

Scharrer, E. 2000. "Tough guys: The portrayal of hypermasculinity and aggression in televised police dramas". 50th Annual Conference of the International Communication Association, Acapulco.

Shanahan, J. and Morgan, M. 1999. *Television and its Viewers: Cultivation theory and Research*. Cambridge: Cambridge University Press.

Shrum, L. J. 1995. "Assessing the social influence of television: a social cognition perspective on cultivation effects". *Communication Research* 24: 402–429.

Signorielli, N. 1990. "Television's mean and dangerous world: A continuation of the cultural indicators perspective. In *Cultivation Analysis: New directions in Media Effects Research*, N. Signorielli and M. Morgan (eds), 85–107, Newbury Park, CA: Sage.

Signorielli, N. 1993. *Mass Media images and Impact on Health: A Sourcebook*. Westport: Greenwood Press.

Signorielli, N. and Morgan, M. (eds) 1990. *Cultivation Analysis: New Directions in Media Effects Research*. Newbury Park, CA: Sage.

Simkin, S., Hawton, K., Whitehead, L., Fagg, J. and Eagle, M. 1995. Media influence on parasuicide. A study of the effects of a television drama portrayal of paracetamol self-poisoning. *British Journal of Psychiatry* 167: 754–759.

Simons, D. and Silveira, W. R. 1994. "Post-traumatic stress disorder in children after television programmes". *British Medical Journal* 308: 389–390.

Smith, S. L., Wilson, B. J., Kunkel, D., Linz, D., Potter, W. J., Colvin, C. M. and Donnerstein, E. 1998. "Part I: Violence in television programming overall: University of California, Santa Barbara Study 3". In *National Television Violence Study 3*, 5–127, Thousand Oaks, CA: Sage.
Smythe, D. W. 1954. "Reality as presented by television". *Public Opinion Quarterly* 18: 143–156.
Snow, R. P. 1974. "How children interpret TV violence in play context". *Journalism Quarterly* 51: 13–21.
Snow, R. P. 1983. *Creating Media Culture*. Beverly Hills, CA: Sage.
Sparks, G. G., and Ogles, R. M. 1990. "The difference between fear of victimization and the probability of being victimized: implications for cultivation". *Journal of Broadcasting and Electronic Media* 34: 351–358.
Sparks, R. 1992. *Television and the Drama of Crime, Moral Tales and the Place of Crime in Public Life*. Buckingham, Philadelphia: Open University Press.
Tamborini, R., Mastro, D. E., Chory-Assad, R. M. and He Huang, R. 2000. "The color of crime and the court: a content analysis of minority representation on television". *Journalism and Mass Communication Quarterly* 77: 639–653.
Tamborini, R., Zillmann, D. and Bryant, J. 1984. "Fear and victimization: Exposure to television and perceptions of crime and fear", In *Communication Yearbook* 8, R. N. Bostrom and B. H. Westley (eds), 492–513. Beverly Hills, CA: Sage.
Van den Bulck, J. 1996. *Kijkbuiskennis, de Rol van Televisie in de Sociale en Cognitieve Constructie van de Realiteit.* Leuven: Acco.
Van den Bulck, J. 1999. "The Miranda effect: data setting as a cultivation effect". Media Systems in Transition on the Eve of the Information Society of the 21st Century IAMCR conference, Leipzig.
Wallack, E. M. and Bingle, G. J. 1996. "Cardiopulmonary resuscitation on television. Correspondence". *The New England Journal of Medicine* 335: 1605.
Wasserman, I. M. 1984. "Imitation and suicide: A reexamination of the Werther effect". *American Sociological Review* 49: 427–436.
Weaver, J. and Wakshlag, J. J. 1986. "Perceived vulnerability to crime, criminal victimization experience and television viewing". *Journal of Broadcasting and Electronic Media* 30: 141–158.
Weimann, G. 2000. *Communicating Unreality: Modern Media and the Reconstruction of Reality*. Thousand Oaks, CA: Sage.
Wicks, R. H. 1992. "Schema theory and measurement in mass communication research: Theoretical and methodological issues in news information processing". In *Communication Yearbook* 15, S. A. Deetz (ed.), 115–145. Newbury Park, CA: Sage.
Wright, J. C., Huston, A. C., Truglio, R., Fitch, M., Smith, E. and Piemyat, S. 1995. "Occupational portrayals on television: children's role schemata, career aspirations, and perceptions of reality". *Child Development* 66: 1706–1718.
Wroblewski, R. and Huston, A. C. 1987. "Televised occupational stereotypes and their effects on early adolescence: Are they changing?" *Journal of Early Adolescence* 7: 283–297.
Zillmann, D. and Wakshlag, J. J. 1985. "Fear and victimization and appeal of crime data". In *Selective Exposure to Communication*, D. Zillmann and J. Bryant (eds), Hillsdale: Erlbaum.

CHAPTER 6

Communication issues in policing family violence*

Mary Anne Fitzpatrick
University of Wisconsin, Madison, USA

America is obsessed with the apparent epidemics of violence, crime, and drug abuse. Vivid media accounts have convinced Americans that violent crimes are committed by juveniles of ever-younger ages and that drug abuse has further contributed to an increase in domestic violence, gang activity, youth violence, child abuse, and various forms of behavioral pathology. Many of these propositions about violence in the street do not hold up to empirical scrutiny. Regardless of the rates and types of violence in American society in general, violence is, however, part of the fabric of American families. And when called into family disputes, police officers are often confronted with complex, dangerous, and unpredictable situations. These situations call for officers to make fast but reasonable decisions about how to respond.

The purpose of these chapter is to highlight the policy implications of basic research on family processes in order give law enforcement professionals a contextual background for dealing with families in distress. Consequently, this chapter considers the nature of the family as well as various contexts and definitions of family violence and subsequently considers the social-legal environment in which the police operate. Finally, a dialectical model of police–citizen encounters is presented in order to describe the interactional and legal constraints on conversational moves in policing family violence.

The nature of family interaction

In dealing with families, police officers need to remember one major organizing principle that undergirds interaction moves in families: that is, relationships are embedded in systems. Individual thoughts and actions are constrained by the fact that people are entrenched in relationships and in families. Families are, in turn, influenced by the societal and cultural niches in which they find themselves. Systems theory views every communication act as simultaneously a stimulus, a response, and a reinforcer, such that interpersonal communication represents a chain of overlapping and interdependent links. Like a wind chime with pieces of various sizes suspended at different levels, one soft wind disturbs a piece which then moves another and so on. In other words, the behavior of one family member impacts on, and is influenced by, all other members of the family (Hinde & Stevenson-Hinde 1988).

Within a given family system, however, families can have remarkably different concepts of how to define roles and duties. There is great variability in who is responsible for what in families as well as who can exercise particular rights. These rights and duties form the rule structure for the family because families are rule-governed, not random or unpredictable. The rules guiding relationships may be, however, explicit (e.g., "Don't talk about money with outsiders") and/or implicit (e.g., "Never tell that Uncle Albert fondled you"). All of these systems (i.e., individual, relationships, family, society, culture) continuously evolve and influence each other over time. And, interaction sequences that occur repeatedly in the family reflect implicit underlying rules for the relationship that are difficult to change.

Two major conceptual dimensions can be used to describe these patterned variations in family systems (Fitzpatrick & Ritchie 1995). Structural traditionalism focuses on the extent to which family members adhere to well-defined role expectations. Because family roles and norms are influenced by the social context in which families find themselves, family roles and the appropriate performance of these roles are legitimated by sources outside the family. Notions of who holds the power or the legitimate monopoly of coercion in the family, conceptions of hierarchy in the family, as well as gender ideologies, are implicated in this conceptual space. Expressiveness focuses on the family's deployment of emotional resources, receptivity to new information, and shared responsibility for coping with daily emotional and social crises. This dimension includes the free and open expression of ideas, information and feelings. These two conceptual dimensions influence one another and define basic family types (Fitzpatrick & Ritchie 1995) which have very different rules for interacting within and outside the family system.

Each marital relationship has a beginning equilibrium point that is set through a variety of individual differences, motivations, and needs and even partner's differential levels of mental health and stability. The marital change that occurs from this baseline is driven by internal communication processes (Karney & Bradbury 1997). Patterns of corrosive conflict which lead to physical violence may indeed erode relational satisfaction and hence stability in the marital system for at least one partner over time. But, the rate and size of the change in the marriage is influenced by the couple's initial equilibrium point. This explanation means that the police officer has no way of knowing where he is entering in the history of the marital or family system. Each system will be unique, as each began at a different point and behaviors may come to have different meanings depending on the family itself.

Within some of these basic family systems, violence can be internalized as a way to handle family conflict. Physical violence may be the way members resolve disputes when they are unable to control their anger and engage in more constructive conflict resolution. Violence may become a lens through which family members see the interaction. Even the very definition of violence may differ between the police officer and the citizen. What outsiders consider a violent act may not have the same meaning for relational participants.

Violence in the family

If one focuses on physical violence in the family, the American Medical Association (1992) estimates that family violence costs the United States from $5 to $10 billion annually in medical expenses, police and court costs, shelters and foster care, sick leave, absenteeism, and non-productivity. Estimates of abuse range from 960,000 incidents of violence against a current or former spouse, boyfriend or girlfriend per year to 4 million women who are physically abused by their husbands or live-in partners per year. The FBI (1997) reports that among all female murder victims, 30% were slain by their husbands or boyfriends. In general, crime victims surveys, police records, and hospital attendance data estimate the rate of violence against women in families at about 3%.

Although federal crime statistics offer an important picture of severe instances of family violence that come to the attention of the criminal justice system, often researchers seek to uncover information about the full extent of family violence in the general population. In what many consider the classic study of the issue, Straus and Gelles (1990) report domestic violence prevalence rates at 10% for men and women, using the Conflict Tactics Scale (CTS). The scale measures asks how many times your partner has engaged in violent acts ranging from throwing something through pushing and shoving to the threat or actual use of a gun or a knife. The debates about the extent of the problem will continue even as controversy surrounds what should be included in a definition of family violence.

Most analysts agree that there are wide variations in the forms, types, and consequences of violence in the family. Abuse in the marital system is often linked to particular styles of family interaction that involve the child (Margolin, John, Ghosh & Gordis 1996). Because of marital violence, children may be ignored, neglected, or maltreated. Children may not be the direct victims of physical abuse but children in violent-prone homes are often the audience for marital violence, causing psychological distress and difficulties (Margolin & Gordis 2000). And, children in these homes are often the target of excessively authoritarian parenting styles (Higgins & McCabe 2000). According to the Spouse Assault Replication Program (SARP) database, young children (0–5 years of age), for example, are disproportionately present in households with violence (Fantuzzo, Boruch, Beriama & Atkins 1997). Thus, more people in relationships are affected by violent acts than those who sustain physical injuries. Given the interconnections in the causes, consequences and remedies for these forms of abuse, many theorists include child abuse, neglect, incest, battering, elder abuse, and psychological abuse under the rubric of family violence (Stith, Rosen, Middleton, Busch, Lundeberg & Carlton 2000).

Regardless of the form or target of the abuse, violent acts can also be defined in terms of their severity and impulsiveness. On the severity continua, abusive behaviors range from mild forms of verbal intimidation, through severe beatings, to extremely violent rapes and homicides. Minor violence includes pushing, grabbing, shoving, hitting with an open hand and other minor injuries. Medium-serious violence includes kicking, beating up, hitting with fists and medium injuries. Serious violence includes serious kicking, serious hitting, beating up, attempts at choking and the use of weapons (Hyden 1994). On the impulsive dimension, violence can range from acts involving sudden emotional outbursts that lead to inflicting injury on others to carefully premeditated and planned attacks (Cahn 1996).

For the police officer, then, it is important to remember that there is a strong potential for emotional spillover in violent families. That is, there is usually not one clearly identified target for violence as the abuse is contagious. And, acts that begin on one end of a severity or impulsiveness continua will probably shift along that continua over time. Impulsive acts of violence, for example, may become "rewarding" as they generate an effect and thus may be repeated in a more thoughtful manner in the future. Less severe acts of violence may also move along the continua over time and become more severe in order to achieve the desired effect.

Myths of family violence

People and their societies invent myths to explain reality. In the case of social reality, there is often some underlying kernel of truth that has been simplified and distorted to cover the complex nature of reality. Myths can be problematic when they blind us to what is actually happening in a given situation. Three powerful myths cloud clear thinking about family violence.

Myth 1: Family violence is about men beating women
There is perhaps no more politicized area than the question surrounding possible gender differences in violent behavior. Two sharply contested viewpoints emerge in the literature: violence involves male perpetrators and female victims, or violence involves a good deal of mutual combat. Feminist researchers typically study samples selected for high levels of partner abuse by men, such as women in shelters or men in treatment programs. Thus, they find that most violence falls into the first category. Family researchers who use representative samples of married, dating, or cohabiting couples uncover the second type of violence which is common couple violence or occasional lapses of control by either partner. Different conclusions are derived from studying different samples (Johnson 1995). Common couple violence must be clearly discriminated from violence involving male batterers and female victims.

One recent review attempted to examine the question of family violence by using meta-analysis. Meta-analysis is a statistical technique that attempts to aggregate the findings across a number of studies in order to develop a firm base of empirical support. Combining research involving samples of over 64,000 individuals, Archer's (2000) study found that women were slightly more likely than men to use one or more acts of physical aggression. Women were also more likely than men to use physical aggression in intimate heterosexual relationships. Female violence does appear, however, to be restricted to the private or personal relationship context rather than the public context: in 1996, 85% of those arrested for violent crimes were men (Frieze 2000). And it can not be ignored that men were significantly more likely to inflict an injury, and overall 62% of those injured were women.

Most of the empirical work available to Archer (2000) for the meta analysis, however, used the Conflict Tactics Scale (CTS) as the measure of violence in the relationship (Straus 1979). Consequently, the conclusions of Archer's analyses are limited by the conceptual underpinnings of the CTS scale. The CTS has been criticized for ignoring the contexts of violent acts (Dobash, Dobash, Wilson & Daly 1992) and not discriminating between mild and severe forms of aggression (White, Smith, Koss & Figuero 2000). Simple frequency counts of violent acts ignore the fact that hitting, for example, may or may not cause sustained and serious physical injury to a victim, depending on a variety of contextual factors.

Attempting to examine the context of marital violence closely, Jacobson and Gottman (1998) studied severely violent couples. They found that whereas not all men who emotionally abuse their wives are batterers, all batterers emotionally abuse their wives. Battering is physical aggression designed to control, intimidate, and subordinate another human being. It is always accompanied by emotional abuse, often by injury, and always associated with fear and terror on the part of the battered woman. Batterers emotionally abuse their wives by "verbal threats, intimidating actions such as the destruction of pets or property, humiliating and degrading remarks directed toward their partners, and attempts to rob their partners of their autonomy as human beings" (p. 23). Once a woman has been battered, emotional abuse can become a proxy for physical abuse as it reminds the woman she can be beaten at any time. A humiliating comment to a woman may, then, actually signify physical violence to her. It is difficult for an outside observer to understand the meaning the remark has for the participants.

Not only is the CTS a measure that ignores the context and the consequences of violence, but it is also a measure that excludes many possible forms of aggression. The CTS ignores a variety of tactics that may be used by males: threatening to hurt partner physically or economically; isolating her; controlling what she does and/or who she sees; and sexual aggression and stalking (clearly criminal acts, see Chapter 8). The scale also leads to an underestimation of possible female violence which may include: passive-aggressive behaviors; property damage; or locking someone outside the house.

Policing family violence requires an understanding of the complex contextual factors that undergird the violent act. And, although male violence may cause more damage, violence is a relational issue (Goodyear-Smith & Laidlaw 1999). Officers should be especially sensitive to emotional abuse that occurs in their presence as it is probably a signal that substantial physical violence is also occurring in the family context.

Myth II: All abusers are alike
Holden and Ritchie (1991) found that abusers, compared to non-abusers, were portrayed by their wives as more irritable, less involved in child rearing, less physically affectionate, less likely to use reasoning, and more likely to use physical punishment and power assertive responses in response to a child's misbehavior. There is a growing realization that a better way to understand the motivations, backgrounds, internal predispositions and so forth of those who abuse is not to assume a homogeneity in that group but to develop typologies based on the individual characteristics. The most general discrimination is that which isolates the individual male who is violent only in the family context in contrast to the individual who is generally violent. Holtzworth-Munroe and Stuart (1994) discriminated three subtypes of males: (a) family only; (b) dysphoric/borderline; (c) generally violent/antisocial. The latter two subtypes of male abuse are caused by serious underlying personality disorders. The borderline condition is intermediate between neurosis and schizophrenia and features impulsiveness, unstable relationships, identity disturbance, unstable moods, and boredom. The generally violent abuser, who is often extraverted and not neurotic, uses violence to resolve difficulties in all types of situations because he is repeatedly at variance with society. He is unable to make deep and stable relationships, lacks concern for others, and is incapable of guilt or remorse. He is likely to have aggressive outbursts in the face of frustrations and delays in the gratification of his wishes.

Jacobson and Gottman (1998) found two types of men who engage in high levels of violence against their wives: Pit Bulls and Cobras. Pit Bulls appear to be driven by insecurity and a high level of unhealthy dependence on their wives. If the wife makes a move toward independence, these men are more likely to become stalkers. Interestingly, counseling may work with these types of men. Cobras, on the other hand, begin a discussion of disagreement by becoming belligerent, contemptuous, or defensive, regardless of how reasonable their wives are in bringing up an issue. Cool and methodical as they inflict pain and humiliation on their partners, Cobras see violence as a part of relational life. The wives of these men are significantly more depressed and frightened yet these couples do not easily separate or divorce. Cobra men are more violent outside the marriage as well and are more likely to suffer antisocial personality disorder.

Typologies like these serve to remind us that the factors underlying and explaining the violent act should cause us to be tentative as we suggest a particular solution to family violence. The low self control that characterizes the borderline personality disordered, the antisocial individual and the Cobra suggests that legal deterrence models for dealing with family violence such as threatening arrest may not be the solution to this situation. The assumption of a rational mind capable of being deterred from engaging in a impulsive act may not be a tenable one in all cases. For the police officer, these types of individuals are the most dangerous as they are more likely to commit extremely violent acts including murder. With good cause, their wives are extremely frightened of them.

Myth III: Violence is an isolated act
Although there may be cases where a violent act has never occurred before in the relationship and will not occur again, violence in the family is almost always part of an ongoing communication process. Communication between people involves the give and take of messages exchanged over time yielding patterns of interactions. The patterns of messages exchanged between partners predict numerous outcomes, including each partners' experienced state of the relationship. Indeed, a physically violent act is rarely the first or only behavior in an exchange.

Many researchers find strong patterns of negative reciprocity in marriage where a negative message is responded to immediately with a negative message. Consider verbally aggressive messages which include: character attacks; competence attacks; physical appearance attacks; background attacks; accusations; profanity; ridicule; threats and nonverbal emblems (Infante, Sabourin, Rudd & Shannon 1990). A verbally aggressive act by one partner is reciprocated with greater intensity over the interaction (Sabourin 1996) and this verbal aggression quickly escalates. Once a given threshold has been reached, verbal aggression serves as a catalyst for physical aggression in couples. We need more research to isolate exactly what the threshold point is in family dialogue that moves negative symbolic behavior into physically violent behaviors. But preliminary evidence suggests that cycles of verbally aggressive messages and responses can easily feed into physical violence.

Indeed such tit-for-tat reciprocity is similar to the problem of resonance in physics, where interacting systems of closely matched frequency give rise to wider and wider oscillations and less self-correction than systems that are further out of synchrony. But perhaps not all systems are reciprocity systems and different rules may undergird these marital systems. Indeed, Hyden (1994) uncovered two different types of marital systems related to marital violence: (1) Symmetrical (similar to Fitzpatrick's [1988] Independents) and (2) Complementary (similar to Fitzpatrick's [1988] Traditionals).

Symmetry (or an attempt to maintain reciprocity and equality in the relationship) was related to seeking a divorce, when there was serious violence in the relationship. This held whether or not the couples were accordant, or shared a number of similar values. Symmetrical or Independent couples engage in open conflict and a high level of sharing of positive and negative emotions in the relationship. There is a concern in these relationships for maintaining a balance of power and equality in the marriage. Common couple violence that is equalized across the relationship may be acceptable for a time, as long as equilibrium can be maintained. When the style of bargaining and negotiation that characterizes these families escalates into unequal amounts of physical violence, these couples leave the relationship.

Conversely, across levels of violence in the relationship, complementary is related to remaining in the relationship, whether or not couples shared a number of similar values. Complementary couples are less likely to directly reciprocate negative messages. Structures of traditionalism give these couples notions of more differentiated gender roles, which may downplay the seriousness of male violence in the family. These values and some limited ability to express their feelings allow these couples to absorb violence and still define the relationship as "satisfactory". Clearly, some marital systems are not overturned by family violence.

Summary

Family relationships have their own internal "psycho-logic" although the police officer may see family actions as irrational adaptations. Families rely on myths and hidden lines of control as well as futile repetitive behaviors and conflicts. Even in the most abusive families, partners are often very connected to one another. At any given point of intervention, the victim in an abusive situation may be dependent, financially or emotionally, on the abuser. And, violence may be a recurring event between individuals in daily contact with one another. Thus, violence may be a central organizing principle of the relationship. The officer needs to develop an appreciation for the variety of family styles. Ready to offer assistance and help, the officer needs to understand that family members often have different definitions of the situation and different constraints on their own behavior.

Police officers need to remember that family violence is widespread, complex, and multi-determined. There is no one profile of victim or aggressor that fits the majority of cases that may be encountered by law enforcement officials. Although it is difficult for a police officer to intervene in family violence at any given point in the couple's history, a few major distinctions based on the research may suggest possible courses of action for a police officer responding to a domestic violence call. The first distinction is: Does this incident represent common couple violence or is this the work of a seriously disturbed husband/partner battering his wife? The second distinction is: Is there one victim or many in the interaction? The third distinction is: How many instances have occurred before and how many do you predict for the future? As we will see in the next section, the answers to these questions suggest different potential courses of action for the police officer.

The nature of the social-legal environment

Although the domestic violence base rate is high compared to other crimes of violence, the police cannot arrest every man or woman who commits a misdemeanor or felony assault against a partner, much less arrest him or her every time it occurs. But in the past thirty years in the United States, there has been a movement in many legal jurisdictions to criminalize domestic violence. This movement has been occurring on three parallel tracks. The first is through mandatory arrest and the use of legal deterrence. The second is through the issuance of restraining orders to protect victims through either criminal or civil procedures. The third is through the increased use of treatment programs.

Mandatory Arrests

Police have traditionally been reluctant to make arrests for domestic violence incidents. Many States have adopted unprecedented statutes mandating arrest in cases of misdemeanor domestic battery, leading to a 70% increase in arrests for minor assaults, heavily concentrated among low-income and minority groups (Sherman, Schmidt & Rogan 1992).

Does arresting the perpetrators stop family violence not only immediately after the arrest but in the future? The classic study on this question was the Minneapolis Domestic Violence Experiment (Sherman & Berk 1984a, b). Police response to domestic violence calls was determined by random assignment. Police could: (1) arrest the suspect; (2) order one of the parties out of the residence; (3) advise the couple. The results of this experiment strongly favored arrest as the solution to family violence. The prevalence of subsequent offending

— assault, attempted assault, and property damage — was reduced by nearly 50% when the suspect was arrested.

Two major issues have come to the foreground as States have proceeded with the implementation of the mandatory arrest policy. First, over time, replications of the Minneapolis experiment failed to produce the same strong support for the mandatory arrest policy. When arrest works, the positive results can best be explained by the stake in conformity hypothesis (Sherman, Smith, Schmidt & Rogan 1992). That is, arrest seemed more likely to deter the married and the employed from engaging in domestic violence. The married and the employed, however, have the most to lose from an arrest. Their arrest seems to instantiate a level of informal social control because of three incurred costs (Williams & Hawkins 1989). The first is an attachment cost because arrest may lead to the loss of valued relationships. Second, arrest may be a stigma; the arrested individual may experience social opprobrium and embarrassment. Third, arrest may incur opportunity costs because the individual may lose a job or other economic benefits because they have been arrested. Thus, mandatory arrest reduces violence against middle-class women but does not necessarily reduce violence against those (often African-American) who are poor (Sherman, Schmidt & Rogan 1992).

The second issue that emerged centered on an indirect effect of the policy. A policy initially proposed to protect women and children from violent men has been used to arrest woman (and at times adolescents). Often, in the disorder and confusion at the scene, police officers arrest both parties. Martin (1997) found that one-third of the arrests in one sample were dual arrests and the women subject to dual arrest were likely to be white, young, urban, unmarried, and employed. The incident was likely to involve alcohol or drug use and physical beating with hands and fists. These dual arrests undoubtedly involve differential use of violence in families (i.e., common couple violence) but also over enforcement of the mandatory arrest policy by some police departments.

In the early studies, many of those arrested did not make it to court and most prosecutors refuse to pursue domestic violence cases following arrest. Martin (1994) examined the nature of prosecution within a State that has a mandatory arrest policy. Using court and police records, 448 cases of intimate family violence were examined: only 14% of the offenders were found to have been prosecuted and convicted. The cases have evidentiary problems and often, for the reasons we have cited, victims refuse to cooperate. Indeed, more experienced police officers seem to adopt a efficiency frame (Can claims be substantiated for successful prosecution?) in contrast to their less experienced counterparts who adopt a normative frame (Who is to blame?) for decision making in domestic assault calls (Stalans & Finn 1995). There may be lurking notions of patriarchy in the criminal justice system which still sees family violence as a private and not a public matter. And variations in treatment across court systems and dual arrests (of both partners) are implementation problems with the mandatory arrest policy.

Schmidt and Sherman (1993) argued that although mandatory arrest decreased domestic violence in some cities, mandatory arrest increased violence in other cities and among the unemployed. These authors urged the appeal of mandatory arrest laws and the substitution of police discretion, warrantless arrest and the issuance of arrest warrants for absent offenders.

Civil protection or restraining orders

These are legally mandated orders for abusers to refrain from contact with victims. Restraining orders are victim-initiated and timely acts and have a relaxed standard of proof. Most orders focus on victim protection and can proscribe a wide range of specific interventions that address extra legal concerns for the safety and economic well-being of the victim. Harrell, Smith and Newmark (1993) found that 60% of the 300 women they interviewed suffered abuse at least once more in the year following a restraining order. In contrast, Carlson, Harris and Holden (1999) examined police records for the two years before and the two years following Civil Protection Orders. These researchers found that prior to filing, 68% of the women reported physical violence and subsequent to filing only 23% reported physical violence. Very low SES women and African American women were more likely to report this re-abuse. Of course, women probably only seek restraining orders against the men who are the most likely to retaliate with violence.

Treatment programs

There is a strong tension in American culture between retributive and rehabilitative justice that is particularly highlighted in cases of family violence. For family members, receiving justice for past acts is often not as important as is achieving peace and family stability. Although public opinion recognizes the victim's need for protection, the public too places great emphasis on family autonomy and harmony. In work by Stalans (1996), the public strongly supported police and courts referrals for family violence to treatment and counseling; only 26% recommended arrest when the wife had moderately severe injuries.

Spouse abuse was ignored by mental health professionals until grass roots efforts by women's groups brought the issue to the attention of legislators and the general public in the seventies. The modal form of treatment for spouse abuse has been gender specific group therapy (O'Leary & Vivian 1990). Men's groups focus on anger management, responsibility for one's actions, and changes in attitudes that lead to aggression against women. Women's groups focus on empowering women to cope with a troubled marriage and seeking alternatives to marriage. When the safety of the partners can be assured, and couples want to remain together, couples therapy is indicated. But comprehensive research still needs to be done to match the family system and the severity of the offense to the correct treatment program.

Summary

Arrest, restraining orders, and treatment programs are not effective in all cases of family violence. Research is beginning to suggest that there is some appropriate match between the offense and the solution, although there are no clear policy directives as yet. In its training program on domestic violence, the Chicago Police Department makes the case that the best way for police units to stop crime is to concentrate effort on family violence (Sullivan 1995). Ten to 15% of all homicides are caused by domestic violence and these deaths may be the most preventable. Thus, a constant attention to even misdemeanor acts of family violence and follow-through in order to decrease the potential for escalation of these situations is time well-spent by the officer.

In responding to a domestic violence call, police are operating under a number of pragmatic constraints. Many jurisdictions have mandatory arrest laws. As professionals, police officers have a series of duties and responsibilities to the community that constrain how they behave and how much situational decision-making power they can utilize. Interestingly, citizens may have more information about the constraints on police officers because they are in a public role than officers have about the roles and rules in a given family situation. As we have seen, families are private cultures with their own specific rules and roles for appropriate behavior and communication. Naturally, there can be potential conflict between the external legal environment and its norms and processes and internal family norms and values about appropriate behaviors. Legal and policing norms may often conflict with internal family norms.

And, both the police and family members are caught between the societal demand for retribution and punishment in contrast to the societal demand for rehabilitation and treatment.

A model of police–citizen interaction

The preceding sections have brought to the forefront some of the myths, contradictions and inconsistencies of legal attempts to deal with the ongoing complexity of family violence. The officer answering a domestic call is confronted with a dilemma: how does he or she balance law enforcement and peace-keeping? I propose that the best model for explaining police–citizen interaction surrounding family violence is a dialectical one (Baxter 1988).

A dialectical model

The relationship between the officer and the family can best be described as one with a major dialectical tension (see Figure 6.1). The fundamental dynamic in police–citizen interaction in a family domestic dispute is that of law enforcement versus peace-keeping. As a police officer, the man or woman called to the scene has a public duty to uphold the laws of the jurisdiction; simultaneously, the officer has an obligation to restore peace and some measure of civility to the family and the surrounding community. The function of the officer is both to protect and assist the public. The relationship between an officer and a citizen requires both law enforcement and peace-keeping (doing no harm). But too much law enforcement may do great harm to family harmony and, conversely,

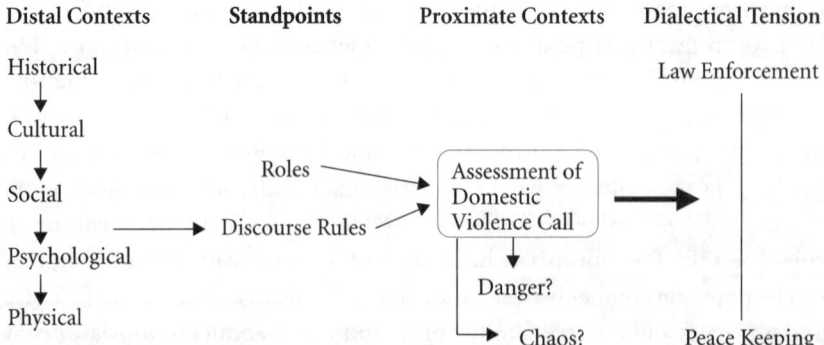

Figure 6.1. A dialectical model of police–citizen interaction

too much peace-keeping may violate the law. Indeed this contradiction is so central to the interaction that, by definition alone, it can be regarded as the principal contradiction in the relationship.

The domestic violence call itself sets in motion this dialectic, for no relationship between the citizen and the officer would exist unless the peace had been disturbed and the law had been violated. The tension between these two poles is real and is experienced by both partners in the exchange. Officers and citizens understand it and may even openly discuss it. But the key question in this section is: how is this dialectic communicatively managed in the encounter? To answer this question, we consider the contexts and constraints on this encounter; the discourse; and the strategies for dealing with the contradictions.

The context and constraints of the encounter

Let us consider the interaction between the police and the family during a call to the home surrounding a violent incident (see Figure 6.1). We focus particularly on the context of the interaction and the roles, rules, and constraints that envelop that the parties. Contexts are the environments and the interweaving of environments. The context of communication affects the expectations of the participants, the meanings that participants assign to messages, and their subsequent behaviors. Context includes the factors that lie outside the interactional partners and relationships but yet can have profound influence on them: in other words, the historical, cultural, social, psychological and physical circumstances that surround a communication episode.

The historical context is the background provided by previous communication episodes between members of the involved group. Police and various citizen groups may have a history of negative interactions functioning as a backdrop against which the current episode is being evaluated. The cultural context is the set of norms, values, and beliefs shared by a large group of people. Examples of cultural contexts that may be involved in police–citizen interaction include, for example, Chicano culture, African-American culture, police culture, gay culture, and so on. The social context is the nature of the relationship than exists between the participants and the psychological context is determined by the moods and feelings that each person brings to the encounter. This encounter will be influenced not only by the beliefs held by communicators about the settings but also by the actual surroundings and the settings. Thus, there is both a demonstrable physical environment and a psychological one.

The context in which this interaction takes place is significantly different for the police officer and the caller. Police culture portrays domestic violence calls as the potentially most dangerous situation for police officers, with elevated risk of injury or death. Although Garner and Clemmer (1986) have shown this fear to be unfounded, it stills exerts a strong influences on officers as they respond to a domestic violence call. Regardless, the very first question for the officer entering the scene must be: is anyone in the family armed and dangerous? Officers are in state of high physiological arousal as they respond to these calls because it is possible that they and others in this situation are in severe, immediate danger. The high level of physiological arousal experienced by officers is liable to negatively affect their ability to process abstract information. And, arousal may hamper his/her questioning and interviewing skills.

The second feature that pervades the context is the chaos that surrounds any heated family argument. According to Sillars and Weisberg (1987), interpersonal conflict episodes in families are ambiguous, disordered, and confusing. Married couples and family members are not like members of the Oxford College Debating Society, where speakers have clear goals and organized patterns of talk to achieve those goals. Particularly for conflicts ending in violence, there can be confusion over what the fight was about, who started it, who is responsible, and even what happened, when. Relationship conflicts are entangled, difficult to isolate, and impossible to define objectively. Although relational conflicts may have structure, such structure may be difficult to discern and impossible to report to an outsider. Conflict is embedded in daily life and may occur at all hours of the day or night, on any occasion, during any activity, for any number of different reasons. And, alcohol or drugs often fuel many chaotic family episodes.

Not only is the officer entering a potentially personally dangerous and chaotic situation, he or she is operating under a number of pragmatic considerations (Williams & Hawkins 1989). As we have seen, many jurisdictions have mandatory arrest laws limiting what the officer can do. Police are also part of a local legal or police culture which has complex patterns of practice that reflect in part the informal norms and expectations that regular players in the system have developed and have come to accept as "how we do things". Police culture socializes new recruits into the appropriate way to "handle" domestic disputes. Police culture includes the norms and attitudes, formal rules, and social relations that influence case outcomes (Fagan 1996). Many feminists view police culture as inherently sexist and unconcerned about violence against women and children. That is, feminists accuse the police, and the legal system in general, of not treating family violence as a serious crime but, rather, as viewing family violence as part of a private, internal family dynamic.

Developing rules for dealing with extremely distressed women and children at the scene is also a major challenge of these encounters. The woman may not be a victim or she may be an equal participant in common couples violence. The children may be victims of violence but they are most certainly the audience for these acts. Adult female victims may enter the discourse fearful of the power of the spouse; anxious that they may lose their children; afraid of leaving the house; and/or fearful of retaliation. Communicating with children presents another large set of interactional difficulties (see Chapter 7). Children may fear, or even fear for, their parents and thus be disinclined to interact with police officers. The chronological and developmental age of the child(ren) makes the interaction between a stranger adult (i.e., the police officer) and the child a situation fraught with possibilities for misunderstanding and problematic talk (Ochs 1991).

Finally, families may come from different cultures than do police officers and consequently, citizens have different values or ways of behaving. Culture influences the content and the form of an interaction. We are all aware when we are in the presence of language differences because language differs in vocabulary, syntax, and sound. But what is less readily apparent are the more abstract components of communication in cross-cultural encounters. Pragmatic structures of language are rule-governed and, therefore, potentially different from group to group. Cultures, for example, often have different rules covering what is polite and how direct or indirect one should be in conversation. In addition, cultures have very different rules for the use of various nonverbal communication cues such as eye gaze, head nods, speaking turn switching, floor time, and so on. The differential use of these cues is very subtle, yet can be very influential in causing communicators to be uncomfortable in one another's presence.

In general, the rules governing the social interaction differ when dealing with a member of a high context or a collective culture (Gudykunst 1991). Collective cultures value indirectness and face-saving; in-group rather than out-group members; and group goals rather than individual goals. When interacting with members of these collectivist cultures, it is important not to rush into the questioning section of the interview. Nonverbally, these cultures value contact, togetherness, and the restrained individual expression of emotion. High context or individualistic cultures value directness and individual goals. Nonverbally, collectivists value space, privacy, emotional expression, and personal choice of nonverbal behavior (Anderson 1998).

The efficacy of police officers depends on their ability to be flexible and to see that communication is a series of choice that our culture as made for us — and that other cultures make different choices. Religious, cultural, and social class differences may make the victim fearful of the police and make the officer uncomfortable interacting with community members. Because, cultures adopt different rules and customs, interactants from different cultures assign different meanings to acts.

In this section, we have covered the standpoints that surround the discourse. The context and the culture of the interactants constrain the dialogue that occurs between them. The material, social, and symbolic circumstances of the lives of the individuals involved in these encounters differ in ways that affect the transactions between them. These disparate circumstances promote distinctive identities, perspectives, priorities, views of social life, and ways of interacting. The first step for the police officer in the face-to-face interaction is to develop rapport. Developing rapport means trying to see the interaction from the point of view of the citizen. Resisting the temptation to evaluate, to judge, to interpret, to criticize, the officer must try to understand and actively listen to what the conversational partner is saying. How the different goals, rules, forms and meanings of communication play out in the encounter is discussed in the next section.

The discourse and the dialectic

Discourse covers all linguistic interactions that serve a discernible function and follow predictable patterns known implicitly or explicitly to participants. The different standpoints discussed in the previous section give each partner in the exchange potentially different goals for the encounter. The officer is balancing the need to enforce the law against the need to be a peace-keeper. At a societal level, this tension is represented in the tension between retributive and rehabilitative justice. These dialectical tensions represent a clash of opposing tendencies. Baxter (1988) argues that there are three major strategies for dealing with these contradictions in conversational interactions: selection, temporal-spatial separation, and integration.

The first strategy for dealing with the dialectical tension is selection. An officer repeatedly selects actions consistent with either the law officer or the peace-keeper polarity. This action is transformative in that one side of the dialectic is the preferred mode of operating in all situations. Police officers concerned with the law enforcement end of the continuum adopt an efficiency frame (Can the claim be substantiated for successful prosecution?). Thus, their major goal is to develop proper investigatory procedures to develop detailed narratives and proper evidence. The officer needs to establish that a crime has occurred and certain facts need to be in the case report. Family members must be separated in order to be interviewed and care should be taken that interviews can be conducted privately. Of course, even the initial discrimination in these interviews between common couple violence and male battering may not be a simple task. But one study (Paternoster, Bachman, Brame & Sherman 1997) found the use of fair procedures when arresting suspects inhibited subsequent assault. Furthermore, the likelihood of arrest was predicted by: offender's presence at the scene when the police arrived; victim preference for arrest; severity of victim injuries; and offender's demeanor toward the police (Feder 1998).

When seeking information about the incident, officers should carefully structure the sequence of the questions. Officers must use questions strategically to achieve the goal of deciding what happened. First, they should build some general rapport and understanding of the situation: ask who is present in the household, has anything like this every happened before, how long has the couple been together, and so forth. After general introductory remarks, the officer should proceed to a discussion of the incident and ask open-ended questions about the incident. Open-ended questions often do not even sound like questions: In your own words, tell me what happened. Open-ended questions allow the respondent to share many details of the incident and allow the officer to follow up as necessary (see, again, Chapter 7). Start to narrow the questions in frame as the interview progresses. Ask questions that assume a given state of affairs. If it is evident that the woman has been assaulted, do not ask: "did he hit you?" Rather ask: "did he hit you with a closed fist or an open hand?" Emphasize that your identity is as a law enforcer, and develop a shared law-abiding identity for the interaction. Use questions that assume a law abiding frame. Do not ask: "will you testify in court?" Ask: "will you tell the truth?" Thus, the structure of the interview should be very discursive at the beginning and with many open-ended questions allowing the citizen to discuss what happened in their own words. Toward the end of the interview, the questions should become more close-ended.

Officers may select the role of peace-keeper and many Americans appear to prefer this end of the dialectic when dealing with family violence. Many Americans prefer the police and the courts handle domestic violence through referrals to marriage counseling. Even when the wife had moderately severe injuries, only 26% favored arrest of the spouse. Most respondents felt that informal methods had a better chance to reduce conflict and achieve fairness for the whole family (Stalans 1996).

The officer attempting to shore up family harmony needs to develop an even stronger understanding of, and sensitivity to, intercultural differences. The law enforcement frame, for example, simply asserts that there are laws governing a given jurisdiction and that everyone must follow them. A peace-keeping frame attempts to bring a family system back into balance along its own lines and values. Thus, this frame demands ethnorelatism, or the tendency to accept, adapt and eventually integrate these cultural differences or standpoints into the existing world view (Bennett 1986).

Women may be attempting to use the police to create a "context of deterrence" within their family or relationship. A female victim may want to end violence and may even want a partner to be arrested, but does not want to follow through with the prosecution of a partner. Mandatory arrest and no drop policies as well as special prosecution units can often work against what the victim wants from the encounter with the legal establishment. Victims may prefer "peace-keepers" not law officers. In other words, victims may want officers to invoke informal social controls in which legal sanctions play only an indirect role (Fagan 1996). For many women, the police represent a deterrent to family violence and a way to bring stability to the situation, without bringing the full extent of the legal system into the equation. Experienced police officers often know that arrest sometimes causes more harm to a female victim as there is always a chance for escalation of violence when the husband is released. And, arresting both individuals when common couple violence occurs does not necessarily quell subsequent violent interactions.

The questioning in the peace keeping encounter should also be open-ended and rather than focusing on who is to blame for the incident, the peace-keeper may focus on the mental states of the communicators, the mutuality or non-mutuality of the violence, and the effects on the children. These factors may help the officer to make referrals to battered women's shelters or to outpatient mental health clinics.

The second strategic way to deal with dialectical tensions is through temporal-spatial separation. Rather than consistently adopting one polarity of the dialectic, some officers may respond to each polarity at separate points in time. He or she may alternate in some cyclic, temporal fashion. For example, the first domestic violence call may provoke a peace-keeping frame whereas subsequent calls move officers in their relationship with the family toward the law enforcement end of the continuum.

Other officers may segment a response in some domain they decide is mutually exclusive from other domains. Following a strict law enforcement paradigm with Cobras or those who have been called the generally violent and anti-social may be the best way to decrease homicides. Apart from objective indicators like past arrest and prosecution records of these men, their conversational style may also be a clue to their identity. These men will employ obloquies and invectives in interactions with their wives and will make demeaning statement about their spouses in their interviews with the police. In turn, their wives are obviously terrified of their husbands as the symbolic abuse is a stand in for physical violence.

The third strategic way to respond to the dialectical tension is through integration. Integration is a very complex and subtle strategy which represents an attempt to resolve dialectical tension by simultaneously responding to both the peace-keeping and the law enforcing ends of the continuum. Officers may need to use ambiguity in their conversations. Some officers may attempt to reframe the contradiction between peace-keeper and law enforcer and attempt to transcend it by working with the family to see actions taken as both enforcing the law and maintaining the peace for the family and the community.

Epilogue

In this chapter, I have discussed the nature of family and of family violence and suggested the basic principles that police officers need to keep in mind as they interact with family members under stressful conditions. Included in these rules are ideologies about gender roles and conformity orientations as well as ideologies about the appropriate levels of openness and expressiveness within the family and outside the family. In addition, we discussed the social-legal context surrounding family violence and the constraints on police officers as they responded to domestic calls. Finally, I proposed a dialectical model of police–citizen interaction.

Future research needs to explore the interactional dynamics of police–citizen interaction using the dialectical model of law enforcement/peace-keeping. The model needs to consider the constraints on communication between the officer and the citizen as well as the various choices that an officer has for a given situation. Capturing in vivo interactions of the type described in this chapter would be difficult and may be unethical. It may be possible, however, to construct various interaction scenarios and simulate the potential interaction routes and outcomes.

It is also extremely important that communication researchers develop linguistic and communicative profiles that may discriminate various forms of family violence. That is, the research does suggest that Cobras are extremely demeaning and abusive toward their spouses. Are there linguistic cues for those who engage in "common couple violence" or any of the other forms of family violence we discussed? The child entering the hospital emergency room constantly stating that their injury is due to a fall and that daddy did not push them is probably an abused child who has been warned over and over again, "tell them it was an accident". Front-line professionals, like officers and doctors, need the help of communication researchers to uncover clues that will help them to look more closely at a particular situation.

Drawing direct practical and policy implementations from basic research is always a difficult exercise. The cautious theorist always wants to wait for better articulated theory and more sophisticated research on larger samples before making any statements. But, the current realities of family life and police work demand that we translate research into some guidelines for practice. This chapter is an attempt to offer a way of thinking about policing family violence incorporating the best advice possible from our current state of knowledge.

Notes

* I would like to thank Anita Vangelisti and Howard Giles for their helpful comments on an early version of this chapter.

References

American Medical Association 1992. *Medical News* January.
Anderson, P. A. 1998. *Nonverbal Communication: Forms and Functions*. Mountain View, CA: Mayfield.
Archer, J. 2000. "Sex differences in aggression between heterosexual partners: A meta-analytic review". *Psychological Review* 125: 651–680.
Baxter, L. A. 1988. "A dialectical perspective on communication strategies in relationship development". In *Handbook of Personal Relationships*, S. Duck (ed.), 257–275. Chichester: John Wiley.
Bennett, M. J. 1986. "A developmental approach to training for intercultural sensitivity". *International Journal of Intercultural Relations* 10: 179–196.
Cahn, D. D. 1996. "Family violence from a communication perspective". In *Family Violence from a Communication Perspective*, D. Cahn, and S. Lloyd (eds), 1–19. Thousand Oaks, CA: Sage.

Carlson, M.J., Harris, S.D. and Holden, G.W. 1999. "Protective orders and domestic violence: Risk factors for re-abuse". *Journal of Family Violence* 14: 205–226.
Dobash, R., Dobash, R, Wilson, M. and Daly, M. 1992. "The myth of sexual symmetry in marital violence". *Social Problems* 39: 71–91.
Fagan, J. 1996. *The Criminalization of Domestic Violence: Promises and Limits.* Washington, DC: NIJ Research Report.
Fantuzzo, J., Boruch, R., Beriama, A. and Atkins, M. 1997. "Domestic violence and children: Prevalence and risk in five major U.S. cities". *Journal of the American Academy of Child and Adolescent Psychiatry* 36: 116–122.
Fitzpatrick, M.A. 1988. *Between Husbands and Wives.* Newbury Park, CA: Sage.
Fitzpatrick, M.A. and Ritchie, L.R. 1995. "Family communication patterns". *Human Communication Research* 20: 123–139.
Feder, L. 1998. "Police handling of domestic and nondomestic assault calls: Is there a case for discrimination?" *Crime and Delinquency* 44: 335–349.
Federal Bureau of Investigation. 1997. *Crime in the United States: Uniform Crime Reports.* Washington, DC: U.S. Department of Justice.
Frieze, I.H. 2000. "Violence in close relationships: Development of a research area: Comment on Archer (2000)". *Psychological Bulletin* 126: 681–684.
Garner, J. and Clemmer, E. 1986. *Danger to Police in Domestic Disturbances: A new look.* National Institute of Justice Research in Brief. Washington, DC: US Department of Justice.
Goodyear-Smith, F.A. and Laidlaw, T.M. 1999. "Aggressive acts and assaults in intimate relationships: Towards an understanding of the literature". *Behavioral Science and the Law* 17: 285–304.
Gudykunst, W.B. 1991. *Bridging Differences: Effective Intergroup Communication.* Newbury Park, CA: Sage.
Harrell, A.V., Smith, B. and Newmark, L. 1993. *Court Processing and the Effects of Restraining Orders for Domestic Violence Victims.* Washington, DC: The Urban Institute.
Higgins, D.J. and McCabe, M.P. 2000. "Multi-type maltreatment and the long term adjustment of adults". *Child Abuse Review* 9: 6–18.
Hinde, R.A. and Stevenson-Hinde, J. (eds). 1988. *Relationships within Families: Mutual Influences.* New York: Oxford.
Holden, G.W. and Ritchie, K.L. 1991. "Linking extreme marital discord, child rearing, and child behavior problems: Evidence from battered women". *Child Development* 62: 311–327.
Holtzworth-Munroe, A. and Stuart, G.L. 1994. "Typologies of male batterers". *Psychological Bulletin* 116: 476–497.
Hyden, M. 1994. *Woman Battering as a Marital Act.* New York: Oxford.
Infante, D.A, Sabourin, T.C., Rudd, J.E. and Shannon, E.A. 1990. "Verbal aggression in violent and non-violent marital disputes". *Communication Quarterly* 38: 361–371.
Jacobson, N. and Gottman, J.M. 1998. *When Men Batter Women: New insights into Ending Abusive Relationships.* New York: Simon and Schuster.
Johnson, M.P. 1995. "Patriarchal terrorism and common couple violence: Two forms of violence against women". *Journal of Marriage and the Family* 57: 283–294.
Karney, B.R. and Bradbury, T. 1997. "Neuroticism, marital interaction, and the trajectory of marital satisfaction". *Journal of Personality and Social Psychology* 72: 1075–1092.

Margolin, G. and Gordis, E. B. 2000. "The effects of family and community violence on children". *Annual Review of Psychology* 51: 445–479.

Margolin, G., John, R., Ghosh, C. M. and Gordis, E. B. 1996. "Family interaction process: An essential tool for exploring abusive relations". In *Family Violence from a Communication Perspective*, D. Cahn and S. Lloyd (eds), 37–58. Thousand Oaks, CA: Sage.

Martin, M. E. 1994. "Mandatory arrest for domestic violence: The courts' response". *Criminal Justice Review* 19: 212–227.

Martin, M. E. 1997. "Double your trouble: Dual arrest in family violence". *Journal of Family Violence* 12: 139–157.

Ochs, E. 1991. "Misunderstanding children". In *Miscommunication and Problematic Talk*, N.Coupland, H. Giles and J. M. Wiemann (eds), 44–60. Newbury Park, CA: Sage.

O'Leary, K. D. and Vivian, D. 1990. "Physical aggression in marriage". In *The Psychology of Marriage: Basic Issues and Applications*, F. Fincham and T. N. Bradbury (eds), 323–348. New York: Guilford.

Paternoster, R., Bachman, R., Brame, R. and Sherman, L. W. 1997. "Do fair procedures matter? The effect of procedural justice on spouse assault". *Law and Society Review* 31: 163–204.

Sabourin, T. 1996. "Cycles of violence". In *Family Violence from a Communication Perspective*, D. Cahn, and S. Lloyd (eds), 21–39. Thousand Oaks, CA: Sage.

Schmidt, J. D. and Sherman, L. W. 1993. "Does arrest deter domestic violence?" *American Behavioral Scientist* 36: 601–609.

Sherman, L. W. and Berk, R. A. 1984a. "The specific deterrent effects of arrest for domestic assault". *American Sociological Review* 49: 261–272.

Sherman, L. W. and Berk, R. A. 1984b. *The Minneapolis Domestic Violence Experiment*. Washington, DC: Police Foundation.

Sherman, L. W., Schmidt, J. D. and Rogan, D. P. 1992. *Policing Domestic Violence: Experiments and Dilemmas*. New York: Free Press.

Sherman, L. W., Smith, D. A., Schmidt, J. D. and Rogan, D. P.1992. "Crime, punishment, and stake in conformity: Legal and informal control of domestic violence". *American Sociological Review* 57: 680–690.

Sillars, A. and Weisberg, J. 1987. "Conflict as a social skill". In *Interpersonal Processes*, M.Roloff and G. R. Miller (eds), 140–171. Thousand Oaks, CA: Sage.

Stalans, L. J. 1996. "Family harmony or individual protection? Public recommendations about how police can handle domestic violence situations". *American Behavioral Scientist* 39: 433–448.

Stalans, L. J. and Finn, M. A. 1995. "How novice and experienced officers interpret wife assaults: Normative and efficiency frames". *Law and Society Review* 29: 287–321.

Stith, S. M., Rosen, K. H., Middleton, K. A., Busch, A. L., Lundeberg, K. and Carlton, R. P. 2000. "The intergenerational transmission of spouse abuse: A meta-analysis". *Journal of Marriage and the Family* 62: 640–654.

Straus, M. A. 1979. "Measuring intrafamily conflict and violence: The Conflict Tactics Scale". *Journal of Marriage and the Family* 41: 75–88.

Straus, M. A. and Gelles, R. J. 1990. *Physical Violence in American Families*. New Brunswick, NJ: Transaction Books.

Sullivan, N. 1995. *Dealing with domestic violence*. Training manual developed for the Chicago Police Department.

White, J.W., Smith, P.H., Koss, M.P. and Figuero, A.J. 2000. "Intimate partner aggression — what have we learned? Comment on Archer (2000)". *Psychological Bulletin* 126: 690–696.
Williams, K.R. and Hawkins, R.1989. "Perceptual research on general deterrence: A critical review". *Law and Society* 20: 545–572.

CHAPTER 7

The discourse of police interviews
The case of sexually abused children

Ann-Christin Cederborg
Linköping University, Sweden

Sweden, as well as every State in the U.S.A., now has formal child abuse reporting laws. This fact can be one explanation for the increased rates of allegations of sexual abuse of children in recent years as well as media attention to, and public awareness of, the problem. This does not necessarily mean an increased prevalence of child sexual abuse but, in Sweden, the number of police reports doubled over the period 1987–1993 (Brottsförebygganderådet BRÅ 1994; Statistiska central byrån 1987–1993). In the U.S.A., a similar trend of increased referrals has emerged, with registered reports increasing for example, threefold from 1980–1986 (National Center on Child Abuse and Neglect 1988). In 1992 and 1993, the U.S.A. had 43 reports per 1000 children less than 18 years of age (U.S. Department of Health and Human Services 1995). Yet, child sexual abuse rates declined to 11% in 1995 from 16% in 1986 (Daro 1995). In Sweden, between one and two police reports are submitted regarding suspected sexual abuse per 1000 children under the age of 15 years (Svedin 1999). The decline implied that, in 1997, the allegations were at the same level as in 1992; that is, slightly more than 2400 allegations per year. This reduction in Sweden has to be contextualized by the fact that the allegations of children between 0–15 years of age, suspected of being sexually abused, actually doubled between 1987–1997. Both in the U.S.A. and in Sweden, a minority of alleged cases is actually taken to court. The statistics are not sufficient but, at the highest, approximately every sixth child investigated by the police in Sweden has its case examined by the court (Diesen 2001). It was, for example, shown in a Swedish study with 193 cases of child sexual abuse that 52 had their cases judged at court. Of those, 33 of the accused denied having sexually abused the children, with the remaining accused pleading guilty (Cederborg 1999).

A satisfactory method providing a sound estimation of the true incidence of child sexual abuse is unfortunately unavailable at the moment (Russell & Bolen 2000). Indeed, there are reasons to believe that the incidence rates are higher than those reported since unrecorded cases are not included. On the other hand, there is no reason to believe that children are at greater risk today than they were during earlier historical periods, even if allegations of abuse have increased since 1960.

Prevalence studies are afflicted with methodological problems and are, therefore, not always reliable and comparable. This means it is almost impossible to indicate clearly the prevalence of child sexual abuse. The estimations of prevalence can range from 3% to 31% for boys and from 6% to 62% for girls (Kuehnle 1996). These estimations can be compared with Swedish studies where the prevalence rates are low compared to the rates reported in studies from the U.S.A. The prevalence of sexual abuse in childhood is estimated to be around 7% to 8% for girls and 1% to 3% for boys (Svedin 2000). The average age of victims is said to be around 8 to 10 years of age (Faller 1989; Martens 1989; Office of Population Census and Surveys 1987), with boys generally being somewhat older than girls when being abused (Faller 1989). Researchers concur that girls are more vulnerable than boys, with the former running to between two and five times greater risk of being the victim of sexual abuse (Finkelhor & Byron 1986; Svedin 1999).

Even though studies of risk factors can have validity problems, an overview of the research shows that age and family factors can have a marked effect on increasing the risk of being sexually abused. Influences such as marital problems, step-parents, other forms of abuse, deteriorating relations between parents and children in the family, or lack of care on the part of parents, stand out as risk factors. Most commonly, the offender seems to be known to the child and is present in the child's immediate surroundings. That does not necessarily mean that the offender is a part of the child's core family. Sexual abuse can imply a feeling of stigmatization and include a sense of powerlessness and betrayal. In addition, sexual abuse of children can have effects on their lives, such as sexual traumatization, impaired self-esteem, and sexual confusion. The child can also become more vulnerable to further abuse because of these psychological consequences (Svedin 2000).

Irrespective of methodological problems, all the rates and the risk factors discussed above, point to the fact that a large number of children, both in Sweden and the U.S.A. — and perhaps elsewhere — may have experienced sexual abuse (including rape) during the years they grew up.

Discourse patterns in police interviews

This chapter concentrates on experiences and knowledge gained from six years of research on children who act as witnesses in cases of child sexual abuse. The data consist of 193-videotaped interviews conducted by six (untrained) officers from one local police district in Sweden over a period of ten years (1986–1995). The data also includes reports from the preliminary investigations and from files for those cases that were taken to court (Cederborg 1998, 1999, 2001; Cederborg, Orbach, Sternberg & Lamb 2000). The general aim of this chapter is to point out how the officer may negatively affect the quality of information obtained from children together with a need for implementing interview methods that can enhance children's abilities to report accurately about their experiences.

Legal prerequisites

Sexual abuse of children is a serious crime. When a suspected sexual offence is reported to the police in Sweden, it is the prosecutor who decides whether to open a pre-trial investigation or not. The police procedure is aimed at investigating a suspected criminal offence with a view possibly to bringing the offender to justice. There has, of course, to be probable cause that a crime has been committed if the police instigate an investigation. When pre-trial investigations are completed, prosecutors decide whether to instigate criminal proceedings or not and they are bound to bring a case to trial if they assume a verdict of guilty. Needless to say, a conviction is only possible if the evidence levied against the accused is very strong and "beyond all reasonable doubt". In many cases, children's reports can be the *only* sources of information available upon which to base these assessments; usually no eyewitness other than the perpetrator and the victim are involved. Moreover, it is not uncommon for the child and the suspected offender to have different opinions about what really happened. Due to the lack of other evidence, too, many police inquiries tend to end in closure or in the prosecutor deciding not to instigate criminal proceedings. According to legal expertise, this is because prosecutors practice excessive caution in the assessment of whether a prosecution could lead to a conviction or not (Diesen & Sutorius 1999).

Swedish legislation states that the court (i.e., the lay assessors and the judge) should be able to presume the innocence and the rights of the accused when it passes a judgment. When there is a doubtful case, as to whether or not there is enough credible evidence to convict a suspect, Swedish court policy is always to give the benefit of doubt to the alleged perpetrator.

As discussed above, there are great difficulties in evaluating the status of evidence in these cases. One legal difficulty is that the child is not always present in court, with the officer's videotaped interview being presented instead. This situation can weaken the child's position because a video interview can, from a legal perspective, have less evidential value than a direct statement in court (Diesen & Sutorius 1999). In addition, the participation of psychological expert witnesses has declined in recent years because the protection of the child's interest in relation to the rights of the suspect and, in accordance with the principles of the legal system, can be difficult to accomplish (Gumpert 2001; Nyström 1996). These issues highlight the need for knowledge about how to elicit the best report possible from the child.

Interviewing children

It is the officer's responsibility to elicit responses from the child that fit into the legal categories of desirable details. Hence, it is the officer who has to fulfill the legal system's expectations of how stories about sexual abuse are supposed to be conducted. Police questioning of children demands a special competence and, clearly, requires the procedure to be adapted to the child's circumstances. If the officers do not exhibit such accommodative skills, their reports are not accepted as providing sufficient proof of sexual abuse.

During a police interview with a sexually abused child, the participants should balance obtaining and providing as much unaffected information as possible. One problem is that the interview situation generates patterns of at least two types of asymmetries. The first relates to an officer's ascribed professional position in defining how the interviews are to be structured. The second built-in asymmetry in police interviews (Linell 1990; Linell & Luckmann 1991) is that police questioning is central to the practice of interviews, and that the quality of the child's answer is dependent on how the questions are designed by the officer. In the words of Goffman (1967, 1983), one can claim that it is officers who "star" in the interview situation as they master the genre and organizes the occasion. On the other hand, children can, to some extent, be said to have a type of predefined authority since they are the ones who can know what happened during the event and can choose to talk about his or her experience of abuse. If the children are afraid of the consequences when telling the truth, they might not be motivated to offer a report. Children can also be in a situation where they are not able to report because of developmental constraints. In addition, they may not previously have experienced this type of conversation, know the communicative codes of a police interview and, hence, may not be aware that they are expected to tell private, sensitive matters to an officer.

In order to restrain inadequate management of children's accounts, and to obtain the best report possible from them, researchers and professional groups have written guidelines that outline the best-practice standards for interviewing children (e.g., American Professional Society on the Abuse of Children 1990; Lamb, Sternberg, Orbach, Hershkowitz & Esplin 1999; Memorandum of Good Practice 1992). Ideally, the officer has to obtain information from the child that can convict an offender or protect the latter from further abuse. In general, it is the officer's task to develop the communication on the basis of getting as much unaffected information as possible from the child. When officers design their interviews, it is important that they strive toward an objective attitude, because the report given by the child should neither be based on subjective values nor assumptions from one single hypothesis (Bruck, Ceci & Hembrooke 1998; Everson 2000; Poole & Lamb 1998).

Researchers recommend that the children should be interviewed as soon as possible after the alleged offences and children should be acquainted with the basic rules of the interview before being questioned about the case. Officers are supposed to explain their roles, the purpose of the interview, and the "ground rules" — these should concern a child's right to ask for clarifications and to say "I don't know" (Warren & McGough 1996). Children also have the right to correct the interviewer when they say something that is inaccurate. It might be easier for especially young children to understand the rules if they are demonstrated through a concrete example. This is because children usually try to *answer* adults' questions and can be reluctant to say, "I don't know" (Hughes & Grieve 1980). For example, if the interviewer says, " My son's name is Sam, isn't it?" the child is supposed to say, "I don't know". If the child says "yes", the interviewer can say, "That is wrong because you do not know my son's name". The point is to encourage the child to say, "I don't know", instead of giving a wrong answer (Poole & Lamb 1998).

In the substantial phase of the interview, it is the officer's task to induce the child to give further and more specific details about events that are forensically relevant. Interviewers are supposed to intrude as little as possible and encourage children to provide information by themselves. Interviewers are urged to use option-posing utterances as sparingly as possible and as late as possible in the interview. This means that option-posing and suggestive utterances are not supposed to be used until the children have had a chance to tell their *own* stories from their own perspectives using open-ended utterances as much as possible (see Chapter 6). If an option-posing question is used, and the child gives relevant information, the officer should strive to return the child to free narrative responding (Lamb, Sternberg, Orbach, Esplin and Mitchell in press).

It is obvious that the way children's information is elicited influences the amount and quality of information they provide (Goodman & Aman 1991; Poole & Lamb 1998). Replicated laboratory analog studies show that information elicited by using open-ended utterances are more likely to be accurate than information elicited using options suggested by the interviewer (e.g., Dale, Loftus & Ratburn 1978; Dent & Stephenson 1979; Goodman, Bottoms, Schwartz-Kenney & Rudy 1991). Ceci and Bruck (1995) claim that the accuracy of a child's report decreases when the child is interviewed in a highly option-posing and suggestive way. The enhanced accuracy of responses to open ended utterances is probably because they force the child to recall information from memory compared to questions that require the child to recognize one or more option suggested by the interviewer (Lamb et al. 2002).

An example of open-ended question that is more likely to elicit accurate information is, "Tell me everything that happened" (Dent 1991; Hershkowitz, Lamb, Sternberg & Eesplin 1997). A definition of an option-posing utterance is that it focuses the child's attention on details or aspects of the alleged incident that the child has not previously mentioned. That is, asking the child to affirm, negate, or select an investigator-given option using memory recognition processes. This type of utterance does not imply that a particular response is expected, but it limits the number of answers from which the child must choose. An option-posing question can be "Did he force you to do this?" Suggestive utterances, however, are stated in such a way that the interviewer strongly communicates what response is expected, for example, "He forced you to do that, didn't he?" Or they assume details that have not been revealed by the child for example: Child: "We laid on the sofa". Interviewer: "He laid on you or you laid on him?" (Cederborg et al. 2000; Lamb et al. 1996).

Accordingly, it is a specific challenge to interview young children because they seem to be dependent on an adult's questions in order to search their memories in an efficient, systematic, and organized fashion (Saywitz, Geiselman & Bornstein 1992). Moreover, studies have shown that pre-schoolers usually do not reject misleading information (Poole & Lamb 1998). Young children are also especially sensitive to social pressures that encourage particular types of answers. Repeated use of suggestive questions with very young children can also create a potential for distortion (Ceci & Bruck 1993). This means that children can fail to give reliable accounts because the officer poses questions that can have a negative influence on the quality of the child's answers. This became obvious in our study of 54 pre-school children (4–7 years old) where officers spoke most of the time. Here, the children had 23%, and the officers 73% of the discourse space; the officers' posed utterances were also highly intrusive. This means that the officer becomes the dominant and, very often, suggestive speaker when the child (for some reason) is not able to tell or did not tell or expand his or her answer (Cederborg 1998).

Researchers in the field have highlighted young children's vulnerability to suggestions, manipulation, and coercion (e.g., Bruck & Ceci 1993, 1995; Ceci & Bruck 1993; Lamb, Sternberg & Esplin 1995; Lamb et al. 1999; Poole & Lamb 1998). The implication is that when pre-school children are supposed to tell sensitive, private, and emotional matters they are, at times, restrained from telling because the strategies for eliciting information do not take into account how these children can express detailed, concrete, and coherent narratives.

There are, of course, a variety of other factors than question types that can influence children's ability to answer the officers. The influences from factors such as the child's developmental level and maturity, previous experiences, general situation in life, and the child's understanding and interpretation of the words and concepts used, can be just as important as in how and what the child recalls. The interview context and degree of stress, and the availability of social support in the interview situation, can also affect the child. This suggests that the accuracy of children's reports is influenced by the child's characteristics versus those of the interview. In other words, all children are unique and one cannot regard sequences from especially young children as objective words used to tell the truth — and nothing but the truth. Particular difficulties arise when, especially, young children have to live up to legal expectations about how a story is supposed to be formulated. In addition, if the child, for various reasons, does not report accurately, it can be very difficult to understand what the child might have gone through. This, in turn, can influence the assessment of what actually happened

This chapter cannot provide a comprehensive review of current understanding of child witnesses' abilities and needs, since the main focus here is on the discourse of the police interview. On the other hand, the issue of children's competence is well-discussed and debated in other sources (e.g., Ceci & Bruck 1995; Poole & Lamb 1998; Saywitz & Goodman 1996).

Influenced utterances

Despite professional consensus regarding desirable interview practices, evaluations of forensic interviews reveal that expert recommendations are, to a large extent, not followed. Researchers have shown that interviewers in Sweden, as well as in Israel, England, and the U.S.A. seldom use open-ended invitations to prompt for information. They tend to rely heavily on option-posing and suggestive utterances (Hershkowitz et al. 1997; Sternberg et al. 1996, 1997; Sternberg, Lamb, Davis & Westcott 2001; Cederborg et al. 2000). The Swedish study, for example, includes 72 first interviews with children who made an allegation and were 4–13 years of age. It showed that 53% of the questions used by the officers were option-posing and suggestive, and that 57% of the children's details were gathered from these problematic utterances. Only 6% of the interviewers' utterances were open-ended invitations, and these elicited only 8% of the information (Cederborg et al. 2000). These problematic requests included questions where the child was supposed to give a "yes" or "no" answer. It can be argued that yes/no questions embody a preference toward an expectation for one pole or another (Pomerantz 1988). Children may feel that they *have* to choose one of the alternatives and we cannot be sure they provide the "right" answer (Poole & Lamb 1998).

When analyzing how children manage to answer these problematic questions, it was found that only 5% of the answers included an "I don't know" answer and 2% "I don't remember". Indeed, 31% of the children's answers rendered an admission of the proposals from the officers. On the other hand, 33% of the answers also indicated a denial of the posed perspectives. It was also obvious that, when the children did not include a yes/no, they tried, instead, to develop their responses in 25% of their answers. In 4% of their answers, the children did not answer the officer's utterances. In addition, in 64% of the cases involved in the Swedish study, the very first question provided the child was option-posing or suggestive. This means that the officers widely initiated how the interviews were to be conducted by thematizing their views of the child's presumed experiences, thereby putting their perspective on what and how the children were supposed to tell. Because this type of (problematic) utterance was introduced so early in the interview, the potential for contamination of information produced later on in the interview is substantial.

In what follows, further details of problematic discourses are discussed. The examples below are brief but are intended to show that untrained officers can improve both the quality of their interviewing as well as the information elicited from the alleged victims.

Perspective setting

Perspective setting is seen as an activity where one participant, in the light of previous knowledge, starts the utterance from his or her adopted hypothesis and develops it in a certain direction. This is achieved in order to render certain points communicated and perhaps also better accepted by the recipient (Linell & Jönsson 1991). If officers use option-posing and suggestive questions, they set perspectives on how the abuse events are supposed to be talked about. The following excerpt is an example of how an officer initiated the first interview with Stina, a 5 year old. She just said that she did not know why she was supposed to talk to the officer. (O = officer and S = Stina).

Perspective setting 1
(1) O: but then I will have to tell you what your mother said
 S: Yes
 O: That your bottom is red and it is impossible that you have hurt yourself with your bicycle.
 S: No
 O: You must have hurt yourself with something else

The officer sets the perspective of possible abuse by introducing the mother's opinion about Stina's bottom. The officer does not say why the bottom was red, but uses the mother's concern to encourage the child to talk about presumed abuse experiences. This type of initiative can induce the child to remember why her bottom is red. The problem is that this initiative also can lead Stina into a position where she has to answer for or against the mother's statement. Certain kinds of questions produce certain kinds of answers and the initiative above implies that the officer has set the perspective for how Stina's report is to be talked about.

Certainly, it can be very difficult to construct an interview situation without shaping its directions; each child is different and so is the circumstance for the case. The role of the officer can be most delicate if the child does not want to tell what happened during the abuse act. Karin, six years of age, can serve as an example of this. In the first interview, she said she did not want to tell anything about her stepfather's activities with her during a weekend she spent with him. The following example shows how the officer finally relinquishes his intent to induce the child to tell him herself and, instead, states what he thinks might have happened to Karin. When the officer says what he thinks happened, Karin just provides confirmatory responses. (O = the officer and K = Karin)

> *Perspective setting 2*
> (2) O: Now I am going, now I am going to say very straight what I think
> K: What did you say?
> O: Now I am going to tell you very straight forward since you are not telling me everything. I believe that your stepfather touched you between your legs
> K: Mm
> O: Am I right?
> K: Mm

Karin did not take the opportunity to give her own version of the event and the officer's intervention did not fulfill the ideals of how a report is supposed to be accomplished. Of course, a child suspected of being abused by her stepfather can be unmotivated to talk about what happened. But this does not mean that suggestive questions are the only option. The problem with such utterances is that the accuracy of the child's information can be called into question, for example, by the suspect's defense lawyer (especially if the child just answers with a "Mm"). This implies that when a child is not motivated or not able to follow the communicative genre of the interview, the implications are that the officer has to weigh for or against the consequences of getting an uncontaminated report of the abuse. For example, if other credible evidence exists that can support the officer's utterances, it might not be so dangerous to support the child with a suggestive utterance. On the other hand, if access to other credible evidence is missing, and the ultimate conjecture is that the child needs suggestions to tell, one has to be aware of the potential for this type of intervention to diminish the accuracy of the answer given by the child.

Coercion

In order to supply the legal system with evidence of abuse, officers can end up in a situation where they use coercive interventions. The problem is that if an especially young child's answer arises from such events, it can be contaminated and might not have been tracked from the child's own experiences (e.g., Everson 1997). An example of this is when Liv, 6 years of age, in her first interview, is asked if she has told the truth about her father's abuse. (O = officer and L = Liv)

> *Coercion 1*
> (3) O: Did you tell the truth when you told me your father did something?
> L: Yes
> O: That was the truth
> L: Yes
> O: Because he would be very sad if this wasn't true, what
> L: No
> O: Do you remember what you told me about what your father did to you?
> L: No

When Liv says she does not remember what she previously said, this can be read as Liv not wanting to say once more what her father did, because she has been confronted with a coercive intervention; that is, the father "would be very sad if this wasn't true". This type of initiative does not take into account that especially young children can feel threatened by an imposed crafting of the unfolding of these events. One has to bear in mind that it can be difficult to allege a crime has been committed by a *close relative*. The child can, for example, be threatened not to tell or be afraid that the suspect will be put in prison. Thus, it is possible that an especially young child like Liv might change the report in order not to harm the abuser or her.

Tor, 12 years old, is another case where the child hardly provided any details by himself about how the stepfather was supposed to have abused him. He produced fragmentary comments and it is noteworthy that the officer believed Tor must have more to tell. Previously, in this first interview, Tor has told the officer that he does not know what happened. (O = officer)

> *Coercion 2*
> (4) O: You can't hide behind it, Tor, that you don't know, because naturally you know what happens, you see, it doesn't work. It doesn't, sort of, may I say like this, it's not fair to step daddy either to say that you don't know, so that we who are watching this and who are supposed to judge this matter get a feeling that something more is happening. We get forced into the idea that OK there was probably more to it, but we don't know what, because you are directing us towards that, you see. It is better to say, this and that happened, and then nothing more happened. Do you see what I mean? What happens apart from

him standing there holding you tight? /*Interval*/ Somewhere deep inside you know what happens, don't you, Tor?

The officer explicitly accuses Tor of concealing important information when he gave the previous "I don't know" answer. By posing a cascade of coercive utterances in the same turn, the officer gives multiple demands for Tor to talk about abuse experiences. It is as if the officer's comments are reprimands. Moreover, the officer proclaims, "It's not fair to the stepfather" for Tor to tell he does not know what happened. This can be understood as a coercion of bad conscience. Tor is actually accused of not fulfilling the expectations of how his presumed report is supposed to be told. The coercion can be seen as an invitation to accomplish a report of abuse. Accordingly, there is a risk that Tor can get confused and say something he has not experienced or that nothing happened, although it did. On the other hand, the best conditions for legal proceedings cannot always overshadow how the children are interviewed. It can actually be the case that a child can keep silent about what has happened but the question is if coercive utterances ever can be useful for the legal system? Of course, one has to weigh for and against the fact that the story about abuse might be contaminated if a child is in some kind of danger. The problem is that the answer from a child may not be accurate if she or he is forced to tell.

Epilogue

Sexual abuse of a child is a serious crime, which means that the child has the right to be protected from such exploitation. The child's interests in safekeeping can be difficult to accomplish because, as above, the alleged victim is often the only available source of information. In order to secure a conviction, it is necessary both for the suspect and the child to achieve an investigation that is as correct as possible. This chapter has its focus on discourse patterns in the interviews. The main point is to show that incorrect interviewing can contaminate the legal accuracy of the child's descriptions of the abuse event with the consequences that it is harder to substantiate abuse cases.

The officers play a very important role in how legal interests are covered in the interviews and failures to accomplish legal evidence can be related to how officers listen to and question especially young children. Both persons involved in the interview situation collaborate when they reconstruct the criminal act, and this is mainly done through question-and-answer sequences (Linell 1990).

The interviewee has to tell his/her story under the conditions defined by the interviewer's directives (Linell & Jönsson 1991). This means that patterns of asymmetries are both predefined and related to the social arrangements in the interview situation. All this can lead to complex dynamics in the dialogical process (Goodwin & Heritage 1990). In other words, the children are put in an unequal position in relation to the officers and the environment they represent, with the consequence that it can be difficult for the child to fulfill the legal expectations of how a report is supposed to be accomplished. This, in turn, makes it very important to be aware of how to reduce the effects of the lack of equality in the interview situation in order to get the best possible report from the child.

Bearing in mind that the parties involved have different opportunities to set perspectives, it is of crucial importance that officers are adept at empowering children to tell as much as possible from their own perspectives. Researchers' agreement on how interviews should be conducted has had little impact on how interviews are conducted in the field. That is why there is a continuing need to translate research knowledge about how to interview children into flexible and effective interview practices. Otherwise, there is a risk that too many police inquires continue to end in closure since the legal system needs facts that are legally defensible.

Questions that set perspectives, for example when the officer defines how the event occurred, or confuses the child by coercive interventions that might force the child to tell, can reduce the child's possibilities to report accurately. Consequently, this enhances the difficulty in interpreting what might have happened to the child. Of course, it is a challenging task to make the child report as accurately as possible, especially if the child is young or if the child is not motivated to talk about it. Studies have shown that American and Israeli 7- to 9 years olds produced significantly more information than 4- to 6-years-olds (see, however, Cederborg et al. 2000). Almost all children respond to open ended prompts and they are able to provide narrative accounts from free recall memory (Orbach et al. 2000; Sternberg et al. 1999, 2001).

If the child for several reasons is not motivated to talk, inappropriate interviewing might be the only way to ask if the child might be in an environment full of risks. On the other hand, if the officers — unreflectedly and unsystematically — use influenced invitations, avoid open-ended invitations and do not listen to, or follow up, what the child previously has said, it can be concluded that the child is being denied the opportunity to be heard and understood in the legal proceeding. In addition, the security of rights for both the child and the suspect can be questioned. In light of these considerations, there is not much we can do about the predefined legal conditions, but the officer can strive towards the best possible requirements for the child to give a report as accurately as possible.

In order to accomplish the best legal report possible, there is a need to supplement the training of officers in how to improve the quality of information provided by young children. Researchers have shown that systematic training, including intensive training, monitoring, and feedback over a period of one year, lead interviewers to accomplish greater retrieval conditions for children, which means considerable improvements in interview quality (Orbach et al. 2000; Lamb et al. in press). This has to be compared with other disappointing findings regarding the impact of specialized training for a shorter period. Studies show that this type of training had little effect on interviewing skills (Aldridge & Cameron 1999; Warren et al. 1999). The conclusion from these different studies is that if interviewers, *continuously* experience different children in different types of situations, spread over several months, and obtain expert supervision on real cases, they can improve their interview skills and integrate expected interview techniques.

Thus, even trained officers cannot protect either the children or the suspect from getting an inaccurate report of sexual abuse as long as we do not know how, for example, therapists expose the children to negative influences parallel with the investigative process. Ceci and Bruck's (1995) position is that therapists should only work with everyday coping strategies before the legal resolution in order not to be accused of creating false memories. The problem, however, is that children exposed to sexual abuse need therapeutic support and a legal resolution both of which can take a long time to accomplish. Since we do not know enough about how therapists can support the children without influencing the accuracy of the legal reports, researchers have to find out what specifically can be understood as a legally acceptable coping strategy in relation to other therapeutic moves.

Many questions as to how to interview children remain unanswered. For example, how to interview children with different disabilities and children who are not mature enough to verbally produce a report. Another important question is how to obtain information about non-existent abuse experiences without using option-posing questions. That said, other questions as to how to interview children have been addressed here and it is clear that, with appropriate planning and sustained training, many problems can be prevented (Aldridge & Wood 1998). In other words, the legal logic of what children are supposed to accomplish in investigative interviews is not possible to improve until the interview procedures are adjusted to international recommendations regarding how to talk to children.

References

Aldridge, J. and Cameron, S. 1999. "Interviewing child witnesses: Questioning strategies and the effectiveness of training". *Applied Developmental Science* 3: 136–147.
Aldridge, M. and Wood, J. 1998. *Interviewing Children: A Guide for Child Care and Forensic Practitioners*. New York: Wiley.
American Professional Society on the Abuse of Children. 1990. *Guidelines for Psychosocial Evaluation of Suspected Sexual Abuse in Young Children*. Chicago, IL: Author.
Brottsförebygganderådet. (BRÅ) 1994. (*National Council for Crime Prevention*). Stockholm: BRÅ.
Bruck, M. and Ceci, S.J. 1993. "Amicus brief for the case of state of New Jersey v. Michaels presented by committee of concerned social scientists". Supreme Court of New Jersey docket # 36,633. (Reprinted in *Psychology, Public Policy, and Law* 1995, 1: 272–322).
Bruck, M., Ceci. S.J. and Hembrooke, H. 1998. "Reliability and credibility of young children's reports. From research to policy practice". *American Psychologist* 53: 136–151.
Ceci, S.J. and Bruck, M. 1993. "Suggestibility of the children: A historical review and synthesis". *Psychological Bulletin* 113: 403–439.
Ceci, S.J. and Bruck, M. 1995. *Jeopardy in the Courtroom: A Scientific Analysis of Children's Testimony*. Washington, DC: American Psychological Association.
Cederborg, A-C. 1998. "Små barns berättelser om sexuella övergrepp" (*Young children's narratives about sexual abuse*). *Socialvetenskaplig tidskrift* 5: 1: 24–44.
Cederborg, A-C. 1999. "The construction of children's credibility in judgments of child sexual abuse". *Acta Sociologica* 42: 147–158.
Cederborg, A-C. 2001. "Where does the story come from? " (submitted).
Cederborg, A-C., Orbach. Y., Sternberg, K.J. and Lamb. M.E. 2000. "Investigative interviews of child witnesses in Sweden". *Child Abuse and Neglect* 10: 1355–1361.
Daro, D.1995. "Current trends in child abuse reporting and fatalities: NCPCAs 1994 annual fifty state survey". *The APSAC Advisor* 8: 5–6.
Dale, P.S., Loftus, E.F. and Ratburn, L. 1978. "The influence of the form of the question of the eyewitness testimony of preschool children". *Journal of Psycholinguistic Research* 74: 269–277.
Dent, H.R. 1991. "Experimental studies of interviewing child witnesses". In *The Suggestibility of Children's Recollections*, J. Ann (ed.), 138–146. Washington, DC: American Psychological Association.
Dent, H.R. and Stephenson, G.M. 1979. "An experimental study of the effectiveness of different techniques of questioning child witnesses". *British Journal of Social and Clinical Psychology* 18: 41–51.

Diesen, C. 2001. "Att utreda sexuella övergrepp mot barn- en lägesbeskrivning ur Stockholmsperspektiv" (*Investigating child sexual abuse — a state description from the perspective of Stockholm*). In *Sexuella övergrepp mot barn* (*Sexual abuse of children*), C. Diesen, C.H. Gumpert, F. Lindblad and H. Sutorius (eds), 73–103. Stockholm: Nordstedts Juridik.

Diesen, C. and Sutorius, H. 1999. "Sexuella övergrepp mot barn. Den rättsliga hanteringen" (*Sexual abuse of children. The legal proceedings*). Expert rapport. Socialstyrelsen (*Expert report, The National Board of Health and Welfare*), art. nr. 36–003.

Everson, M.D. 1997. "Understanding bizarre, improbable, and fantastic elements in children's accounts of abuse". *Child Maltreatment* 2: 134–149.

Everson, M.D. 2000. "Good ethics vs. Good practice: reconciling role conflicts in treating abused children". Paper presented at the International conference about abused children in August in Salt Lake City. National Institute of Child Health and Human Development.

Faller, K.C. 1989. "The myths of the "collusive mother". Variability in the functioning of mothers of victims of intrafamilial sexual abuse". *Journal of Interpersonal Violence* 3: 190–196.

Finkelhor, D. and Byron, L. 1986. "High-risk children". In *Sourcebook on Child Sexual Abuse*. D. Finkelhor l (ed.), 60–88. Beverly Hills, CA: Sage.

Goffman E. 1967. *Interaction Rituals. Essays on Face-to-Face Behavior*. New York: Pantheon Books.

Goffman. E. 1983. "Felicity conditions". *American Journal of Society* 89: 1–53.

Goodman, G.S. and Aman, C.J. 1991. "Children's use of anatomically detailed dolls to recount an event". *Child Development* 61: 1859–1871.

Goodman, G.S., Bottoms, B.L., Schwartz-Kenney, B.M. and Rudy, L. 1991. "Children's testimony about a stressful event: Improving children's reports." *Journal of Narrative and Life History* 1: 69–99.

Goodwin, C. and Heritage, J. 1990. "Conversation analysis". *Annual Review of Anthropology* 19: 283–307.

Gumpert, H.G. 2001. *Alleged Child Sexual Abuse: The Expert Witness and the Court*. (Disertation). Stockholm: Repro Print.

Hershkowitz, I., Lamb, M E., Sternberg, K.J. and Esplin, P.W. 1997. "The relationships among interviewer utterance type, CBCA scores, and the richness of children's responses". *Legal and Criminological Psychology* 2: 169–176.

Hughes, M. and Grive, R. 1980. "On asking children bizarre questions". *First Language* 1: 149–160.

Kuehnle, K. 1996. *Assesing Allegations of Child Sexual Abuse*. Sarasota, FL: Professional Resourse Press.

Lamb, M.E., Hershkowitz, I., Sternberg, K.J., Esplin, P.W., Hovav, M., Manor, T. and Yudilevitch, L. 1996. "Effects of investigative utterance types on Israeli children responses". *International Journal of Behavioral Development* 19: 627–637.

Lamb, M.E., Sternberg, K.J. and Esplin, P.W. 1995. "Making children into competent witnesses: Reactions to the amicus brief". *Psychology, Public Policy, and the Law* 1: 438–449.

Lamb. M. E., Sternberg. K. J. Orbach. Y., Esplin. P. W. and Mitchell. S. in press. "Is ongoing feedback necessary to maintain the quality of investigative interviews with allegedly abused children?" *Applied Developmental Science.*

Lamb, M. E., Sternberg, K. J., Orbach, Y., Hershkowitz, I. and Esplin, P. W. 1999. "Forensic interviews of children". In *Handbook of the Psychology of Interviewing*, A. Memon and R. Bull (eds), 253–277. New York: Wiley.

Lamb. M. E., Sternberg. K. J., Orbach. Y., Hershkowitz. I., Horowitz. D. and Esplin E. P. (2002). "The effects of intensive training and ongoing supervision on the quality of investigative interviews with alleged sex abuse victims". *Applied Developmental Science* 6: 35–51.

Linell, P. 1990. "The power of dialogue dynamics". In *The Dynamics of Dialogue*, I. Markova and K. Foppa (eds), 147–177. Harvester Wheatsheaf: Hemel Hempstead.

Linell, P. and Jönsson, L. 1991. "Suspect stories: on perspective setting in an asymmetrical situation". In *Asymmetries in Dialogue*. I. Markova and K. Foppa (eds), 75–100. Harvester Wheatsheaf: Hemel Hempstead.

Linell, P. and Luckmann, T. 1991. "Asymmetries in dialogue: some conceptual preliminaries". In *Asymmetries in Dialogue*, I. Markova and K. Floppa (eds), 1–20. Harvester Wheatsheaf: Hemel Hempstead.

Martens, P. L. 1989. "Sexualbrott mot barn. Presentation och diskussion av några centrala teman inom forskningsområdet" (*Sexual crimes against children. Presentation and discussion of some specific theme*). BRÅ-rapport, 1. Stockholm: BRÅ.

Memorandum of Good Practice. 1992. London: Her Majesty's Stationery Office.

National Center on Child Abuse and Neglect. 1988. *Study findings: Study of National Incidence and Prevalence of Child Abuse and Neglect.* Washington, DC: U. S. Department of Health and Human Services.

Nyström, I. 1996. Sakkunnig i domstol (*An expert witness in court*) In Rättspsykologi (*Forensic psychology*), S-Å.Christianson (ed.), 344–357. Stockholm: Natur och Kultur.

Office of Population Census and Surveys. 1987. "Mid 1986 population estimates for England and Wales". *OPCS Monitor PPI 87/1.*

Orbach. Y., Hershkowitz. I., Lamb, M. E., Sternberg, K. J., Esplin, P. W. and Horowitz, D. 2000. "Assessing the value of scripted protocols for forensic interviews of alleged abuse victims". *Child Abuse and Neglect* 24: 733–752.

Pomerantz, A. 1988. "Offering a candidate answer: An information seeking strategy". *Communication Monographs* 55: 360–373.

Poole, D. A. and Lamb, M. E. 1998. *Investigative Interviews of Children: A Guide for Helping Professionals.* Washington, DC: American Psychological Association.

Russell, D. E. H. and Bolen, R. M. 2000. *The Epidemic of Rape and Child Sexual Abuse in the United States.* Thousand Oaks: Sage.

Statistiska central byrån. Rättstatistisk Årsbok. 1987–1993. (*Statistics Sweden Year book of Judicial Statistics 1987–93*). Stockholm: SCB.

Saywitz, K., Geiselman, R. E. and Bornstein, G. K. 1992. "Effects of cognitive interviewing and practice on children's recall performance". *Journal of Applied Psychology* 77: 744–756.

Saywitz K. and Goodman, G. S. 1996. "Interviewing children in and out of court". In *The APSAC Handbook on Child Maltreatment*, J. B. Briere, L. Berliner, J. A. Bulkley, C. Jenny and T. Reid. (eds), 297–318. Thousand Oaks: Sage.

Sternberg, K. J., Lamb, M. E., Davis, G. M. and Westcott, H. L. 2001. "The Memorandum of Good Practice: Theory versus application". *Child Abuse and Neglect* 25: 669–681.

Sternberg, K. J., Lamb, M. E., Esplin, P. W., and Baradaran, L. B. 1999. "Using a structured interview protocol in investigative interviews: A pilot study". *Applied Developmental Science* 3: 70–76.

Sternberg, K. J., Lamb, M. E., Esplin, P. W., Orbach, Y. and Hershkowitz, I. 2001. "Using a structured interview protocol to improve the quality of investigative interviews". In *Memory and Suggestibility in the Forensic Interview*, M. Eisen, J. Quas and G. Goodman (eds), Mahwah, NJ: Erlbaum

Sternberg, K. J., Lamb, M. E., Hershkowitz, I., Esplin, P. W., Redlich, A. and Sunshine, N. 1996. "The relation between investigative utterance types and the informativeness of child witnesses". *Journal of Applied Developmental Psychology* 1: 439–451.

Sternberg, K. J., Lamb, M. E., Hershkowitz, I., Yudilevitch, L., Orbach, Y., Esplin, P. W. and Hovav, M. 1997. "Effects of introductory style on childrens' abilities to describe experiences of sexual abuse". *Child Abuse and Neglect* 21: 1133–1146.

Svedin, C-G. 1999. "Sexuella övergrepp mot barn. Definitioner och förekomst" (*Sexual abuse of children Definitions and prevalence*). *Socialstyrelsen. (The National Board of Health and Welfare). Article # 36–004*.

Svedin, C-G. 2000. "Sexuella övergrepp mot barn. Orsaker och risker". (*Sexual abuse of children. Causes and risks*). *Socialstyrelsen (The National Board of Health and Welfare). Article # 36–006*.

U. S. Department of Health and Human Services, National Center on Child Abuse and Neglect. 1995. *Child Maltreatment 1993: Reports from the States to the National Center on Child Abuse and Neglect*. Washington, DC: U. S. Government Printing Office.

Warren, A. R. and McGough, L. S. 1996. "Research on children's suggestibility: Implications for the investigative interview". *Criminal Justice and Behavior* 23: 269–303.

Warren, A. R., Woodhall, C. E., Thomas, M., Nunno, M., Keeney, J., Larson, S. and Stadfeld, J. 1999. "Assessing the effectiveness of a training program for interviewing child witnesses". *Applied Developmental Science* 3: 128–135.

Chapter 8

In the shadow of the stalker
The problem of policing unwanted pursuit

Brian H. Spitzberg
San Diego State University, San Diego, USA

There are crimes, and then there are crimes. In the popular parlance and stereotypes of the public at large, there is a common distinction between "relational problems" and "crimes" (Straus 1999). Unwanted pursuit, harassment, date rape, relational aggression, and the like, illustrate problems that are often considered more matters between persons than matters of state. These problems are not easily equated with actions such as robbery, vandalism, arson, breaking and entering, aggravated assault, or murder. Yet, with the exception of murder, which itself is often an end-product of relational problems, these traditional crimes are far less likely to have significant and enduring traumatic effects on quality of life than relational problems.

The policing of relational problems has encountered a host of problems in attempting to apply traditional models of law enforcement to the private world of relationships (Fyfe, Klinger & Flavin 1997). Legislation and law enforcement have experienced long learning curves in areas such as domestic violence (see Chapter 6) and rape. Mandatory arrest policies in cases of domestic violence and rape reform legislation have sounded a significant sea change in the degree of interest the State accepts in maintaining relational civility. Perhaps as an extension of such recognition of State interests, combined with the political weight of feminist interests in securing a safe public environment for women, and combined with salacious media interests in crime, it is not surprising that stalking has become the next horizon of law enforcement. This move to construct stalking as a crime, and the various problems this crime creates for policing, are the subject of this chapter. Specifically, it will examine the nature of stalking, the ways in which it creates problems for law enforcement, and some of the ways in which threat management can be facilitated. Throughout, stalking itself, and the ways in which victims and police attempt to manage the crime, are revealed to be largely communicative and interactional phenomena.

The nature of stalking

Stalking is widely recognized as an old behavior but a *new crime*. Themes of stalking and pursuing the object of one's affection have appeared in popular culture since the beginnings of the literary tradition (Lee 1998; Meloy 1999; Skoler 1998). Until 1989, however, neither the term, nor the crime, was commonly associated with the process of continued, unwanted pursuit, and harassment. However, the murder of actress Rebecca Schaeffer, and several women in Southern California who had restraining orders against their attackers, led to momentum in the mass media to give a name to this phenomenon. Stalking became a common moniker for the process of stealthy, unwanted pursuit and harassment, and was soon associated with the interpersonal terrorism of women and celebrities (Best 1999; Cadiz & Spitzberg 2001; Holmes 1993; Keenahan & Barlow 1997; Leets, de Becker & Giles 1995; Lowney & Best 1995; Saunders 1998). In 1990, the first anti-stalking statute took effect in California, and stalking entered the legal lexicon (McAnaney Curliss & Abeyta-Price 1993).

"Stalking describes a constellation of behaviors in which one individual inflicts on another repeated unwanted intrusions and communications" (Pathé & Mullen 1997:12). More specifically, stalking is a process of "willful, malicious, and repeated following and harassing of another person" (U.S. Department of Justice 1998:5). There is inconsistency in particular provisions of statute, but most U.S. State penal codes define stalking as involving the following three elements:

– A pattern of willful or intentional harassing or annoying/alarming conduct such as repeat messages, following, vandalism, and other unwanted behaviors
– Infliction of credible explicit or implicit threats against a victim's safety or that of her family
– Actual and reasonable victim fear of the stalker resulting from this behavior (Miller 2001:8)

In a veritable avalanche of political momentum, within a decade of California's anti-stalking statute, all 50 U.S. States, the U.S. Federal government, Canada, Australia, and Great Britain had passed some form of stalking legislation. Such legislation continues to be modified and refined. In the U.S., 11 States define first offense stalking as a felony, 25 allow some discretion to prosecute as a misdemeanor or felony, and 14 define first offense as a misdemeanor (Miller 2001). All 50 U.S. States permit orders of protection from domestic violence and 27 States permit civil protection orders against stalking (Miller 2001). Such laws are generating extensive legal testing; as of early 2001, there were 508 State and Federal stalking-related cases in the U.S., mostly surrounding constitutional issues such as vagueness and claims of being over-broad. Most legislation to date has been upheld. Miller's (2001) review shows that legislative reform efforts continue to expand penalties, provide broader scope (e.g., cyberstalking, harassment), extend protections (e.g., civil or criminal protection orders, confidentiality programs), and intervention options (e.g., offender treatment programs). As a legal construct, stalking appears prepared to stay.

These legalistic issues have been modified in some ways by the social scientific literature, which has tended to take two distinct but overlapping approaches: clinical and interactional (Spitzberg & Cupach in press). The clinical literature has tended to pathologize stalking as an attachment disorder or as representing underlying pathologies or incompetencies (Mullen, Pathé & Purcell 2000). The interactional literature has tended to view stalking as most often arising from failed relationships and distorted conceptions of communication in courtship (e.g., Cupach & Spitzberg 1998; Cupach, Spitzberg & Carson, 2000; Emerson, Ferris & Gardner 1998). In both approaches, however, most stalking is recognized as a persistent process of unwanted and targeted communications and intrusions that a reasonable person would find fearful. To understand the ways in which stalking may be considered threatening, it is important to examine its prevalence, and its typological and tactical topography; that is, the types of stalkers and the ways in which stalkers stalk.

Prevalence

Two large-scale representative surveys have been conducted in the U.S. to ascertain the prevalence of stalking in society. The Tjaden and Thoennes (1998) study surveyed 16,000 respondents (8,000 males, 8,000 females). Using a strict definition, they concluded that 8% of women and 2% of men have been stalked in their lifetime. Using a more liberal definition in which minimal fear is required, these estimates were 12% and 4% respectively. The Fisher, Cullen and Turner (1999, 2000) study surveyed over 4,400 college women randomly selected from student lists at colleges of over 1000 students. They estimated that

13% of college women had been stalked since the college year began. In Australia, a representative sample of 1,844 Victoria residents indicated a lifetime incidence of 23%, and an incidence in the previous year of almost 6% (Purcell, Pathé & Mullen 2000). In their sample, 75% of lifetime victims were female, but there was no sex difference in victims in the previous year. In Great Britain, the Home Office conducted a representative sample of 14,947 adults, concluding that almost 12% of adults had been stalked at some point in their lifetime, and almost 3% in the previous year (Budd & Mattinson, 2000). Spitzberg and Cupach (in press) averaged estimates across 25 studies and concluded that 21% of the adult population has been stalked. In terms of the ratio of male to female victimization, most research indicates that between 60 and 80% of victims are females, and 20 to 40% of victims are males (Spitzberg & Cupach in press).

An aspect of stalking that is often overlooked is the sheer duration of the crime. Tjaden and Thoennes (1998) found that the average victim claimed to have been stalked for 1.8 years. Similarly, across 13 studies reviewed by Spitzberg (2001), the average duration of stalking was 1.4 years. Across studies stalking cases are identified that range from days to decades (Spitzberg & Cupach 2001). Such durations suggest not only the extended and indeterminate horizon the victim faces, but also the effort and investment potentially required of law enforcement. Furthermore, short of arrest and conviction, there is never any certainty that the stalking, once relapsed for a period of time, might not begin again.

The extent to which such stalking results in violence is difficult to estimate, given that violence can co-occur with stalking and yet also be incidental to it. Across 10 studies of clinical and forensic cases of stalking, the mean rate of violence was 30%, and the rate was 50% in cases in which there had been a prior sexually intimate relationship (Meloy in press). While the existence of threats by the stalker do appear to predict violence, the effect size is small (betas ranging from .15 to .26), and the false positive rates tended to be greater than 50%, with false negative rates below 25% (Meloy, in press). In contrast to strictly forensic and clinical studies, research on victims reveals a range from 3 to 89% rates of violence (Spitzberg & Cupach 2002). Recognizing widely divergent operationalizations in the 20 studies reviewed by Spitzberg and Cupach, the average rate of physical violence of some sort is 32.6%. In the largest scale victim study yet reported, Tjaden and Thoennes (1998) found that of the half of women victims stalked by a former partner, 80% had been physically assaulted at some point in their relationship, although this assault cannot be directly linked to the stalking itself. To date, the best predictor of violence in stalking cases appears to be the nature of the prior relationship. Compared to stalking by strangers and acquaintances, victims who had a prior sexual relationship with their pursuer face greatly elevated risks of suffering violence at the hands of their pusuer (Farnham, James & Cantrell 2000; Meloy, in press).

Another form of violence, sexual assault and rape, also seems intimately involved with stalking (Spitzberg, Marshall & Cupach 2001; Spitzberg & Rhea 1999). Across 10 studies in which sexual assault, coercion, or rape were studied, the range of victim experience was 3 to 32%, with an average of 13.8% (Spitzberg & Cupach 2002). In the Tjaden and Thoennes (1998) study, of the half of female victims of stalking by a former partner, 31% had been sexually assaulted at some point in their relationship. In the Home Office study in Great Britain, 9% of female victims, and 3% of male victims, of stalking, reported a forced sexual act in the context of the stalking (Budd & Mattinson 2000).

Even when stalking does not result in violence, research is clear that stalking tends to result in significantly diminished victim quality of life. Stalking victimization has been associated with anxiety, stress, sleep disorder, appetite disturbance, aggression, paranoia, distrust, loss of faith, depression, suicide ideation, and physical illness (Spitzberg & Cupach in press). The vast majority of victims of stalking experience extensive changes in lifestyle as they significantly alter their telephone numbers, security measures, jobs, schedules, routine activities, residence, city, and sometimes, even identities to escape the ongoing campaign of intrusion. Collectively, the evidence on symptoms and violence suggests that stalking is a potent negative force in victims' lives. "Although the phenomenon of stalking is just as grave as issues of rape and domestic violence, stalking does not have the same stigma attached to it" (Lee 1998:404).

Stalking may be as serious as rape and domestic violence, but it also may not receive such accord from society and law enforcement. For example, in one study about half of women entering a battered women's shelter did not contact the police. When the police were contacted, it was most likely to occur when there was physical abuse rather than emotional, and "perpetrated by someone other than an ex-partner" (Coulter, Kuehnle, Byers & Alfonso 1999:1296). Stalking simply may not rise to many people's threshold of threatening and illegal. Stalking is clearly a complex and variegated phenomenon. Just as clearly, therefore, it is likely to present a number of problems for law enforcement and threat management. An examination of some of these problems reveals stalking to be a relatively unique and challenging crime to manage.

A topography of stalking

Stalking takes on an enormous diversity of tactical approach. In part, the types of stalking activity will depend on the type of stalker. One of the most developed typologies of stalker types identifies five types of stalker, and three related categories of activity (Mullen et al. 1999; Mullen et al. 2000). The *rejected stalker* is one who pursues a prior partner after the break-up of a pre-existing relationship (Langhinrichsen-Rohling, Palarea, Cohen & Rohling 2000). The motive can be reconciliation, revenge, or both. Rejected stalkers demonstrate among the most persistent and variable ranges of pursuit tactics of the stalker types. The *resentful stalker* engages in a campaign of retaliation for perceived wrongs. Such wrongs can range from the humiliation of being fired to the humiliation of being rejected as a relational partner. The *predatory stalker* engages in planning and preparation for an attack upon the victim. This type of stalker perhaps best fits the public and media stereotypes of stalkers, and are least likely to make their presence known until the attack. These latter two types reflect a distinction made by a study of threats upon public figures, which differentiated "howlers," who threaten and complain but rarely act on their invectives, and "hunters," who rarely threaten but are likely to act on their agenda (Calhoun 1998). *Intimacy-seeking stalkers* are obsessed with the object of their affection. They idealize and fantasize about the object. These stalkers also are likely to be quite persistent; in one study, the intimacy-seekers stalked their object for an average of over three years (Mullen, Pathé, Purcell & Stuart 1999). *Incompetent suitor stalkers* lack social skills and, therefore, tend to pursue intimacy in awkward ways. Where the intimacy seeker views the object of affection as the fulfillment of destiny, the incompetent simply wants a date, and will tend to display one of the shortest durations of stalking.

Mullen et al. (1999; Mullen et al. 2000) also point to three phenomena that reflect rather specialized types of stalking-related activity. One of the most stereotypical pathologies associated with stalking is *erotomania*, or the delusional belief that self is loved by another who, in fact, has no such feelings. Erotomania is generally associated with other pathologies such as schizophrenia, and is obviously likely to motivate stalking activities. *Same-gender stalking* does occur, but does not reveal many significant differences from opposite-sex stalking (Pathé, Mullen & Purcell 2000). Same-gender stalkers appear less likely to result from prior intimate relationships and more from workplace contacts. Same-gender stalkers are also less likely to harass through following and approaches than opposite-sex stalkers. *Stalking by proxy* involves other people or agencies in contacting or observing the object of pursuit. It is one of the least studied and understood types of stalking activity (see also Sheridan in press; Sheridan, Davies & Boon 2001).

Finally, *false victimization* represents a small but potentially important percentage of stalking cases. The only estimate available suggests that approximately 2% of stalking cases presented to the police are false (Mohandie, Hatcher & Raymond 1998). Given the potential relevance of this particular activity on policing, it bears closer examination. The motives for a person falsely claiming to have been stalked are varied, but appear to fall into at least four patterns (Pathé, Mullen & Purcell 1999). First, stalkers sometimes attempt to preempt their victim's anticipated legal efforts by charging the victim as being the stalker. Second, mental disturbance can lead someone to fabricate a delusion of being persecuted or stalked. Third, persons who have been stalked or otherwise victimized before may develop a hypersensitive or paranoid view of the world in which innocent actions are misinterpreted as stalking. Finally, factitious and malingerer types of stalking represent attempts to achieve the sick role so as to elicit material gain or sympathies from significant others. These cases can present as legitimate stalking cases and tie up considerable administrative and law enforcement resources as well as impair the reputation of innocent persons.

There are several other typologies that have been developed to diagnose stalker types (e.g., Hargreaves in press; Harmon, Rosner & Owens 1998; Holmes 1993; Spitzberg & Cupach 2002; Zona, Palarae & Lane 1998). Such typologies assist in identifying stalkers, and in anticipating their patterns of behavior. However, to date, these typologies have revealed rather extensive overlap of actual behaviors. Therefore, one of the more diagnostically useful approaches to stalking is to identify the tactical profile of a stalker.

As there are different types of stalkers, stalkers employ different types of tactics in the pursuit of their targets. As of this writing, over 70 studies of stalking and stalking-related activities have been conducted (see Spitzberg & Cupach in press, 2001, 2002 for review). Of these, 34 examined tactics in a quantitative manner in which the percentage of victims experiencing a certain type of tactic, or pursuer engaging in a certain type of tactic, was assessed. Over 250 separate tactic labels were reduced to five tactical clusters of stalking activity, which are reproduced in Table 8.1.

Table 8.1 A synthesis of stalking tactic studies*

I. **Hyperintimacy tactics:** Function: to communicate affection/attraction
   1. affection, exaggerated messages of;
   2. intrusion in interactions;
   3. invasion of personal space;
   4. involvement in activities;
   5. telephone calls (just to talk, to express interest);
   6. computer messages: (e-mail; internet);
   7. dating coercion: (e.g., manipulate or coerce into dating);
   8. expose self;
   9. gifts/objects: (flowers, gifts);
   10. letters: (notes/messages, inappropriate sexually explicit);
   11. sexual coercion, contact (kissing/caressing of victim, forced);
   12. sexual proposition;

II. **Pursuit (proximity) tactics:** Function: to monitor and communicate control, persistence, commitment to course of action
   13. approaches (in public; in threatening or harassing manner);
   14. contact: (forced confrontation; at residence, work, physical, through third party);
   15. drive by: (home, workplace, past the target);
   16. follow: (followed, to car);
   17. lying in wait: (neighborhood, prowling, workplace, home, showing up at places);
   18. move residence closer to where target lives or places target frequents;
   19. visitation: (home, school, workplace, places target frequents);
   20. watch: (from afar, observed, waiting/standing and staring);

III. **Invasion tactics:** Function: to obtain information/tokens and communicate power
   21. breaking and entering (home, auto); attempted;
   22. breaking and entering (home, auto); actual;
   23. intrusion upon/involvement with friends/coworkers/family;
   24. telephone calls: (workplace; anonymous; hang-ups; obscene, threatening, or mysterious);
   25. invasion of computer (cyberstalking, planting virus, obtaining information);
   26. surveillance: (of home, watching, via friends/family);
   27. surveillance: (monitoring, photographed target without target knowledge);
   28. surveillance: (covertly obtaining information);
   29. theft: (intercepting mail/deliveries, stolen/read, valued possessions, property);
   30. trespass: (on victim's property);

IV. **Intimidation tactics:** Function: to communicate power, deterrence, incentive
   31. contempt of court order;
   32. gifts/objects: (bizarre or sinister items);
   33. harassment: computer (e-mail, cyberstalking);
   34. harassment: economic (canceling victim's credit cards, etc.);
   35. harassment: interpersonal (telling lies to victim's friends, family, co-workers);

36. harassment: legal (regulatory harassment, spurious legal actions);
37. harassment: written (signs, letters, etc.);
38. harassment; discredit: (letters, slandering; sabotaging employment; spread gossip);
39. obscenity: (offensive language, sexual);
40. property damage: (valued possessions, vandalism, ramming victim's car);
41. rage/anger: (displayed, aggressive/insulting upon seeing the target out with others);
42. threats: mode (via intermediaries, firearm/weapon, implied/overt physical, verbal);
43. threats: target (third parties, family and/or friends; new partner; pet; property);
44. threats: type (physical injury, to kill, violence);
45. verbal messages: (aggression, verbal abuse/mild).

V. **Violence:** Function: to communicate power, commitment to goals, to fuse through annihilation

46. assault/violence, actual: (physical injury, sexual, attack, battery, hit or beat, physical abuse, with weapon);
47. assault, attempted: (attempted harm; attempted sexual);
48. assault, third-parties: (child abuse, friends, family, associates, 'rival,' etc.);
49. murder, actual;
50. murder, attempted;
51. murder, solicitation to commit;
52. pet: (killed or injured);
53. restraint: (confined or kidnapped, physically restraining);
54. self-harm: (attempt hurt self; threatened, threatening suicide).

Note

* Table is a synthetic summary of approximately 250 separate tactics across 34 studies, the list of which is available from the author. Tactics were synthetically extracted by (1) presuming behaviors as unwanted, excessive, and repeated, (2) splitting compound tactics (e.g., extreme harm such as sexual or physical assault); (3) eliminating redundant terms; (4) combining like concepts (e.g., physical harm, physical assault); and (5) removing unobservable or overly ambiguous concepts (e.g., "deceptive").

The first cluster represents *hyper-intimacy tactics*, which are exaggerated forms of courtship. A single rose given face-to-face is likely viewed as courtship; two-dozen roses laid out on one's car in a deserted parking lot will more likely viewed as "creepy." Research suggests that one of the ways stalkers often delay outright rejection is through the infusion of courtship cues into their pursuit (Dunn 1999). Such hyper-intimate actions capitalize on the ambiguities of flirtation, flattery, and the presumed persistence involved in cultural models of courtship (Lee 1998).

The *pursuit and proximity tactics* category includes attempts to observe, follow, and be near the object of pursuit. This is perhaps the most stereotypical activity of stalking, and also the closest to the etymology and historical uses of the term (Spitzberg & Cupach in press). Driving by, lying in wait, approaching in public, visiting work or home, and watching from afar all reflect the stalker's fascination with the object of pursuit, and their need to have information about the object of pursuit so as to guide future potential contacts.

Some stalkers stop with pursuit and proximity tactics. Others go further and intrude directly into the object's personal or territorial privacy. Such *invasion tactics* include actions such as trespass, breaking and entering, inveigling into the person's social life, informational surveillance of mail or computer, theft, and one of the hallmarks of contemporary stalking, incessant telephone calls. These tactics range from the merely annoying and harassing (e.g., telephone calls) to the more threatening and clearly illegal (e.g., trespass, breaking, and entering).

At times, the motive underlying stalking shifts from amorous to coercive. *Intimidation tactics* are attempts to frighten, threaten, or otherwise influence the object of pursuit. Sometimes such influence is intended to coerce the person into giving the relationship a chance whereas, other times, it will be part of a more elaborate campaign of terror designed to hurt the object of pursuit. Actions such as leaving bizarre objects or gifts, harassing the person legally or economically, damaging valued possessions, or making threats all represent communicative attempts to intimidate the object, and to make the object more malleable for future manipulation.

Finally, a stalker can engage in *violent tactics*. The issue of violence in stalking is complex, and the subject of considerable speculation and investigation. Violence is not the same thing as stalking. Law enforcement has a considerable armamentarium for coping with violence and assault. However, violence is also clearly bound up in, and often instrumental to, the activity of stalking (Sheridan, Gillett & Davies 2000). As such, it is important to recognize that "physical assault" does not exist a priori distinct from stalking, except in the rhetorical and normative constructions of the legal system. In somewhat the same sense, wielding a weapon to enact a rape is clearly aggravated assault, but also clearly an act of violence in order to perpetrate another form of violence, which just happens to be sexual in nature. Physical violence, therefore, is part of the tactical topography of the stalking process. It may not occur, but its possibility is ever present, and is clearly one of the potential threats to be managed in any stalking cases.

The problematics of unwanted pursuit

Stalking occupies an intriguing nexus between traditional notions of crime on the one hand, and culturally-endorsed conceptions of courtship, on the other (Lee 1998). Whereas stalking threatens, frightens, intrudes, invades, and is potentially endangering, enforcement of stalking laws also potentially restricts movement in public spaces, access to various organizations, and communication through legitimate media. Such clashes of core values of freedom of speech and movement versus privacy and safety produce dilemmas of public policy. Some of the unique difficulties of the crime itself are examined next, after which the tensions these difficulties create for police are explored.

The challenges of the crime

The crime of stalking presents a variety of legally problematic aspects. Among other things,

> "stalking is often an illusive crime. It starts, stops, starts again, and ends, at least temporarily, again. Similarly, the locations where stalking occurs vary, ...The methods used by stalkers to stalk can constantly change, ...investigation and prosecution of stalking rely on prospective evidence collection..."
> (Miller 2001:63)

Such a crime can tax the resources of even highly motivated law enforcement. Therefore, an enumeration of some of the troublesome features of the crime is in order.

Stalking presents at least five challenges to law enforcement. First, there is no "there" there. That is, there is relatively little "crime scene" to investigate. Second, law enforcement must rely very heavily on the victim to play investigator and evidence collector. Third, the harms of stalking are often primarily subjective rather than objective. Fourth, as a product of relationship decay or disjunctive relationships, stalking often becomes a crime of "he said, she said," diminishing the value of testimony alone. Finally, stalking mimics many relatively normal processes of relationship decay. If stalking is viewed as a "relational" matter, it may seem inappropriate for legal intervention. Each of these challenges is elaborated below.

The typical crime has a crime scene. The crime scene is a physical location at which the crime occurred, and presumably at which there are likely to be perpetrator(s) or forms of evidence. As such, most crimes tend to consist of a single incident, in a single scene, in which evidence and testimony is collected, and the case is then investigated along further leads for purposes of possible intervention and prosecution. In contrast, stalking does not have a clear beginning, as the crossover from courtship to stalking may well be ambiguous. Stalking often has no particular location, as it occurs through various media of communication and across various times and locations of pursuit. Furthermore, stalking has no definitive endpoint. The crime extends into an indefinite future, and the collection of evidence is likely to require an eye toward this horizon. As such, criminal investigation often faces the unusual situation of thinking about the crime in future rather than past tense.

Stalkers tend to be highly creative. Indeed, studies of forensic samples indicate that stalkers are more intelligent than their non-stalking clinical or forensic cohorts (Meloy 1998). As such, stalkers are often mindful of evidentiary concerns. The police cannot maintain constant surveillance of either the victim for protection or the stalker for enforcement. Given that stalkers seek contact with the object of pursuit, it follows that police must often relinquish much of the process of evidence collection to the victim. This creates a rather ironic context in which the victim becomes a pursuer, as the victim systematically keeps logs or diaries of incidents, recordings, notes, gifts, encounters, property damage, thefts, and so forth. Indeed, some victims even hire private investigators, follow their follower, make inquiries, and engage in their own campaign of surveillance so as to better gauge the nature of their pursuer and the threat of that pursuit. All the while that evidence is being amassed, however, the victim is enduring the process of pursuit, invasion, intrusion, and fear. "In virtually no other crime is the investigation and prosecution so dependent upon the victim for evidence collection. Nor are there many other crimes where victim safety is so threatened over such a long period of time" (Miller 2001: 64).

Crimes of violence are exactly that: violent. As such, these crimes tend to leave signs of violence (e.g., injury, blood) or potential for violence (e.g., weapons). Stalking, as indicated above, is occasionally but far from always violent. The crime consists of contacts, notes, intimidations, harassments, and the like. As such, the violence tends to be psychological and, therefore, not particularly evidentiary by ordinary crime standards. According to a survey of police officers "Many officers believed that bodily harm must have been committed or that the perpetrator must be a stranger to classify an incident as stalking" (Farrell, Weisburd & Wyckoff 2000: 164). Yet, stalking laws do not require physical injury. Instead, they tend to require that a reasonable person would experience *fear* if faced with the pattern of pursuit and harassment experienced. Indeed, a survey of police in Victoria, Australia, found that over 30% reported "problems obtaining evidence of intent to harm" and almost 22% "experienced problems in obtaining evidence concerning the harmful effect of the stalking behaviour on the victim" (Dussuyer 2000:77).

Much stalking mimics, and indeed is, a process of courtship, however deviant or disturbed. Many stalking cases proceed as a disjunctive relationship in which one person takes on the role of spurned or would be lover (Cupach et al. 2000). As such, there are likely to be divergent stories from the pursuer and object of pursuit. Both accounts are likely to share some commonality, and yet also likely to represent incompatible accounts of the nature of the relationship. Such crimes, especially when the evidence is often elusive or seemingly benign, are particularly difficult to pursue legally.

Stalking can enact many different motives, expressive and instrumental (see Chapter 6), amorous and predatory (Spitzberg & Cupach in press). However, most stalking emanates from the remains of previous relationships (Spitzberg & Cupach in press; Tjaden & Thoennes 1998). In the context of a relationship gone wrong, police may be inclined to view stalking, especially in the early stages, as little more than a series of misunderstandings or merely a case of unrequited love. Indeed, much current theorizing conceptualizes most stalking and stalking-related phenomena as the product of distorted or disturbed courtship (e.g., Cupach & Spitzberg 1998; Emerson et al. 1998; Sinclair & Frieze 2000; Spitzberg & Cupach 2002). If stalking is viewed as a product of passion gone awry, there may be an inclination to treat it as a *private* matter rather than a matter for the law.

The challenges of police response

Contacting the police is one of the common responses victims of stalking attempt, although police may be viewed by the typical victim as the coping response of last resort. Bjerregaard (2000) found that only 35% of female and 10% of male victims called the police. Blackburn (1999) reported that 35% of victims "approached" the police. Other studies show higher percentages, ranging from 60 to 89% (Blackburn 1999; Brewster 1998; Kohn, Flood, Chase & McMahon 2000; Pathé et al. 2000). Some of these differences represent sample differences, for example, between college students versus battered women. In Tjaden and Thoennes' (1998) large-scale survey, 55% of female victims and 48% of male victims of stalking claimed their stalking was reported to the police. However, most studies reveal that victims engage in a wide variety of coping responses, most of them informal and interactional in nature (e.g., having a talk with the pursuer, talking to friends, trying to avoid pursuer, etc.). Tjaden and Thoennes (1998) found that when asked why they did not contact the police, stalking victims mentioned such reasons as it not being a police matter (20%), that the police would not be able to do anything about it (17%), that the stalker might seek reprisals (16%), that the police would not believe the victim (7%), and that they did not want the police or courts involved (5%), among other reasons. Further, a study of stalking cases that came to the attention of Victoria, Australia, police found that stalking "had been occurring for some time before it was brought to the attention of the police and courts" (Dussuyer 2000:68). Communicating with the police therefore, may represent a coping response at an end of a continuum of threat when the more convenient, less formal means of coping have been exhausted. If so, it makes the nature of the police contact with victims all the *more* important. Yet, presuming a victim does contact the police, there are a number of potential challenges to police management of stalking cases.

Lack of obvious injury
Police have three primary tasks when confronted with a stalking report: to assess the stalker, gather evidence, and manage risk. The former two are the more classic police roles (Wells 2001), whereas the latter is increasingly viewed as part of victim services, which are sometimes housed in law enforcement but, at other times, are handled primarily through private, generally nonprofit organizations. Assessing the stalker is problematic for several reasons, including that threats rarely predict actual violence, and that there are many types of stalkers, with many types of motives, posing highly variable levels of potential risk to the victim (Meloy 2000). Gathering evidence involves taking statements, examining tokens, artifacts, recordings, and possibly searches and surveillance. Implicit in evaluating the stalker and gathering evidence is an assessment of the veracity and psychological state of the victim. Stories and accounts may diverge significantly, and some victims may be malingering, factitious, or even delusional. Given that stalking cases can endure for months and even years, it is important to ascertain that a victim is, indeed, a legitimate victim. But this means treating with skepticism a person who may already be very traumatized by a legitimate campaign of interpersonal terrorism.

Among the implications of these assessments is that police face several subtle thresholds in their decision-making process, all of which depend importantly on the outcome of police communication with victim and suspect. At what point is it clear that the victim is telling the truth, or to what extent is the victim telling the truth? At what point does the victim's reality raise to the legal level of "fear?" At what point does the stalker represent a legitimate threat as determined by the legal standard of the "reasonable person?" At what point should the victim be referred to victim's services? At what point does the victim's experience raise to the level of prosecution rather than less formal interventions? At what point, if the case does not appear prosecutable, would it be, and to what extent does waiting for evidence accumulation endanger the victim's safety? Finally, "many victims develop coping behaviors that may, on the surface, appear to undercut the seriousness of the threat faced by the victim and her fear of the stalker" (Miller 2001:75). Thus, at what point do police attempt to intervene into the victim's life to micro-manage his or her behavior? Such questions all imply decisional continua upon which there are no clear demarcations. Some imply skepticism of the victim in a context in which the victim is most in need of sympathy and proactive response and, some imply hyper-sensitivity to a situation that is unlikely to amount to anything more. Such decisional and communicative tensions are part of the fabric of everyday police assessments (see Chapter 6), but the crime of stalking presents rather unique issues compared to more many more traditional crimes.

Lack of specialized knowledge
Stalking was criminalized throughout the 1990s. However, criminalizing a behavior does not bring with it funding, specification of departmental procedure, training, or additional officers. Thus, it is little surprise that the vast majority of stalking cases are assigned to detective units or domestic violence units within existing departmental structures. A survey of Florida police agencies revealed that 56% engaged in in-service training on stalking, but most of this occurred during roll-call briefings (Tucker 1993). A survey of 162 urban law enforcement agencies across the U.S., replicated a year later among 151 agencies, found that, by far, most stalking cases are assigned to detective or DV units and that recruit training typically occurs as part of domestic violence training (Miller 2001). "Significantly, over one-third provided no in-service training to their officers," although more than half provided in-service training on stalking to detectives (Miller 2001:30–31). About 60% of agencies reported having written policies and procedures for stalking cases, typically as part of their domestic violence protocols. Only 11 of the 162 agencies had protocols specifically tailored to stalking. A survey of Australian police officers revealed that their knowledge of stalking was based on "their own reading" (84%) or colleagues (39%), suggesting a lack of systematic training (Dussuyer 2000).

Perhaps training is not common because training is not needed. Unfortunately, this seems unlikely (Schell & Lanteigne 2000). A survey of almost 250 police officers found that "Half of all patrol officers (48%) did not know whether the police department had a written policy on stalking" and 18% said it did not (Farrell et al. 2000: 164). Furthermore, when asked to identify stalking as a crime, "Only 18% of police officers defined stalking in a manner consistent with the State statute" (Farrell et al. 2000: 164). Even two-thirds of the officers admitted that "their department did not deal with stalking cases particularly well" (Farrell et al. 2000: 166). The evidence suggests that police are largely untrained and uninformed about the crime of stalking, and that what training occurs tends to be brief and framed within a context of "domestic" violence rather than stalking in its own right.

Further evidence of the importance of such training and education is provided by a study of victim service agencies. The survey asked what the priorities for stalking victims were. Criminal justice training was the second most commonly noted need for intervention in stalking cases. Of those agencies reporting the need for criminal justice training of victims, 75% noted the need for "law enforcement officers to either gain a better understanding of stalking, be able to recognize stalking cases, or be more sensitive to victims" (Spence-Diehl & Potocky-Tripodi 2001:91). Several responses also indicated a recognized need for

> better law enforcement identification and tracking of stalking cases, increased prosecution ... speed[ing] up actions taken when protective orders are violated [and] the development of specialized stalking units in police departments""
> (Spence-Diehl & Potocky-Tripodi 2001:91)

There are additional structural challenges that are likely to present police with obstacles to responding to stalker needs.

Lack of clear jurisdiction
Stalking is a crime of pursuit. But the object of pursuit is typically mobile, and the means of contact are frequently capable of communication across a distance. Stalking tends to cross over a variety of jurisdictions (e.g., city, county, state, federal) and agencies (e.g., city attorney, district attorney, domestic violence, stalking unit, probation). Thus, "no single law enforcement agency has jurisdiction over all the stalking locations" (Miller 2001: 83). Although some agencies have worked to develop cross-jurisdictional procedures by designating "key" cases of stalking to a primary office and with a commonly identifiable

case number, such efforts are by far the exception to the rule (Miller 2001). Consequently, much of the law enforcement response is uncoordinated due to lack of clear jurisdictional prerogative.

Momentum of the familiar
Given a lack of training, there is a proclivity for police officers to treat stalking in the context of the familiar. This tendency is exacerbated by the fact that stalking often involves more traditional crimes as incidental to the stalking. Thus, crimes such as trespassing, criminal threat, harassment, and assault are likely to be the **preferred** case management response. A study of over 250 police officers presented two scenarios, one involving an ex-husband harassing his ex-spouse causing substantial emotional stress and, another, in which a work acquaintance trespasses more than once on a woman's property and harasses with calls causing discomfort (Farrell et al. 2000). A quarter of officers thought the first scenario should be reported as domestic violence, 44% thought the second scenario deserved a trespass report, and 67% and 49% thought the scenarios reflected harassment. Slightly over half of officers thought either scenario should be reported as stalking, even though both have clear elements of stalking. Even more discouraging was a study of 1,785 domestic violence reports in Colorado Springs in 1998 (Tjaden & Thoennes 2000). Almost 17% ($N=285$) of police reports had narrative elements of stalking. Of these, only a single case actually recommended a charge of stalking.

Another momentum toward the familiar is suggested by Tjaden and Thoennes' (1998) finding that police were significantly more likely to arrest alleged perpetrators and refer the victim to services when the victim reporting the stalking was female. The traditional stereotype of females as the sex most at threat of predatory crimes, and the more recent association of stalking with domestic violence (e.g., Bernstein 1993; Burgess et al. 1997; Coleman 1997; Jordan 1995; Kurt 1995; Logan Leukefeld & Walker 2000; Mechanic, Weaver & Resick 2000; National Institute of Justice 1996; U.S. Department of Justice 1998; Walker & Meloy 1998), suggest that police may not take *male* victims of stalking as seriously as female victims, or dating or friendship cases of stalking as seriously as domestic cases.

The momentum of the familiar may combine in unfortunate ways with other enduring interpersonal and bureaucratic factors. One small-scale study of battered women who had multiple encounters seeking police intervention noted any of four styles of problematic interaction (Stephens & Sinden 2000). Some officers minimized the situation by downplaying the seriousness of the woman's complaint (e.g., "Well, what do you want me to do about it? He'll just be back tomorrow."). Other officers merely disbelieved the victim. For example, some victims' claims to have a protective order were discounted, even in one case after the victim produced a copy. Third, some officers demonstrated apathy in the form of lack of concern, indifference, lack of compassion, affect, and sympathy. Finally, some police were characterized by a macho or insolent style. One "participant was stunned when an officer suggested that she must be 'awfully good in bed' for her ex-husband to continue his stalking and harassment of her" (p. 541). These were not universal experiences of the women contacting police. They do, however, illustrate the possibility that when faced with an awkward and relational crime, officers may often fall back on their personal scripts and styles of interaction to avoid contending with the problems of the crime itself.

These problems of police response to stalking suggest that victims will often be met with mixed results. Indeed, 43% of victims in one study who contacted the police claimed that the police "met their needs" (Brewster 1998). Victims gave police the highest ratings for "response time" and "politeness" and the worst ratings for "sympathy" and "living up to victim's expectations," although all ratings were in the neutral to positive range, including helpfulness (Brewster 1998:54). Another study of victims found that police "officers received an average rating of *somewhat successful*" (Spence-Diehl & Potocky-Tripodi 2001:90). Still another study noted that calling the police was rated from .95 for females and .1 for males, where 0 was never used, and 1 was "tried but wasn't effective" (Fremouw, Westrun & Pennypacker 1997). Finally, Tjaden and Thoennes (1998) found that 50% of victims were satisfied with the actions taken by the police, 54% believed the situation improved upon contacting the police, and 51% believed the police did everything they could. Victims who contacted the police were significantly more satisfied when their pursuer was arrested (76%) than when the pursuer was not arrested (42%). It may be that the trappings of the law enforcement establishment provide some sense of substance and efficacy that is comforting to many victims, especially if most prior coping responses have been informal and unsystematic. Indeed, when victims of domestic violence do not contact the police, they often regret it (Fry & Barker 2001), suggesting that even when victims are disappointed with police response, they might be just as disappointed by not contacting them. Nevertheless, this analysis suggests that there is a significant need for additional training, expertise, specialization of departments and programs, and even a change of organizational culture such that stalking becomes a higher priority in the law enforcement establishment.

Facilitating threat management

Presuming that police departments significantly increase their attention to stalking as a policing priority, there are a number of reforms that could be enacted. Many of these reforms could simply incorporate resources and models of procedure and assessment available in government reports (e.g., U.S. Department of Justice 1998), institutional reports (e.g., Miller 2001), training conference reports (e.g., San Diego District Attorney's Office 2001), and websites (e.g., Stalking Assistance: www.StalkingAssistance.com; www.stalkingvictims.com; National Center for Victims of Crime: http://www.nvc.org; National Crime Victims Research and Treatment Center: http://www.musc.edu/cvc; National Violence Against Women Prevention Research Center: http://www.nvaw.org). Among the priorities for police is to develop departmental procedures that include brief legislative histories and relevant statutes, stalker typology descriptions, procedures for victim reporting and evidence gathering, victim services, and threat management (e.g., Wells 2001). The police response will typically be only part of a larger domain of coping responses that the victim will need to mobilize.

Victim coping

A review of 17 studies of coping with stalking, as well as a review of coping responses to other types of interpersonal trauma (e.g., domestic violence, privacy invasion) indicates five basic modes of victim response, most of which are communicative or interactional in nature (Spitzberg & Cupach 2001). *Moving inward* responses are intended to cope by focusing on self (e.g., ignore or deny the problem, seek therapy, engage in meditation, use drugs, etc.). *Moving outward* responses involve mobilizing the support or intervention of others (e.g., seek sympathy or emotional support, obtain protection or deterrence from others, seek legal intervention, contract private investigator, etc.). *Moving away* responses entail efforts to avoid the stalker (e.g., minimizing interactions with the stalker, restricting accessibility through telephone options, changing one's schedule of activities, change address, etc.). *Moving toward or with* responses are actions that attempt to negotiate an end to the unwanted behavior (e.g., defining the relationship as 'just friends,' bargaining with the stalker, accepting promises of restraint, attempting to deter future behavior by talking about self-defense training or need to be alone, etc.). Finally, *moving against* responses cope by attempting to intimidate the stalker (e.g., humiliating stalker, seeking restraining order or charging stalker with violating the law, threatening, using violence, etc.). To date, avoidance seems to be the preferred tactic for both police and threat management experts, but there is little empirical data upon which to base such judgments. Regardless, none of these coping responses has sufficient proven effectiveness for police to rely upon them to assure the victim's safety, and many of them seem likely to exacerbate the victim's plight (e.g., threatening the stalker). When the victim's standard coping responses do not appear to be sufficient, the police would be well-advised to consider two additional recommendations for victim action: Victim assistance and protective orders.

Victim assistance

Victims often experience trauma and tangible needs while being stalked, or perhaps in association with legal intervention, which police often cannot provide directly. In such cases, police will need to facilitate victim access and referral to such services. A study of victim service providers found that the five most highly needed services in relation to stalking were assistance in applying for and obtaining restraining orders, psychological face-to-face counseling, information on how to negotiate the criminal justice system, legal advocacy, and emergency shelter (Spence-Diehl & Potocky-Tripodi 2001). The need for these services is suggested by the finding that stalking services for victims currently are relatively unavailable for certain populations of victims. Specifically, 15% of victim service agencies "reported they did not provide services to any victims of stalking, 83% provided services to victims of domestic stalking, and 45% served victims of nondomestic stalking" (Spence-Diehl & Potocky-Tripodi 2001:89).

Such services need to be coordinated with the law enforcement response. One such approach is to develop a multi-agency task group to meet regularly with representatives from various concerned departments of law enforcement and victim service agencies as well as experts involved in threat management and assessment. For example, the case assessment group of the Stalking Strike Force in the San Diego District Attorney's Office meets regularly with victims and the police in charge of the cases. The small, but diverse, group represents members from victim services, probation, detective units, psychological counseling, threat assessment, and scholars. The cases are discussed with an eye to coordinating services and intervention strategies across agencies and assess needed services within the resource parameters of the various agencies. Such meetings help: achieve consistency in policies and procedures across agencies; make policies and procedures fresh and responsive to victim needs; keep various agencies apprised of what is possible; and mobilize the full resources the municipality has to offer the victim.

Protective orders

In many cases, police are inclined to recommend the victim obtain a protective order, and victims of partner violence who experience stalking appear more prone to seek protection orders than victims who do not experience stalking (Wolf, Holt, Kernic, & Rivara 2000). The protective order, whether criminal or civil, is often sought by police more to expand prosecutorial options than to protect the victim. This motive is not entirely misguided because if an order is violated, it generally permits subsequent stalking charges to be enhanced such that the stalker could be imprisoned for a longer period of time if prosecuted and found guilty. Indeed, violation of restraining orders has been found to be a significant factor in police decisions to arrest violent partners (Kane 1999, 2000), even if the decision to arrest is still a relatively rare occurrence (Rigakos 1997). However, the research on restraining orders reveals a very mixed picture of effectiveness. In Tjaden and Thoennes' (1998:12–13) study, 23.6% of stalking victims sought protective orders. Of these, "less than 1% said the stalking stopped because they obtained a restraining order against their stalker." A review across 25 studies in which some estimate was available of the extent to which restraining orders were violated is provided in Table 8.2. It should be noted that these represent very different jurisdictions, times, and for the most part, represent domestic violence victims who may or may not have been stalked. Across the studies, encompassing 23,580 cases or respondents, the range of restraining order violation ranged from 3 to 79%, with a mean of almost 43%. In nine studies, the noncompliance estimate had a component consisting of victims who claimed that violence or stalking increased after, or as a result of, the restraining order. Across these studies, almost 23% claimed that the situation got worse subsequent to the restraining order. Thus, restraining orders may provide more prosecutorial options and may seem a natural extension of law enforcement interests, but they do not appear to be particularly effective, and may often exacerbate the victim's plight. Nevertheless, for many victims it is the feeling of doing something that *sometimes* provides a needed sense of efficacy.

Table 8.2 Gross noncompliance estimates from studies of protective orders

Study	Sample (Type of Order)		Noncompliance	Escalation
1. Adhikari et al. (1993)	41	domestic violence victims (PO)	56.0	17.0
2. Blackburn (1999)	83	F stalking victims (RO)	48.5	18.5
3. Brewster (1998)	19	F stalking victims (TRO)	63.0	21.0
	96	F stalking victims	62.0	16.0
4. Buzawa et al. (1998)	356	F DV victims (RO)	26.0	
5. Carlson et al. (1999)	210	F (Civil PO) applicants	23.0	
6. Chadhuri & Daly (1992)	30	F (TRO) applicants	37.0	10.0
7. Fischer & Rose (1995)	287	F DV victims (PO)	60.0	60.0
8. Gill & Brockman (1996)	601	criminal harassment cases (RO)	18.0	
9. Grau et al. (1985)	270	DV (RO) cases	56.0	
10. Hall (1997)	145	F stalking victims	52.0	21.0
11. Harmon et al. (1995)	78	stalking cases	51.0	
12. Harmon et al. (1998)	175	stalking cases	66.0	
13. Harrell & Smith (1996)	355	F DV victims (TRO) applicants	75.0	
14. Horton et al. (1987)	820	DV victims & (TRO) applicants	46.0	
15. Kaci (1992)	224	DV victims (TRO) court records	18.0	22.0
16. Kaci (1994)	42	DV (TRO, Permanent ROs)	21.0	2.5
17. Keilitz (1997)	177	F (PO) applicants	16.0	
18. Kienlen et al. (1997)	25	stalkers	36.0	
19. Logan et al. (2000)	130	college stalking victims	3.0	
20. Marshall & Castle (1998)	1855	DV and (RO) applicants (Australia)	15.5	
21. Meloy et al. (1997)	200	domestic civil (PO) defendants	18.0	
22. Nicastro et al. (2000)	55	stalking (PO) cases	67.0	
23. Sheridan et al. (2000)	19	stalking victims (CI)	79.0	
24. Tjaden & Thoennes (1998)	182	stalking (PO) victims	70.0	
Sum	23,580			
Range			3–79	2.5–60
Mean			42.78	22.94
sd			21.71	14.39

Note

PO = Protective Order, TRO = Temporary Restraining Order, RO = Restraining Order, CI = Civil Injunction.
F = Female, M = Male

Epilogue: Shedding light on the shadowy stalker

The world of stalking still lies very much in the shadows of public consciousness. In the societal psyche, stalking is seen as something that happens to celebrities and public figures (Best 1999; Cadiz & Spitzberg 2001; Leets et al. 1995; Lowney & Best 1995). But studies reveal that these cases are, by far, the minority. The most typical victim of stalking is the typical person. Police occupy a *unique* position from which to vanguard the public safety from stalking. Such protections are not likely to come easily. Stalking presents a particularly elusive profile from the perspective of law enforcement. It is a crime that extends over an indeterminate but generally lengthy horizon of time. It is a crime that by its very nature tends to be stealthy, calculated to target a victim by being privately but not publicly obvious. It is a crime that strikes in unpredictable, often bizarre ways, and capitalizes on the openness of space and media that society demands. It can rapidly become a nightmare for victims who otherwise may show no overt signs of injury. It is often a deviant product of the most private and cherished domain of romantic relations and, yet, is simultaneously difficult to distinguish from the more normative forms of this relational prototype. In short, stalking represents a particularly problematic crime from the perspective of policing public safety.

The social science of Communication has only recently begun to make inroads into this previously uncharted territory. The maps of this territory to date are rough and error-prone. Most police departments are exploring this territory armed with little more than experience and analogy. As research accumulates, this territory should become more navigable for both police and victims. This chapter has provided a rudimentary guide to some of the obstacles to expect along the way.

References

Adhikari, R. P., Reinhard, D. and Johnson, J. M. 1993. "The myth of protection orders". In *Studies in Symbolic Interaction* 15. N. K. Denzin (ed.), 259–270. Stamford, CT: JAI Press.
Bernstein, S. E. 1993. "Living under siege: Do stalking laws protect domestic violence victims?" *Cardozo Law Review* 15: 525–567.
Best, J. 1999. *Random Violence: How we talk about new crimes and new victims*. Berkeley, CA: University of California Press.
Bjerregaard, B. 2000. "An empirical study of stalking victimization". *Violence and Victims* 15: 389–406.
Blackburn, E. J. 1999. *"Forever Yours": Rates of Stalking Victimization, Risk Factors and Traumatic Responses Among College Women*. Doctoral dissertation, Boston, MA: University of Massachusetts — Boston.
Brewster, M. P. 1998. *An Exploration of the Experiences and Needs of Former Intimate Stalking Victims* [Final report submitted to the National Institute of Justice, NCJ 175475]. Washington DC: U. S. Department of Justice.

Budd, T. and Mattinson, J. 2000. *Stalking: Findings from the 1998 British Crime Survey* (Research findings No. 129). London: Home Office.

Burgess, A. W., Baker, T., Greening, D., Hartman, C. R., Burgess, A. G., Douglas, J. E. and Halloran, R. 1997. "Stalking behaviors within domestic violence". *Journal of Family Violence* 12: 389–403.

Buzawa, E., Hotaling, G. and Klein, A. 1998. "The response to domestic violence in a model court: Some initial findings and implications". *Behavioral Sciences and the Law* 16: 185–206.

Cadiz, M. and Spitzberg, B. H. 2001. "Stalkers and streetwalkers: The media construction of stalking myth". Paper presented at the Association for Women in Psychology, Los Angeles, CA.

Calhoun, F. S. 1998. *Hunters and Howlers: Threats and Violence Against Federal Judicial Officials in the United States, 1789–1993* [USMS No. 80]. Washington, DC: U. S. Department of Justice United States Marshals Service.

Carlson, M. J., Harris, S. D. and Holden, G. W. 1999. "Protective orders and domestic violence: Risk factors for re-abuse". *Journal of Family Violence* 14: 205–226.

Chadhuri, M. and Daly, K. 1992. "Do restraining orders help? Battered women's experience with male violence and legal process". In *Domestic Violence: The Changing Criminal Justice Response*, E. S. Buzawa and C. G. Buzawa (eds), 227–252. Westport, CT: Greenwood.

Coleman, F. L. 1997. "Stalking behavior and the cycle of domestic violence". *Journal of Interpersonal Violence* 12: 420–433.

Coulter, M. L., Kuehnle, K., Byers, R., and Alfonso, M. 1999. "Police-reporting behavior and victim-police interactions as described by women in a domestic violence shelter". *Journal of Interpersonal Violence* 14: 1290–1298.

Cupach, W. R. and Spitzberg, B. H. 1998. "Obsessive relational intrusion and stalking". In *The Dark Side of Close Relationships*, B. H. Spitzberg and W. R. Cupach (eds), 233–263. Hillsdale, NJ: Lawrence Erlbaum.

Cupach, W. R., Spitzberg, B. H. and Carson, C. L. 2000. "Toward a theory of stalking and obsessive relational intrusion". In *Communication and Personal Relationships*, K. Dindia and S. Duck (eds), 131–146. New York: John Wiley and Sons.

Dunn, J. L. 1999. "What love has to do with it: The cultural construction of emotion and sorority women's responses to forcible interaction". *Social Problems* 46: 440–459.

Dussuyer, I. 2000. "Is stalking legislation effective in protecting victims?" Paper presented at the Stalking: Criminal Justice Responses Conference, Australian Institute of Criminology, Sydney, Australia.

Emerson, R. M., Ferris, K. O. and Gardner, C. B. 1998. "On being stalked". *Social Problems* 45: 289–314.

Farnham, F. R., James, D. V. and Cantrell, P. 2000. "Association between violence, psychosis, and relationship to victim in stalkers". *Lancet* 355: 199.

Farrell, G., Weisburd, D. and Wyckoff, L. 2000. "Survey results suggest need for stalking training". *The Police Chief* 67: 162–167.

Fischer, K. and Rose, M. 1995. "When 'enough is enough': Battered women's decision making around court orders of protection". *Crime and Delinquency* 41: 414–429.

Fisher, B.S., Cullen, F.T. and Turner, M.G. 1999. *The Extent and Nature of the Sexual Victimization of College Women: A National-Level Analysis* [Final Report submitted to the National Institute of Justice, NCJ 179977]. Washington DC: U.S. Department of Justice.

Fisher, B.S., Cullen, F.T. and Turner, M.G. 2000. *The Sexual Victimization of College Women*. Washington, DC: National Institute of Justice, Bureau of Justice Statistics, Department of Justice.

Fremouw, W.J., Westrup, D. and Pennypacker, J. 1997. "Stalking on campus: The prevalence and strategies for coping with stalking". *Journal of Forensic Sciences* 42: 664–667

Fry, P.S. and Barker, L.A. 2001. "Female survivors of violence and abuse: Their regrets of action and inaction in coping". *Journal of Interpersonal Violence* 16: 320–342.

Fyfe, J.J., Klinger, D.A., and Flavin, J.M. 1997. "Differential police treatment of male-on-female spousal violence. *Criminology* 35: 455–473.

Gill, R. and Brockman, J. 1996. *A Review of Section 264 (Criminal Harassment) of the Criminal Code of Canada* [Working document WD 1996–7e]. Canada: Research, Statistics and Evaluation Directorate, Department of Justice.

Grau, J., Fagan, J. and Wexler, S. 1985. "Restraining orders for battered women: Issues of access and efficacy". In *Criminal Justice Politics and Women: The Aftermath Of Legally Mandated Change*, C. Schweber and C. Feinman (eds), 13–28. New York: Haworth.

Hall, D.M. 1997. *Outside Looking In: Stalkers and their victims*. Ph.D. dissertation, Claremont Graduate School, Claremont, CA.

Hargreaves, J. in press. "Stalking behaviour". In *Profiling Rape and Murder*, D.V. Canter and L. Alison (eds), 1–16. Aldershot, England: Ashgate.

Harmon, R.B., Rosner, R. and Owens, H. 1995. "Obsessional harassment and erotomania in a criminal court population". *Journal of Forensic Sciences* 40: 188–196.

Harmon, R.B., Rosner, R. and Owens, H. 1998. "Sex and violence in a forensic population of obsessional harassers". *Psychology, Public Policy, and Law* 4: 236–249.

Harrell, A. and Smith, B.E. 1996. "Effects of restraining orders on domestic violence victims". In *Do Arrests and Restraining Orders Work?* E.S. Buzawa and C.G. Buzawa (eds), 214–242. Thousand Oaks, CA: Sage.

Holmes, R.M. 1993. "Stalking in America: Types and methods of criminal stalkers". *Journal of Contemporary Criminal Justice* 9: 317–327.

Horton, A.L., Simonidis, K.M. and Simonidis, L.L. 1987. "Legal remedies for spousal abuse: Victim characteristics, expectations, and satisfaction". *Journal of Family Violence* 2: 265–279.

Jordan, T. 1995. "The efficacy of the California Stalking law: Surveying its evolution, extracting insights from domestic violence cases". *Hastings Women's Law Journal* 6: 363–383.

Kaci, J.H. 1992. "A study of protective orders issued under California's domestic violence prevention act". *Criminal Justice Review* 17: 61–76.

Kane, R.J. 1999. "Patterns of arrest in domestic violence encounters: Identifying a police decision-making model". *Journal of Criminal Justice* 27: 65–79.

Kane, R.J. 2000. "Police responses to restraining orders in domestic violence incidents: Identifying the custody-threshold thesis". *Criminal Justice and Behavior* 27: 561–580.

Keenahan, D. and Barlow, A. 1997. "Stalking: A paradoxical crime of the nineties". *International Journal of Risk, Security and Crime Prevention* 2: 291–300.

Keilitz, S. L. 1997. "Victims' perceptions of effectiveness of protective orders as an intervention in domestic violence and stalking". In *Domestic Violence and Stalking* 37–44 [Second Annual Report to Congress under the Violence Against Women Act]. Washington, DC: Office of Justice Programs, U.S. Department of Justice.

Kienlen, K. K., Birmingham, D. L., Solberg, K. B., O'Regan, J. T. and Meloy, J. R. 1997. "A comparative study of psychotic and nonpsychotic stalking". *Journal of the American Academy of Psychiatry and Law* 25: 317–334.

Kohn, M., Flood, H., Chase, J. and McMahon, P. M. 2000. "Prevalence and health consequences of stalking — Louisiana, 1998–1999". *Morbidity and Mortality Weekly Report* 49: 653–655.

Kurt, J. L. 1995. "Stalking as a variant of domestic violence". *Bulletin of the Academy of Psychiatry and the Law* 23: 219–213.

Langhinrichsen-Rohling, J., Palarea, R. E., Cohen, J. and Rohling, M. L. 2000. "Breaking up is hard to do: Unwanted pursuit behaviors following the dissolution of a romantic relationship". *Violence and Victims* 15: 73–90.

Lee, R. K. 1998. "Romantic and electronic stalking in a college context". *William and Mary Journal of Women and the Law* 4: 373–466.

Leets, L., de Becker, G. and Giles, H. 1995. "Fans: Exploring expressed motivations for contacting celebrities". *Journal of Language and Social Psychology* 14: 102–123.

Logan, T.K, Leukefeld, C. and Walker, B. 2000. "Stalking as a variant of intimate violence: Implications from a young adult sample". *Violence and Victims* 15: 91–111.

Lowney, K. S. and Best, J. 1995. "Stalking strangers and lovers: Changing media typifications of a new crime problem". In *Images of Issues: Typifying Contemporary Social Problems* [2nd ed], J. Best (ed), 33–57. New York: Aldine de Gruyter.

McAnaney, K. G., Curliss, L. and Abeyta-Price, C. 1993. "From imprudence to crime: Anti-stalking laws". *Notre Dame Law Review* 68: 819–909.

Marshall, J. and Castle, C. 1998. "Restraining orders and stalking offences in 1995 and 1996". *Information Bulletin* 6: 1–16.

Mechanic, M. B., Weaver, T. L. and Resick, P. A. 2000. "Intimate partner violence and stalking behavior: Exploration of patterns and correlates in a sample of acutely battered women". *Violence and Victims* 15: 55–72.

Meloy, J. R. 1998. "The psychology of stalking". In *The Psychology of Stalking*, J. R. Meloy (ed.), 2–24. San Diego, CA: Academic Press.

Meloy, J. R. 1999. "Stalking: An old behavior, a new crime". *Forensic Psychiatry* 22: 85–99.

Meloy, J. R. 2000. "Violence risk and threat assessment". San Diego, CA: Specialized Training Services.

Meloy, J. R. in press. "Stalking and violence". In *Stalking and Psychosexual Obsession*, J. Boon and L. Sheridan (eds), London: Wiley.

Meloy, J. R., Cowett, P. Y., Parker, S. B., Hofland, B. and Friedland, A. 1997. "Domestic protection orders and the prediction of subsequent criminality and violence toward protectees". *Psychotherapy* 34: 447–458.

Meloy, J. R. and Gothard, S. 1995. "Demographic and clinical comparison of obsessional followers and offenders with mental disorders". *American Journal of Psychiatry* 152: 258–263.

Miller, N. 2001. *Stalking Laws and their Implementation: What Stalking Investigators and Prosecutors Do — A Problem Solving Perspective*. Alexandria, VA: Draft Report, Institutefor Law and Justice.
Mohandie, K., Hatcher, C. and Raymond, D. 1998. "False victimization syndromes in stalking". In *The Psychology Of Stalking*, J.R. Meloy (ed), 225–256. San Diego, CA: Academic Press.
Mullen, P.E., Pathé, M. and Purcell, R. 2000. *Stalkers and their Victims*. Cambridge: Cambridge University Press.
Mullen, P.E., Pathé, M., Purcell, R. and Stuart, G.W. 1999. "Study of stalkers". *American Journal of Psychiatry* 156: 1244–1249.
National Institute of Justice. 1996. *Domestic Violence, Stalking, and Antistalking Legislation* [Annual Report to Congress under the Violence Against Women Act, NCJ 160943]. Washington, DC: U.S. Department of Justice.
Nicastro, A.M., Cousins, A.V. and Spitzberg, B.H. 2000. "The tactical face of stalking". *Journal of Criminal Justice* 28: 69–82.
Pathé, M. and Mullen, P.E. 1997. "The impact of stalkers on their victims". *British Journal of Psychiatry* 170:12–17.
Pathé, M., Mullen, P.E. and Purcell, R. 1999. "Stalking: False claims of victimization". *British Journal of Psychiatry* 174: 170–173.
Pathé, M., Mullen, P.E. and Purcell, R. 2000. "Same-gender stalking". *Journal of the American Academy of Psychiatry and the Law* 28: 191–197.
Purcell, R., Pathé, M. and Mullen, P.E. 2000. "The incidence and nature of stalking victimization". Paper presented to the Criminal Justice Responses Conference, Australian Institute of Criminology, Sydney, Australia.
Rigakos, G.S. 1997. "Situational determinants of police response to civil and criminal injunctions for battered women". *Violence Against Women* 3: 204–216.
San Diego District Attorney's Office 2001. *Stalking the Stalker 2001 Conference Proceedings*. San Diego, CA: San Diego District Attorney's Office.
Saunders, R. 1998. "The legal perspective on stalking". In *The Psychology of Stalking* J.R. Meloy (ed), 25–50. San Diego, CA: Academic Press.
Schell, B.H. and Lanteigne, N.M. 2000. *Stalking, Harassment, and Murder in the Workplace*. Westport, CT: Quorum Books.
Sheridan, L. in press. "The course and nature of stalking: An in-depth victim survey". *Journal of Threat Assessment*.
Sheridan, L., Davies, G.M., & Boon, J.C.W. 2001. "The course and nature of stalking: A victim perspective". *Howard Journal of Criminal Justice* 40: 215–234.
Sheridan, L., Gillett, R., & Davies, G. 2000."' Stalking' — Seeking the victim's perspective". *Psychology, Crime and Law* 6: 267–280.
Sinclair, H.C. and Frieze, I.H. 2000. "Initial courtship behavior and stalking: How should we draw the line?" *Violence and Victims* 15: 23–40.
Skoler, G. 1998. "The archetypes and psychodynamics of stalking". In *The Psychology of Stalking*, J.R. Meloy (ed.), 85–112. San Diego, CA: Academic Press.
Spence-Diehl, E. and Potocky-Tripodi, M. 2001. "Victims of stalking: A study of service needs as perceived by victim services practitioners". *Journal of Interpersonal Violence* 16: 86–94.

Spitzberg, B.H. 2001. "Taking stock of stalking science". Powerpoint presentation to the Rutgers Research Conference on Stalking. New Brunswick, NJ.

Spitzberg, B.H. and Cupach, W.R. in press. "What mad pursuit: Conceptualization and assessment of obsessive relational intrusion and stalking-related phenomena". *Aggression and Violent Behavior: A Review Journal.*

Spitzberg, B.H. and Cupach, W.R. 2001. "Paradoxes of pursuit: Toward a relational model of stalking-related phenomena". In *Stalking, Stalkers and their Victims: Prevention, Intervention, And Threat Assessment*, J. Davis (ed), 97–136. Boca Raton, FL: CRC Press.

Spitzberg, B.H. and Cupach, W.R. 2002. "The inappropriateness of relational intrusion". In *Inappropriate Relationships*, R. Goodwin and D. Cramer (eds). Mahwah, NJ: Lawrence Erlbaum.

Spitzberg, B.H., Marshall, L. and Cupach, W.R. 2001. "Obsessive relational intrusion, coping, and sexual coercion victimization". *Communication Reports* 14: 19–30.

Spitzberg, B.H. and Rhea, J. 1999. Obsessive relational intrusion and sexual coercion victimization. *Journal of Interpersonal Violence* 14: 3–20.

Stephens, B.J. and Sinden, P.G. 2000. Victims' voices: Domestic assault victims' perceptions of police demeanor. *Journal of Interpersonal Violence* 15: 534–547.

Straus, M.A. 1999. "The controversy over domestic violence by women: A methodological, theoretical, and sociology of science analysis". *Violence in Intimate Relationships*, In X. Arriaga and S. Oskamp (eds), 17–44. Thousand Oaks, CA: Sage.

Tjaden, P. and Thoennes, N. 1998. *Stalking in America: Findings from the National Violence Against Women Survey* [NCJ 169592]. Washington DC: National Institute of Justice and Centers for Disease Control and Prevention.

Tjaden, P. and Thoennes, N. 2000. "The role of stalking in domestic violence crime reports generated by the Colorado Springs Police Department". *Violence and Victims* 15: 427–441.

Tucker, J.T. 1993. "Stalking the problems with stalking laws". *Florida Law Review* 45: 609–707.

U.S. Department of Justice. 1998. *Stalking And Domestic Violence* [Third Annual Report to Congress under the Violence Against Women Act; NCJ 172204]. Washington DC: Violence Against Women Grants Office, U.S. Department of Justice.

Walker, L.E. and Meloy, J.R. 1998. "Stalking and domestic violence". In *The Psychology of Stalking*, J.R. Meloy (ed.), 139–161. San Diego, CA: Academic Press.

Wells, K. 2001. *Training Manual On Stalking.* San Diego, CA: San Diego Stalking Strike Force.

Wolf, M.E., Holt, V.L., Kernic, M.A. and Rivara, F.P. 2000. "Who gets protection orders for intimate partner violence? *American Journal of Preventative Medicine* 19: 286–291.

Zona, M.A., Palarea, R.E. and Lane, J.C. 1998. "Psychiatric diagnosis and the offender-victim typology of stalking". In *The Psychology Of Stalking*, J.R. Meloy (ed.), 69–84. San Diego, CA: Academic Press.

CHAPTER 9

Signs and cultural messages of bias motivated crimes
Analysis of the hate component of intergroup violence

Edward Dunbar
University of California, Los Angeles, USA

Intergroup violence, as any student of history knows, is a chronic social problem. It is as old as the efforts of society to resist it. The study of anti-social behavior, as Raine (1997) has suggested, incorporates a variety of biological, anthropological, and symbolic components. This latter issue will be considered in regard to bias motivated crimes. I will consider how intergroup violence incorporates signifiers or attributional "signs," which reveal the hate motivation of the offense, as well as cultural meta-messages that serve as exemplars of ingroup bias. The behavioral and cognitive elements of these attributional signs will be considered in terms of crime report data collected by a law enforcement agency in a large metropolitan setting.

The anthropological study of culture has emphasized the role of common history and experience as a condition of ingroup membership. As Kluckhohn (1951) has observed, social group membership is signified by engagement in behaviors consistent with the values and assumptions of the ingroup. This includes the utilization of symbols, namely artifacts and language, that connote ingroup membership, and in turn, enhance social identity and individual self-esteem (Tajfel 1982). The use of attributional signs can be observed with criminal gang behavior, for example, in which members often communicate their group affiliation via distinctive dress, restricted language codes, graffiti, and kinesthetic or non-verbal communication. While signs of ingroup identity are often in the service of prosocial ends, they can also demonstrate the shared group animus towards outgroups, as well.

Hate crimes and the problem of determining bias motivation

Hate crimes are offenses to property and persons motivated by the perpetrators' outgroup hostility (Levin 1999). As many in law enforcement know all too well, these laws have been an issue of controversy. Classifying a crime as being hate-motivated relies upon determination of the perpetrator's motivation. This issue has been a significant stumbling block for criminologists, who frequently argue that there is substantial within-group variation amongst hate offenders. Accordingly, clearly defining this "bias component" can help law enforcement to understand whether a crime is biased motivated or not.

Crimes motivated by prejudice have only been recognized as a separate criminal offense in the U.S. since the passage in 1990 of the Federal Hate Crime Statistics Act. Federal and state hate crime laws have defined the legal criteria for employment of penalty enhancements for crimes motivated by outgroup hostility. The state of California hate crime law states in part that the offense is "any act of intimidation, harassment, physical force or threat of physical force directed against any person, or family, or their property or advocate, motivated either in whole or in part by the hostility to the real or perceived ethnic background, national origin, religious belief, sex, age, disability, or sexual orientation, with the intention of causing fear and intimidation." As indicated by this statute, hate crime laws are evidently broad in their scope and can be open to interpretation as to how bias motivation "either in whole or in part" may be determined. As Jacobs and Potter (1998), two opponents of hate crime laws, have commented, "Prosecuting a bias crime requires proving the defendant's bias motivation beyond a reasonable doubt. Even in seemingly clear-cut cases of bias motivation, prosecutors have failed to obtain convictions" (p. 103). The effective documentation of the how and what of bias crimes is clearly needed if the concerns of critics of these laws are to be effectively answered.

Hate crime laws and the role of police work

Hate crime laws can be thought of as both a tool in the prosecution of markedly violent criminals and as a suppression strategy employed by policy makers to prevent the escalation of bias-based ideological groups, which are inherently anti-democratic. While hate crime laws may be relatively clear as to their intent, how they are enforced is quite another matter. For example, the question of how regions of the United States which were historically bastions of slavery, systematic racial segregation, and organized hate-based groups such as the Ku Klux Klan can report a virtual absence of bias crime activity is incomprehensible. From the most recent federal government statistics, the Southern states of Alabama, Mississippi, and Louisiana, for example, reported no hate crime offenses for calendar year 1999. The problem with the base rates in the reportage of bias crimes is compounded by an absence of predictive evidence of risk (i.e., probability) for bias crime victimization. To date, there is limited information which predicts the intentions of bias crime offenders. Berk, Boyd and Hammer (1992) have noted, "Very little is known about risk factors for hate-motivated crimes. Even in the case of race, where skin color and other physical features are relevant, no quantitative estimates exist that separate the impact of race from other related risk factors" (p. 137). As such, our comprehension of why victims of bias crimes are selected, what the motives of the offender are, and how this can be determined in the process of crime analysis is largely hypothetical on the one hand, and not uniformly enforced on the other.

What are the implications for police work? As will be argued throughout, law enforcement needs to make every effort possible to apply the standards established under these laws as equitably as possible. Beyond this, and related to this critical issue, law enforcement plays a critical role in terms of both operational and strategic issues in the improvement of intergroup relations. Indeed, through effective enforcement of hate crime policies, law enforcement agencies can do a great deal for themselves to improve their credibility with ethnic minority groups who have frequently been the target of police harassment and ethnic violence.

In addition, through the systematic analysis of hate crime activity, law enforcement can provide otherwise unavailable information about patterns of intergroup violence in urban communities. The tracking of hate crime activity can identify "hot spot" communities where there may be rapid escalation of intergroup violence which, in some instances, may lead to the proliferation of copycat offenses, particularly in communities with established criminal gangs. Only law enforcement agencies can effectively track emergent patterns of bias motivated violence. Other stakeholder groups, such as public human relations organizations and community-based organizations, typically review hate crime activity on an annual basis, meaning that frequently analysis of community intergroup issues is considered 12 to 18 months after the crime has been reported. The rapid response efforts of larger policy departments across the U.S. illustrate how crime data may be employed for prevention of the escalation of intergroup violence in at-risk communities. This clearly places law enforcement in a role not only to suppress bias-motivated violence, but additionally to inform policy makers and community leaders about the need to intervene in communities as intergroup problems are emerging. This shift from suppression to prevention not only re-casts the role of policing in the community but also saves valuable human and financial resources that can be re-directed if effective intervention is provided by other stakeholder groups. This, of course, all is contingent upon the comprehensive analysis and reportage of bias crimes to begin with, which is the focus of the methodology described here.

Attributional signs of bias: Behavioral, ideational, and ideological signifiers

As Allport (1954) noted half a century ago, prejudice can be conceptualized as a hierarchy that extends from an internalized dislike of social outgroups to the systematic extermination of entire minority populations. Accordingly, as prejudice increases in its intensity, its manifestation is elevated from a belief to an aggressive, and ultimately violent, behavior. While Allport considered prejudice in terms of level of intensity, the issue of bias motivation in intergroup aggression, in light of contemporary human rights and criminal laws, has not been systematically studied. Dunbar (1999) has recently proposed that this "bias component" can be examined via a multi-dimensional approach that incorporates cognitive, behavioral, and historical factors. Such a strategy can provide greater clarity and specificity than is found in the legal definition of hate criminality.

The signifier variables or "attributional signs" of the offender's hate motivation include: (1) articulated beliefs of ingroup superiority, (2) affiliation with social cohorts who embrace a hate-based worldview, (3) the vociferation of hate speech during the commission of the index offense, (4) the offender's use of symbols which communicate this worldview (dress, tattoos, iconography, and art), and (5) the prior enactment of bias-motivated aggression. These identified bias signifiers may be of value not only from a descriptive standpoint, but as predictors of future offender behavior, and arguably, the capacity to benefit from rehabilitation. From a heuristic standpoint, these bias signifiers may also help to elucidate differences amongst bias offenders. Levin and McDevitt (1993) for example, have proposed a thrill-seeking, a reactive, and an ideological or "mission" type of bias criminal. It could be that the attributional signs may reveal within-group differences amongst a criminal population about which little is otherwise known.

Crime-related hate speech
The presence of hate speech during the commission of the index offense is, on its face, the most common factor resulting in the classification of a crime as being bias-motivated. In the review of 976 reported bias crimes in Los Angeles County during 1995, hate speech was reported to be an indicator of the bias motivation of the offender in 62% of the cases (Dunbar, 1999). A variant form of hate speech is written hate speech and hate graffiti. These were found in 20% and 16% of the 1995 hate crimes in Los Angeles County, respectively. Amongst convicted offenders in Los Angeles County during the mid-1990s, 87% were identified as evidencing hate speech in the commission of the index crime. As such, the presence of hate speech is by far and away the most common factor in the classification of a crime as being bias-motivated.

While hate speech may be the most common characteristic of bias crimes, there is also reason to consider it a poor indicator of hate motivation. This is due to the fact that the presence of hate speech — in the U.S. at any rate — is in and of itself not a criminal offense. Hate speech is criminal only if it is accompanied by a plausible threat of harm to a person, group, or institution. In these instances, hate speech may constitute a terrorist threat. Furthermore, hate speech uttered by an offender during the commission of a crime may simply represent the activation via impulse of a shared social prejudice of the offender's ingroup. The role of popular culture to incorporate hate speech into comedy, advertising, and public discourse further obfuscates the meaning of the message from the sender to the receiver. There is theoretical support for this observation in the laboratory research of Dovidio and Gaertner (1986) in the study of aversive racism. In aversive racism, individuals maintain a belief of intergroup equality, fueled in part by social pressures not to appear biased, while encountering discomfort in even benign inter-racial and intergroup contact experiences. Further experimental study shows that alcohol intoxication can invoke biased behaviors, including the use of hate speech, in otherwise socially conforming subjects (Reeves & Nagoshi 1993). As such, experiences of anxiety and tension in ingroup conflict and impulse disturbance may together result in the utterance of hate speech even in the absence of a discernible bias ideology. The role of impulsivity is clearly important in terms of individual risk for violence generally (Webster & Jackson 1997) as well as expression of outgroup hostility with non-violent individuals (Dunbar 1998).

A particular dilemma concerns hate speech and its relevance to the commission of a crime. Consider, for example, a fight that erupts on the campus of a public secondary school between two racially different young women. As the fight escalates from personal hubris to physical aggression, one of the assailants shouts out a racial epithet. If this event were witnessed by other credible persons, it might easily place a school administrator, as the first respondent to the incident, in the role of decision-maker as to whether the assault was a hate crime or otherwise bias-motivated, even if it is not a criminal offense. In cases such as this, the utterance of hate speech during the commission of a crime may be inconsequential to the incident. Defining a crime as bias-motivated solely due to the presence of hate speech heightens the probability of false-positive or "type one" error in perpetrator classification. If, however, it were considered whether the individuals belonged to racialized gangs, or had been involved in other inter-racial offenses, the probability of the bias-motivation of the offense might accordingly be quite different.

It is worth noting that hate speech now includes communication in cyberspace. A recent example of this involved a former student of the University of California Irvine (UCI). In this landmark case, the threat of physical harm to the victims was carried out solely via email. The offender identified via the campus internet students whom he presumed were of Asian-Pacific descent and sent them messages indicating his intent "To hunt down and kill all of you stupid asses." He was convicted under the federal hate crime statute for the violation of the civil rights of students attending a public institution of higher education. The UCI case provides an example of the power of technology to make a singular hate message a threat to an entire community.

Articulated hate ideology of the offender
The offender's stated belief in a hate-based ideology or "worldview" is arguably the singularly most important signifier of a true bias motivation. A freely articulated hate-based worldview is significantly independent of the utterance of hate speech. As Kluckhohn and Strodtbeck (1961) suggested, an individual's worldview constitutes a schema by which behaviors and cognitions are organized. Worldviews incorporate both values and shared assumptions by which the individual defines their group membership. Typically a bias-based worldview emphasizes ingroup superiority vis-à-vis designated outgroups or is linked to the theme of ingroup victimization and need for retribution. That is, a biased-based worldview is not only the preference for the behaviors and values of one's ingroup, but additionally the strongly held belief that the mores of the ingroup must be emphasized, protected and enforced in such a way as to dominate denigrated outgroups. In talking with hate crime offenders, this ideology is, when present, frequently ill-defined, gratuitous, and exaggerated.

The responding officer and crime scene investigator should not expect to find a complex bias ideology, so much as a series of thinking errors by which hostility toward outgroup persons is legitimized. The belief systems of bias-motivated criminals are rarely made sense of by classic dialectical reasoning. The belief system is rather an organizing principle that is both simple and effective. The social psychological literature on the adherence to stereotypes to simplify belief systems — what Allport referred to as the principle of least effort — and to guide intergroup interactions is exemplified by the hate beliefs of many offenders.

A clear example of this bias ideology variable may be found in the case of RL, a young member of a hate gang. RL was arrested for the commission of a bias-motivated offense against a young man who had been identified as a member of an ethnic minority group. At the time of investigation, while RL was being held, he was asked if he believed in "White Power." RL quickly answered, "Of course I do, I know it is right, it is what I have to do." RL was subsequently convicted and incarcerated, and upon his release from prison he engaged in a racially motivated homicide. This offense was likewise an unprovoked attack against a victim — in this case an elderly minority person — unknown to the assailant. RL, when interviewed by investigators, stated he had perpetrated this crime to gain status with his hate group.

The ascription to a bias-based worldview may or may not co-occur with hate speech in the commission of a crime. Often investigating law enforcement personnel may presume the presence of a hate ideology from the utterance of hate terms in the perpetration of the index crime. Again, a powerful means to communicate a bias-based worldview is via the internet. Hate-oriented websites are found in abundance and are an issue of concern for human relations groups. To date, however, there is no empirical evidence to support a relationship between the operation of a bias-oriented website and the commission of hate aggression, irrespective of how appealing such a presumption may be, nor is there indication that persons who visit such sites are members of hate groups. In the U.S., at present, hate beliefs transmitted via electronic media of any sort are within the scope of the rights guaranteed under the First Amendment. This is not to say that the use of the internet to harass or threaten *individuals* is not per se criminal, nor that the endorsement of violence against social *outgroups* may not be criminal.

Affiliation with bias-identified social cohorts
The involvement of the offender with social cohorts who embraces a hate-based worldview provides additional information concerning the bias motivation and

orientation of criminal offenders. Involvement in hate groups implicitly reveals the risk of intent to enact various forms of hate behavior. As noted by Allport (1954), organized hate aggression is a more extreme and egregious form of prejudice. Groups that perpetrate hate violence often evidence instrumental — that is, planned and goal-oriented — aggression.

In his ethnographic research of members of hate groups, Ezekiel (1995) noted a variety of motives for membership in bias-identified groups. As he notes, motivation for involvement in leadership roles may be significantly linked to extrinsic reward, such as by raising money from persons attracted to hate movements — i.e., for a small group of individuals, belonging to a hate group may have a financial incentive. Ezekiel noted that, more frequently, persons affiliated with hate-based groups were absent an alternative ideological basis from which to view intergroup issues, leading many young men with limited economic and social resources to find a sense of belonging to a group that was at once socially reinforcing and at-odds with the larger social context from which they felt excluded, if not betrayed. Frequently, these group members were absent any serious psychiatric disturbance. Indeed, Ezekiel noted for some individuals the worsening of a drug or alcohol problem resulted in members "graduating out" of these hate groups.

An additional motivational factor of individuals to join bias-oriented groups can be found in the racialized criminal gangs in the U.S. today. While not inherently motivated by racial animus, membership in criminal gangs is commonly based upon ethnic and/or racial group factors. This in turn may lead to not only to conflict with racially different rival gangs, but also to the perpetration of violence against any person of a racial outgroup residing in their community. This issue will be considered further in terms of the meta-messages of bias aggression, below.

Adoption of bias-identified symbols
The presence of symbols which communicate a bias belief system may be represented via dress, tattoos, iconography, and art. These symbolic signifiers have importance in terms of potentially revealing future activity — violent and otherwise — that is motivated by, if not organized around, a bias-based worldview. The presence of hate-based music — typically the metal music of skinhead bands — is also a clear indicator of a bias-based worldview.

The imagery associated with organized hate groups spans the cultural history of Euro-American culture. The hooded Klansmen and the black-shirted fascist have given way to the skinhead members of hate gangs and the camouflaged members of para-military groups. As Ezekiel (1995) has noted, there is a small cottage industry in the sale of hate literature — from the notorious Turner Diaries to home-printed broadsides against racial minority groups — and related hate paraphernalia. The use of symbols as a means of organizing bias-belief groups may include both national political movements (Payne, 1998) as well as neighborhood gangs.

In the author's community, for example, a white hate gang that engaged in inter-racial violence called themselves the "Polar Bears." They developed their own symbol or "placa" — gang iconography found in the graffiti of Latino gangs — which found its way into local schools and the surrounding neighborhoods. The use of these symbols organized what had been a loosely organized group of young violent men. As one of their victims stated "Polar Bears, you don't have think to hard too get the message, white and violent."

Prior enactment of hate aggression
The prior enactment of bias-motivated aggression provides additional evidence of the risk for subsequent bias aggression. As the familiar adage in psychology goes "past behavior is a good predictor of future behavior." Careful examination of this issue is especially important in that the offender may not otherwise wish to communicate or represent their actions as being hate-oriented.

In the record review of convicted bias offenders, there is no singular rule-of-thumb condition that explains why some violent offenders engage repeatedly in hate aggression. There are as many differences as similarities among offenders who have a history of bias recidivism. For example, some repeat bias offenders may demonstrate a clear ideological basis for on going hate criminality. For some, this may constitute their entire criminal history; for others, repeat bias crimes may be embedded in a series of diverse convictions. Individuals with more personal or idiographic patterns of interpersonal violence may also re-offend, due to a bias ideology. Some of these mission-type offenders, to use the Levin and McDevitt model, may fail completely to see their behavior as inappropriate. For some gay bashers, for example, the idea of equal rights for their victims is rejected out of hand. Such individuals pose numerous challenges for the criminal justice system and provide little evidence of being capable of benefiting from rehabilitation efforts.

Cultural meta-messages of bias aggression

Hate crimes frequently appear as odd or unwarranted to the average citizen. The offenses are often absent a viable criminological need. Material needs and wants are rarely satisfied through the commission of a bias crime. All the same, there is indeed something to understand in the offense. The absence of other competing reasons for the offense all the more warrants that we understand what the message is, what it is the offender wishes us to understand. This is disturbing to many of us; bias offenders are not thought of as credible commentators on our society. Yet it is exactly this that we ought to consider. The bias crime carries within it a larger message about our social conditions and dilemmas. The bias offender often demonstrates palpably the further extensions of widely adhered to fears and frustrations concerning intergroup problems. While the manifestation of bias through violence is often seen as reprehensible, it also can provide a warning as to the risk of societies that tolerate and condone institutional and de facto forms of discrimination. As Allport would argue, prejudice moves from an internalized disdain to overt forms of aggression which, for some individuals, elevates into violent behaviors. Comprehending the meta-message of the bias offense is therefore important in the documentation of bias crimes. The narrative recounting of the motivation for the event can assist in the ultimate prosecution and penalty decision-making that occurs. It also allows us to look at the shared assumptions which our social groups maintain, and which in turn provide a rationale for others to perpetrate violence against members of denigrated outgroups.

Herek has commented (Herek & Berrill 1992) that bias criminality serves a symbolic function that is independent of conventional criminal motives. As Herek and others have proposed (Herek, Gillis, Cogan, & Glunt, 1997), hate violence is perpetrated in opposition to an entire social outgroup. The hate element of the crime is frequently unrelated to the targeted individual, in that the victim is often randomly selected. As such, bias crimes are at once highly specific as to what the offender desires to communicate via commission of the offense, and at the same time de-individuated, that is, de-personalized. In his study of aggression against lesbians and gay men, Herek has asserted that the perpetrator is acting on a value generally ascribed to by the majority culture, namely heterosexist bias. That is, the offenders of bias crimes against gays and lesbians are not, per se, acting upon a deviant belief, nor are they communicating a belief that is rejected by the majority of society (Herek & Capitano 1996). Herek's research makes the point that bias motivated offenders, while demonstrating behavior that is criminal, are adhering to beliefs, i.e., hostility toward gays and lesbians, that many socially conforming individuals ascribe to as well. This is important to consider in that many of the beliefs of hate crime perpetrators are typically represented in popular culture as deviant. Herek's research underscores the inaccuracy of demonizing perpetrators of bias crimes as being alien to mainstream society. As will be suggested below, bias crime offenders actually serve a role in how society contends with intergroup conflict and the issue of universal human rights.

If we take seriously the proposition that bias aggression serves a symbolic function in intergroup relations, then examination of both the sign (the bias element) and the cultural meta-message, needs to be considered. I am proposing that the meta-message can be considered on a continuum in terms of its congruence with the ascribed values of the offending individuals' ingroup. At one polar point, the highly congruent meta-message serves as an exemplar of the biases of the ingroup. Warfare provides a clear example of how the cultural meta-message of violence against individuals of social outgroups is supported institutionally by the ingroup. Bias aggression between Palestinians and Israelis provides an example of overt aggression that is wholly congruent, if not sanctioned, by the ingroup, for example. By contrast, the bias-motivated homicide of a professional woman, which the offender ascribes to his belief that women should not be in the workplace can be considered incongruent, if not deviant in the U.S., even if a significant number of men are ambivalent about opportunities for economic equity of women. In this case, the meta-message is essentially incomprehensible with proscribed behaviors of the offender's ingroup. In examining intergroup harassment in school settings, and in some instances even hate crime cases, it is evident that in many cases the cultural message is neither deviant ("You don't kill women because they get uppity") nor serves as an exemplar of ingroup bias ("I will kill the enemy of my people and be a hero in heaven"). Rather, the meta-message contains culturally congruent and incongruent (idiographic) beliefs or actions.

The meta-message of bias crimes may likewise reveal the ambivalence of the ingroup toward outgroups. It is the ambivalent and less extreme cases of intergroup aggression that are most problematic for law enforcement and policy makers. For example, it is obvious that most Americans were appalled by the bias-motivated torture and murder of Matthew Shepard, a gay college student, who was beaten to death by four young men and women. It is equally obvious that many Americans tolerate humor that is heterosexist when directed at the lives of gay men and lesbians. Whereas the former meta-message of the Shepard murder is deviant, the use of hostile gay and lesbian humor is arguably an exemplar, at worst, or ambivalent, at best. Under periods of significant cultural change, the determination of the comprehensibility of the cultural message of outgroup hostility is most complicated. For example, the internment of U.S. citizens of Japanese ancestry during the Second World War reflects the ambivalence of the larger society at the time — i.e., was the war with a foreign government or persons of a distinct ethnic heritage?

A typology of meta-messages

The following typology summarizes five culturally congruent and two culturally incongruent (or "idiographic") meta-messages of bias-motivated violence.

Defended neighborhoods

Green and his colleagues (1997) have discussed the pattern of community violence directed against visible ethnic minorities, typically by residents of a racially homogenous ingroup, geographically situated in a clearly defined community. These bias offenses typically are spontaneous and occur in the course of benign intergroup contact. As Green notes, these offenses may reflect a substantial symbolic or message component, one in which the offender is keeping their community and social group safe from outside ethnic group members.

The defended neighborhoods message may occur as a singular acute event or conversely may result in a pattern of escalating violence. An example is provided by recent crime patterns in Hawaiian Gardens, an impoverished urban community of 15,000 largely Latino residents, in Los Angeles County. From 1995 through 1997, over 40 reported hate crimes were committed against African Americans in this one square mile community. Initially, the assailants were exclusively members of an established Latino criminal gang; however, over time the pattern of bias crimes included copycat violence, perpetrated against African Americans who traveled into the community. The violence escalated to a point where a series of homicides were committed that included the death of two African American adolescents. In reviewing the crime reports, it was clear that many of these incidents were spontaneous in nature; the assailants had no prior relationship with their victims, the contact was random, and the evidence did not suggest a planned action by the offenders. The factors of poverty, a dominant ethnic group, and an entrenched criminal gang presence, all contributed to the pattern of violence found in this community.

In a different context, the defended neighborhoods component of bias crimes is found in recurring hate activity in a neighborhood by a "lone wolf" (i.e., singular) offender. Over the course of several months, the offender committed numerous acts of vandalism to the homes of Southeast Asians and distributed hate literature denigrating Indochinese at a local community college. The offender, when apprehended, stated he was trying to discourage the integration of his community, as a way to prevent the insurgence of Indochinese gangs, who he felt would bring crime to his community.

Retributional violence
Unlike the defended neighborhoods crime, acts of retributional violence are characterized by a series of ongoing intergroup conflicts, which may escalate to widespread violence. The cultural message here concerns the continuance of intergroup violence between groups that view one another as adversarial. Behaviorally, the sequence of conflict possesses a tit-for-tat pattern of reciprocal aggression. Illustrations of this pattern of violence are readily found in international settings such as Northern Ireland and the Middle East. More commonly, the pattern of bias-motivated retributional violence is found at the intracommunity level. It is frequently related to criminalized gangs and may include examples of copycat or pseudo-vigilante activity of members of the community.

A very interesting issue in terms of legal and political theory concerns the relationship of hate criminality to that of war crimes. Clearly, how this is to be considered in the proposed world court for human rights will be significant for policy makers and legal scholars and may, in turn, spawn a renewed interest in the role of social psychological issues in the area of international intergroup relations.

Perceived economic threat
There has been significant presumption that economic factors underlie the perpetration of intergroup aggression. With respect to hate crimes, this assumption is essentially un-tested in terms of either social psychological or sociological evidence. Still, individuals who perpetrate hate crimes often believe they are reacting to unfair economic behavior by other social or national groups. U.S. anti-Japanese attitudes found in the late 1980s and early 1990s have been considered as a factor in harassment of Asian-Pacific victims. Likewise, the anti-immigrant surge in the U.S., as exemplified by passage of Proposition 187 in the State of California, resulted in a rise in hate activity against Latinos. The notion of economic threat may also reflect the protection of illicit markets by racialized criminal gangs.

Social dominance
Bias aggression, in both laboratory and naturalistic settings, has been linked to social dominance. Sidanius and his colleagues (Sidanius & Pratto, 1996) have described social dominance as a common if not universal social phenomenon, one that accentuates the need for power and control of social outgroups. Social dominance (SD) varies amongst both individuals and (hypothetically) cultures. In more socially benign contexts, social dominance is evidenced in the attitudes of fans of sport teams, as well as in the trappings of organizational life. With respect to intergroup violence, recent examples of social dominance include terrorist bombings in gay and lesbian bars in England and Germany and the "ethnic cleansing" of the Balkans wars of the 1990s.

The role of social dominance in hate violence is pervasive. That is, while there may be other core components of the cultural message, the intent to assert the dominance of the ingroup is frequently present. What is striking about many hate crimes is the selection of victims who are particularly vulnerable targets. This is in part due to the anonymity of the majority of bias crimes, in that the victim does not perceive a threat of violence, in many instances, prior to the index offense. This element of surprise obviously enhances the sense of control for the bias offender. Frequently, bias crimes are characterized by a victim who is not of similar physical strength, number, or readiness with their assailant. While this may be true for many forms of criminal activity, the issue of bias crimes is interesting in that frequently the offender creates an impression of having to fight back against their victim. This is seen in defended neighborhood crimes as well as the idiographic crimes of homosexual panic and racial paranoia (see below). As such, while the offender often describes feeling victimized by members of the outgroup, they infrequently engage in conflict in situations where they themselves are truly vulnerable. As with other meta-messages of hate crimes, the offender indeed may be demonstrating a belief ascribed to by members of their ingroup. However, the forms of outgroup bias (to consider Allport's model of prejudice again as a continuum) endorsed by the offender's ingroup do not often extend to violent behavior. The message to the victim of "You are less worthy to be in our community than we are" is linked with the offender's thinking error of "I am right to harm this person, to show everyone of their group that they don't belong here." It can be argued that other members of the offender's ingroup find more socially sanctioned means to convey social dominance, be it through discrimination in hiring practices, support of political agendas that create barriers to equal protection under the law, or by efforts to establish de facto intergroup segregation. Anecdotally, it is worth noting that frequently the acting out of this social dominance message is perpetrated by the more disenfranchised and alienated members of the ingroup.

Punishment of deviancy
Intergroup violence may also communicate an intolerance for diversity, due to perceived "deviant" qualities of the social outgroup. Bias crimes of anti-Semitism and assaults against gay men and lesbians constitute two classic examples of this. Thematically, the offender often evidences authoritarian and/or religious faith-based ideological motives. Again, the escalation of shared ingroup denigration of an outgroup to a level that is at once violent and criminal underlies the perpetration of many such bias crimes.

Authoritarian ideology and the proposed Authoritarian personality described by Adorno and his colleagues (1950) after the Second World War emphasized the need for punishment of inferior and deviant others as a means to address internal psychological conflicts. Today, Altemeyer (1997) and others have emphasized the social psychological aspects of authoritarianism, suggesting that the core dimensions of the belief system consist of conventionalism, submission to authority, and tolerance of aggression to punish deviancy. Numerous survey studies of authoritarianism with university samples have demonstrated its relationship to bias against minority groups. Kecmanovic (1996) has proposed that an "Authoritarian Syndrome" is an organizing principle of the ethno-nationalist movements in central and Eastern Europe.

Protecting individuals and institutions that the responding law enforcement officer does not have empathy for is problematic, if not unique to the issue of hate crimes. As such, a significant dilemma for law enforcement concerns the enforcement of hate crime laws when the underlying social bias — hostility against gay men and lesbians, for example — is shared by the mainstream culture. This is exacerbated by situations in which the law itself is not adequately articulated nor supported institutionally. The law enforcement professional as with other stakeholder professionals, may be confronted with situations in which their efforts to enforce hate crime laws are in conflict with their ingroup's values.

Idiographic persecutory defense
The role of a core cultural message in the commission of a bias-motivated crime has been considered in terms of how shared ingroup biases serve to fuel the aggression of the offender. Bias criminals often feel they are acting on behalf of the needs of their ingroup, or that their actions are reasonable, in perpetrating violence against members of social outgroups. In some cases, however, the

offender is operating substantially upon their own internalized social presumptions that are contrary to their ingroup. These bias offenses will be referred to here as "idiographic" messages. Two examples of the idiographic cultural message are found in "Homosexual Panic" and "Racially Induced Paranoid Delusion Disorder (RIPDD)."

From a psychological perspective homosexual panic — also called the "Portsmouth Defense," in the United Kingdom — constitutes an acute terror response, based on the offender's supposed fear of sexual solicitation by their same-sex victim. Traditionally, homosexual panic referred to the aversive response to a repressed and latent homosexuality of the individual (Chuang & Addington, 1988). This theory has been largely supplanted in legal defense cases to propose the offender was acting in self-defense. In a homicide in the suburbs of Washington D.C., for example, the assailant of a gay man was acquitted of first- and second-degree murder charges due to the supposed sexual demands made by the victim, who had supplied the assailant with crack cocaine. After the murder, the assailant stole the victim's car and was in possession of the vehicle a month later when he was charged with the crime. The assailant claimed he panicked and in self-defense stabbed his victim, an opinion found credible by the jury.

The relationship between severe psychiatric disturbance and violent bias crime has been represented by the controversial "Racially Induced Paranoid Delusion Disorder (RIPDD)" condition. Essentially a legal defense, it has been employed in the highly publicized Bernard Goetz case (*People vs. Goetz 1986*). RIPDD constitutes a legal interpretation of a psychiatric condition — paranoia — that has not been demonstrated via research to contain a racial or bias component. Still, RIPDD may reflect the idiographic and distorted ideation of some hate crime perpetrators, though this figure is likely quite small.

Idiographic identity diffusion
A second idiographic meta-message is referred to as the "Idiographic Identity Diffusion." Psychologically, disturbance of the self-image is a long-recognized indicator of serious interpersonal problems (McGlashan, Levy & Carpenter 1975; Brown, Scheflin & Hammond 1998) and positive racial and ethnic identity formation (Carter, 1995). Idiographic Identity Diffusion is characterized by a persistent discomfort about one's cultural heritage or social groups, including race. The individual experiences uncertainty about issues relating to his or her ethnic identity, friendship patterns, moral values, and group loyalties.

In identity diffusion cases, perpetrators are particularly prone to aggress against victims of their own social ingroups and do not, as such, reflect a normative struggle with one's ethnic or sexual identity. The case of RL (see above), a skinhead gang member who was himself of Mexican-American heritage, provides an example of this identity diffusion condition. In a prior bias crime, he was convicted of assault with a deadly weapon against a Latino youth. RL's rejection of his identity with his Latino heritage reinforced his need to identify with an Anglo hate ideology. RL's hate ideology fueled his identification with his skinhead gang and paved the way for his attaining greater status within the group through his subsequent murder of a Black man.

The role of bias signs in violence risk assessment

While recurrent hate behavior may occur throughout the spectrum of hate criminality, from nuisance offenses of threats of hate violence between teenagers to the perpetration of mass homicides, the most important issue for the criminal justice system concerns the ability to define the risk for ongoing aggression against outgroup victims. Of particular concern is whether the attributional signs may provide evidence as to the potential for future violence. A variety of characteristics can be found, via criminal investigation, which distinguish bias offenders from other offenders (between-group differences) and which are related to the strength or prominence of the bias motivation amongst this offender group (within-group differences). These factors are summarized as: (1) planful versus reactive aggression, (2) goals of social dominance versus material pursuit, (3) interpersonal distance (relationally proximal versus distant), and (4) psychological intactness versus marked disorganization of the offender.

These attributional signs were employed in the study of 46 hate-motivated homicide offenders. Dunbar, Krop and Sullaway (2000) found that the prominence of the bias motivation, using the criteria described previously, was related to both historical and post-offense indicators of risk for violence. Higher bias ratings were related to offender problems in their relationships and work performance, failure to benefit from prior remediation efforts to mitigate against recidivism, and limited insight into problem behavior. Bias homicide offenders who evidenced higher bias motivation ratings were more goal-directed and methodical in carrying out the index crime. Qualitatively, many of the bias homicide offenders evidenced idiographic — though rarely psychotic — meta-messages, rather than defended neighborhood or retributional violence aggression. That is, many of the bias-motivated murders were less obviously linked to comprehensible social biases. With this sample, when compared to other non-bias homicide offenders, psychological test data found that bias offenders were more impulsive, paranoid, and prone to emotional and cognitive disorganization, socially alienated, and pre-disposed to a prejudiced worldview in general.

In a second study conducted via file review with 58 convicted hate crime offenders, Dunbar (1999) found that one or more of the attributional signs described above were prominent — i.e., clearly documented in the body of the crime report — for 26% of the sample. Analysis of the presence of a discernible hate motivation, indicated that 13.8% (n=8) of the perpetrators belonged to an organized hate gang or group, that 22.4% (n=13) possessed hate paraphernalia/iconography (books, graphic images, or had hate tattoos on their body) at the time of their crime, and that 10.3% (n=6) had a history of prior hate violence. Results revealed offenders who clearly evidenced one or more of the bias signs engaged in more instrumental (i.e., predatory and premeditated) crimes rather than emotionally spontaneous or "reactive" crimes. The bias-prominent offenders evidenced greater goal orientation and were less likely to have had any prior relationship with their victims; they also exclusively engaged in race/ethnic-motivated crimes rather than sexual orientation or gender-motivated crimes. Correlations for the prominent bias signs and violence risk assessment ratings, based upon the Hare (1991) Psychopathy Check List: Short Version (PCL:SV) and HCR-20 (Webster et al., 1997; Douglas et al., 1998) rating systems, were not significant. As such, the bias motivation of the offender does not indicate an explicit relationship to dangerousness per se, and should not be subsumed by such violence assessment ratings by crime investigators.

Attributional signs in hate crimes perpetration: Community findings

The role of law enforcement in making hate crime laws "work" is of course critical. It was therefore of interest to apply the methodology to a community sample to determine whether the analysis of the attributional signs provided useful information about hate crimes. The sample consisted of 518 bias crimes reported to a metropolitan law enforcement agency in California in 1999. Three specific issues were examined in the review of hate crime reports with a metropolitan police department. The questions examined were: (1) Are the proposed bias signs found in crime reports, — i.e., do officers provide such information, routinely in documenting bias crime activity, (2) are these attributional signs related to differences in victim selection, specifically ethnic/race versus sexual orientation crimes, and (3) does the prominence of these bias signs reveal differences in the behavioral manifestation of intergroup hostility?

As suggested by prior research of violent bias offenders, differences in patterns of aggression may help to clarify the motivation for future hate violence of bias perpetrators. These within-group differences reveal important information concerning the offender's motivational patterns of criminality (Cornell, Warren, Hawk, Stafford, et al., 1996). Berkowitz (1993) has described patterns of aggression that he describes as "reactive" and "instrumental." Cornell et al. (1996) reported that perpetrators of instrumental crimes were more likely to meet the criteria for psychopathy, an individual difference factor related to violence and recidivism generally. To return to Allport (1954), more extreme and egregious forms of prejudice are often instrumental, that is, are planned and goal oriented. On the other hand, the young men in criminal gangs in Hawaiian Gardens — who often did not evidence a prominent bias motivation — committed hate crimes that were significantly more likely to demonstrate a reactive form of aggression. Again, simply classifying a crime as being bias-motivated may be less revealing of the motives of the offender than considering the patterns of aggression found in the offense.

Methodology and analysis

Several specific factors were examined in the crime reports. These included whether the index offense was classified by the responding officers as being bias-motivated; if so, was the specific bias motivation (religion, sexual orientation, national origin, for example) identified. Additionally, offender characteristics of race/ethnicity and gender were coded. Victim race, gender, and sexual orientation were also recorded. We also considered whether the physical dress or appearance of the offender was routinely identified, and whether the index offense was classified as being related to gang activity. Data were content-analyzed by members of a research team composed of 6 trained psychology students. The behavioral characteristics of the hate crimes were evaluated in terms of a variety of behavioral and demographic factors. These ratings served to assess the crime in terms of form of aggression, severity of violence, and the estimated victim impact. The three methods of analysis are summarized as follows.

1. *Offender Demographic Characteristics*: The research methodology incorporated content analysis of the behavioral and socio-demographic (e.g., victim race/ethnicity and gender) characteristics of all reported hate crimes for the

January to June 1999 period. Each hate crime case was coded in terms of age, gender, and ethnicity/race of the victim(s) and perpetrator(s).
2. *Cornell Aggression Index* (Cornell Warren, Hawk, Stafford, et al., 1996): This rating scale examines the instrumental and reactive features of a single criminal event. The Cornell Aggression Index has been employed to evaluate mixed offender groups with both adults and adolescents. The scale produces 9 dimensions, of which the primary dimension rates the crime on a 4-point scale as "clearly instrumental" to "clearly reactive." This dimensional scale is based on the overall evaluation of a particular incident. The remaining 8 dimensional ratings consider specific characteristics of aggression that aid in distinguishing between instrumental and reactive criminal behavior. For example, planning and goal-directedness are typically related to instrumental crimes, whereas provocation, arousal, and lack of planning are features of reactive aggression.
3. *Bias Motivation Profile* (Dunbar, 1999): The Bias Motivation Profile (BMP) is a 5-item rating system developed to assess bias motivation of criminal offenders. It may be scored via interview and/or record review. Items are coded on a 3-point (2=yes/prominent, 1=somewhat/secondary, and 0=no/absent) scale, and reflect observable, behavioral, or historical evidence of bias, based on (for example) reports of victims and eye witnesses, police or detective reports, and criminal record where available. Ratings include Hate Speech present during commission of the offense ($m = 1.84$, $s.d. = 1.57$), Hate Paraphernalia ($m = 1.64$, $s.d. = 1.01$, inter-rater kappa $= .86$), Hate Group Membership ($m = 1.63$, $s.d. = .74$), Hate Ideology ($m = 2.95$, $s.d. = 1.17$), and Prior Bias-Motivated Aggression ($m = 1.4$, $s.d. = 1.06$). The sum of these ratings produced an overall scale score for the bias component ($m = 5.44$; $s.d. = 1.56$, coefficient alpha $= .82$).

The bias offender sample consisted primarily of men (86.5%), with 13% women, and less than 1% men and women together. The offender's median age was 25 years ($m = 29.09$, $s.d. = 13.02$, range $= 13$ to 62). In 69% of the cases, the race/ethnicity of the offender was identified, with the remaining ($n = 162$) cases having no identified perpetrator. For the identified perpetrator cases, the race/ethnic breakdown included African American (20.5%), Asian-Pacific (2.7%), Euro-White (42.3%), Latino (31.4%) and multi-racial (2.7%). The victim demographic characteristics indicated that 64% were men, 25% were women, less than 1% were men and women together; and 10% consisted of institutional/property crime damage. The victim median age was 35 ($m = 37.45$,

Table One. Relationship of bias motivation profile scores with victim group classification

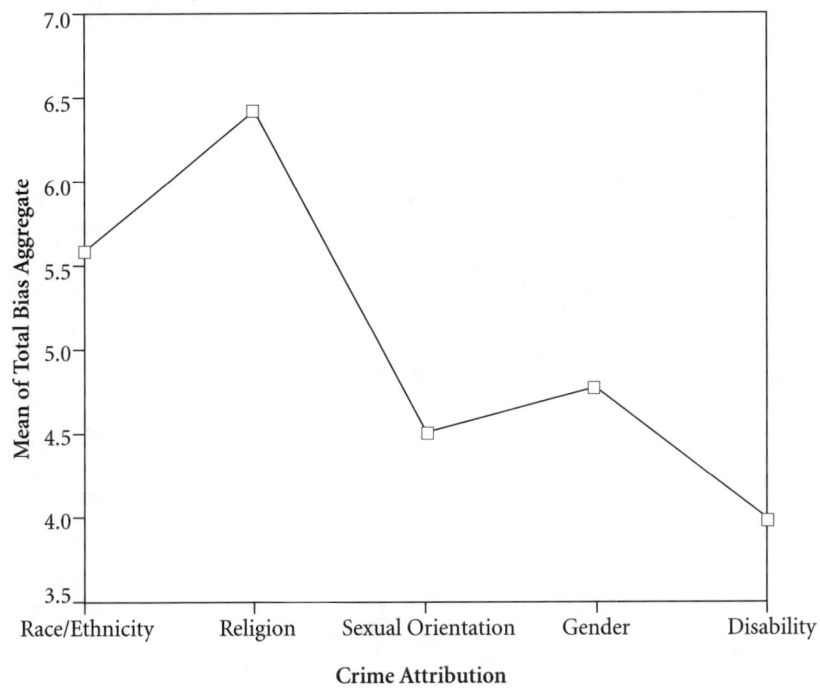

	Mean	SD
Race/ethnic motivation	5.06	3.16
Religious motivation	6.42	1.83
Sexual orientation motivation	4.51	2.16
Gender motivation	4.78	1.56
Disability motivation	4.00	0.00
Group Mean	5.42	2.24

s.d. = 18.38, range = 13 to 62). Classification of victim race/ethnicity was as follows: African American (27.8%), Asian-Pacific (8.4%), Euro-White (38.8%), Latino (16.8%), and multi-racial (2.6%). The sample included 357 bias offenses (69%) related to race/ethnicity, 105 (20%) sexual orientation, 43 (8%) religion, 11 (2%) gender, and 1 case relating to disability. The most frequent offenses reported included verbal threat of harm (29%), vandalism (28%), and assault with a deadly weapon (17%).

Table Two. Relationship of bias motivation profile scores with offender age

[Graph: Mean of Total Bias Aggregate vs Perpetrator Age. Values approximately: 18 and under ≈ 5.65; 19 thru 25 ≈ 5.06; 26 thru 35 ≈ 4.63; over 35 ≈ 4.89]

	BMP Scores			
	Mean	SD	F Value	p
			3.74	.05
Under 18	5.65	2.61		
19 through 25	5.06	2.41		
26 through 35	4.53	2.11		
35 and over	4.98	1.91		

The presence of attributional signs, based upon the BMP values, revealed that the prominence of bias motivation varied by victim group. In Table One, the BMP scores for each victim category are reported. The crimes classified as motivated by racial/ethnic bias (m = 5.51) had significantly higher BMP ratings than did sexual orientation (m = 4.51) bias crimes (t = 3.90, p < .001); multiple-perpetrator offenses (m = 5.33) also had slightly higher BMP ratings than single offender (m = 4.81) crimes (t = 1.18, p < .07). There were no differences in the offender BMP scores by gender, however.

Table Three. Relationship of bias motivation profile scores with offender aggression patterns

[Chart: Mean of Total Bias Aggregate plotted against Cornell I/R categories: Reactive hostile agg. (~5), Primarily reactive (~7), Primarily instrument (~7.8), Clearly Instrumental (~8.8)]

	BMP Scores			
	Mean	SD	F Value	p
			24.42	.001
Reactive/hostile aggression	3.27	2.08		
Primarily reactive	4.86	1.77		
Primarily instrumental	5.38	1.98		
Instrumental aggression	6.26	2.29		

The offenders were clustered by age into categories of 18 years of age and under, 19 to 25, and over 35. Results indicated that there were differences by these offender age groupings for the BMP scores ($F=3.74$, $p<.05$). The age grouping value differences are found in Table Two. Findings reveal that for younger and (surprisingly) older offenders, the bias motivation ratings were greater than that of young adult men in their twenties and early thirties.

In examining the aggression characteristics using the Cornell system, it was found that 46.4% of the offenses demonstrated clearly instrumental aggression.

That is, nearly one-half of the offenses indicated a premeditated and organized approach to the commission of the offense. Only 7.6% of the offenses indicated a clearly reactive or spontaneous form of aggression. In an analysis of variance of the aggregate bias score by the Cornell aggression ratings (1X4), it was found that there was a significant relationship (F=24.42, p<.001). This is reported in Table Three. Pearson correlations for the Cornell Aggression Index dimensions and the BMP ratings revealed that the bias motivation was correlated with greater goal orientation (r=.31, p<.02) and pre-event planning (r=.47, p<.001). Higher bias motivation ratings were also negatively correlated with (lower) levels of arousal (r=−.16, p<.005) and (lower) levels of pre-event provocation (r=−.14, p<.02).

In summary, for the identified hate crime perpetrators, bias aggression includes more than hate speech; however, hate utterances constituted the singularly most common indicator of offender bias motivation. The prominence of the bias component was related to more pre-meditated acts of aggression and varied by the targeted victim group. These findings indicate that law enforcement can effectively assess and evaluate bias aggression from a multidimensional approach that includes the analysis of behavioral and meta-communicative elements, as reflected in the attributional signs described above.

Reporting bias crimes: Issues in law enforcement effectiveness

"A couple of fruits get bashed — that's not a crime. That's normal. There are just two kinds of crime — dope and cars. The rest is just stupidity. I say dope and stolen cars are the only crimes worth my time. Not fruit bashing and not these domestic calls. That's just too bad."
Los Angeles Police Officer (Boyd, Berk & Hammer 1996)

The role of law enforcement in enforcing hate crime laws is obviously critical. Most metropolitan police departments provide peace officer training concerning how to report bias incidents. The effectiveness of such training has not been seriously examined, due in part to the feelings of many in law enforcement that the laws are difficult to enforce. In an important study, Nolan (1997) examined differences among law enforcement agencies that encourage (versus discourage) hate crime reporting. He found that organizational policies and practices varied significantly across the agencies he studied. Nolan identified several factors that affect the reporting of hate crimes. These included perceived organizational support of officers to report bias crimes, existence of effective community relations programs, organizational stability, and allocation of resources to investigate hate crimes. He also found that individual attitudes, i.e., responder attitudes and beliefs influenced how effectively hate crime laws were perceived to be enforced.

The issue of motivation to enforce hate crime laws needs be considered as an independent and critical issue from that of technical knowledge of the bias characteristics — i.e., the attributional signs — of the offense. Law enforcement attitudes concerning bias crimes largely reflect the social attitudes toward the victim groups of such offenses. Differences in cultural attitudes concerning crimes against visible racial and ethnic minorities, immigrant groups, gay men and lesbians, as well as religious minority groups will influence how vigorously law enforcement personnel respond to hate crimes.

Along with the question of such "soft" issues as the reduction of personal biases of the responding officer, the technical or cognitive component of how to investigate, document, and communicate about the bias component is critical. Developing skill to respond to bias crimes incorporates two distinct factors, one of which reflects the ability to know how to evaluate the bias component, and the second of which concerns accurate knowledge of the scope of the laws themselves. As has been proposed in the study of expertise, these factors, referred to as operational knowledge and declarative knowledge, are both required for competent policing in response to intergroup violence. Operational knowledge concerns the "knowing how" (Johnson 1987) in responding to a bias crime. This includes the self-awareness of the responder's cultural biases and skilled behaviors to elicit and document information from suspects, victims, and witnesses. Declarative knowledge references the possession of accurate, factual information concerning the scope of federal and local hate crime statutes, the process of reporting bias crimes — i.e., the chain of command in the reporting process — and the ability to document all forms of evidence related to the crime and the varying motivational characteristics, including the attributional signs and cultural message of the offense. The declarative knowledge component of bias crime investigation encompasses the knowledge and skill (the "what" of the offense) in identifying the bias component of the hate crime.

The skill issues in responding to bias crimes are summarized in Table four, in which three core dimensions of the crime response are considered. These are: (1) the responding officer's self-awareness and knowledge, (2) the officer's interaction with the offender, and (3) the interaction of the officer with the victim. As detailed in Table Four, officer awareness of socio-cultural attitudes of victims — which may include attitudes concerning law enforcement and/or

Table Four. A proposed model of expertise in bias crime response

	Operational knowledge	Declarative knowledge
Responder-Focused	1. comfort & awareness of personal biases 2. comfort in addressing hate violence 3. motivation to enforce hate crime laws	1. accurate knowledge of federal and state legal standards 2. understands the chain of command in bias crime reportage
Offender-Focused	1. skilled inquiry of offender regarding criminal and bias motivations 2. descriptive & thorough documentation of crime scene indicators of bias signs	1. determines the presence of attributional bias signs in the index crime 2. conceptualizes message component of bias motive
Victim-Focused	1. skill in asking about bias components of the index crime 2. implements appropriate victim triage activities concerning bias components of the index offense	1. awareness of socio-cultural attitudes and experiences with law enforcement 2. knowledge of victim service resources 3. aware of socio-linguistic factors in victim discussion of bias aggression

expectations of how violence is tolerated in some non-U.S. cultures — may be critical in gathering information, specifically as related to the attributional signs that have been discussed above. It is a sad fact that some victims find it extremely difficult to volunteer information that would reveal that they were targeted because of prejudice against their social group. Additionally, officers must be skillful in asking suspects about bias attitudes and assumptions, as well as gathering evidence that may support the bias motivation of the offense,

The analysis of bias crimes has been considered in terms of the attributional signs of the offense. These signifiers, when aggregated, reveal the prominence of bias motivation of the offender. This dimensional approach can be employed empirically, as demonstrated in the community data for bias crimes. Using this method of analysis, within-group differences amongst bias offenders were found for the degree of instrumental aggression, victim target, and interestingly, the difference in age of the offender. In addition, the meta-message of bias crimes has been articulated via a descriptive typology. This includes both culturally congruent as well as idiographic messages of outgroup hostility. These meta-messages constitute a descriptive methodology, one that with refinement may provide a basis for future study. As has been argued through the examples of individual cases, and as has been supported empirically, differences between bias offenders are important for both crime suppression and subsequent rehabilitation. It is hoped that the model employed here may be extended by others in criminology, communication and psychology, in the effort to control hate crimes in our society.

References

Adorno, T. W., Frenkel-Brunswik, E., Levinson, D. J., & Sanford, R. N. (1950). *The Authoritarian Personality*. Oxford, England: Harpers.
Allport, G. (1954). *The Nature of Prejudice*, Reading MA: Addison-Wesley.
Altemeyer, B. (1997). *The Authoritarian Specter*. Cambridge: Harvard University Press.
Berk, R. A., Boyd, E. A., & Hamner, K. M. (1992). "Thinking more clearly about hate-motivated crimes." In G. M. Herek & K. T. Berril (Eds.), *Hate Crimes: Confonting Violence Against Lesbians and Gay Men* (pp. 123–143). Thousand Oaks, CA: Sage Publications.
Berkowitz, L. (1993). *Aggression: Its Causes, Consequences, and Control*. Philadelphia: Temple University Press.
Boyd, E. A., Berk, R. A., & Hamner, K. M. (1996). "Motivated by hatred or prejudice": Catagorization of hate-motivated crimes in two police divisions. *Law & Society Review, 30*, 4, 819–850.
Brown, D., Scheflin, A. W., & Hammond, D. C. (1998). *Memory, Trauma Treatment, and the Law*. New York: W. W. Norton & Co., Inc.
Carter, J. H. (1995)."Psychosocial/cultural issues in medicine and psychiatry: Treating African Americans". *Journal of the National Medical Association, 87*, 12, 857–860.
Chuang, H. T. and Addington, D. (1988). "Homosexual panic: A review of its concept". *Canadian Journal of Psychiatry, 33*, 7, 613–617.
Cornell, D. G., Warren, H. J., Stafford, E. O. and Pine, D. (1996). "Psychopathy of instrumental and reactive violent offenders". *Journal of consulting and clinical psychology, 64*, 783–790.
Douglas, K. S., Klassen, C., Ross, D., Hart, S. D., and Webster, C. D. (1998). "Psychometric properties of HCR-20 violence assessment scheme in insanity acquittees". Paper presented at the 103rd annual American Psychological Association, San Francisco, CA.
Dovidio, J. F. and Gaertner S. L. (1986). "Prejudice, discrimination, and racism: Historical approaches". In J. F. Dovidio and S. L. Gaertner (Eds.) *Prejudice, Discrimination, and Racism*. New York: Academic press.
Dunbar E. (1999). Toward a Profile of Violent Hate Criminals: Aggressive, Situational, and Ideological Signifiers of Bias Motivated Offenders. Unpublished manuscript.
Dunbar E. (1999). "Defending the indefensible: A critique and analysis of psycholegal defense arguments of hate crime perpetrators". *Journal of Contemporary Criminal Justice, 15*, 1, 64–78.
Dunbar E. (1998). The relationship of DSM diagnostic criteria and Gough's prejudice scale: Exploring the clinical manifestations of the prejudiced personality. *Cultural Diversity and Mental Health 3*: 247–258.

Dunbar, E. Krop, H. and Sullaway M. E. (2000). "Behavioral, Psychometric, and Diagnostic Characteristics of Bias-Motivated Homicide Offenders". Unpublished manuscript.

Ezekiel, R. S. (1995). *The Racist Mind: Portraits of American Neo-Nazis and klansmen*. New York: Viking.

Green, D. P., Strolovitch, D. Z., and Wong, J. S. (1997). *Defended neighborhoods, integration, and hate crime*. Unpublished paper.

Hare, R. D. (1991). *The Hare Psychopathy Checklist-Revised*. Toronto: Multi-health systems.

Herek, G. M. and Capitano, J. P. (1996). "Some of my best friends: Intergroup contact, concealable stigma, and heterosexuals' attitudes toward gay men and lesbians". *Personality and Social Psychology Bulletin 22*: 412–424.

Herek G. & Berrill, (1992). *Hate crimes: Confronting Violence Against Lesbians and Gay Men*. Newbury Park: Sage Publications.

Herek, G. M. Gilles, R. Cogan, J. and Glunt, E. (1997). "Hate crime victimization among lesbian, gay, and bisexual adults". *Journal of interpersonal violence, 12*, 2, 195–215.

Jacobs J. B. and Potter K. (1998), *Hate Crimes: Criminal Law and Identity Politics*. New York: Oxford university press.

Johnson, S. D. (1987). "Knowing that versus knowing how: Toward achieving expertise through multicultural training for counseling". *The Counseling Psychologist 15*: 320–331.

Kecmanovic, D. (1996). *The Mass Psychology of Ethnonationalism*. New York: Plenum Press.

Kluckhohn, C. (1951). "Values and value orientations in the theory of action". In T. Parsons & E. A. Shils (Eds.), *Toward a General Theory of Action*. Cambridge: Harvard University Press.

Kluckhohn, F. R. & Strodbeck (1963). *Variations in Value Orientations*. Westport, Conn.: Greenwood Press.

Levin, B. (1999). "Hate crimes: Worse by definition". *Journal of Contemporary Criminal Justice 15*: 6–21.

Levin, J. and McDevitt, J. (1993). *Hate Crimes*. New York: Plenum.

McGlashan, T. H., Levy, S. T., & Carpenter, W. T. (1975). "Integration and sealing over". *Archives of General Psychiatry, 32*, 10, 1269–1272.

Nolan, J. J. (1997). Law Enforcement Participation in Hate Crime Data Collection: Assessing the Field of Forces. Temple U, USA. UMI Order Number: AAM9724263. Dissertation Abstracts International Section A: Humanities & Social Sciences, 1997 Sep, v58 (n3-A):1102.

Payne, S. G.(1995) *A History of Fascism 1914–1945*. Madison: University of Winsconsin press.

Raine, A. (1977). *The Psychopathology of Crime: Criminal Behavior as a Clinical Disorder*. San Diego: Academic Press.

Reeves S. B. and Nagoshi, C. T. (1993). "Effects of alcohol administration on the disinhibition of race prejudice". *Alcoholism: Clinical and Experimental Research 17*, 1066–1071.

Sidanius, J. and Pratto, F. (1996). *Social Dominance: An Intergroup Theory of Social Hierarchy and Oppresion*. New York: Cambridge University Press.

Tajfel, H. (1982). *Social Identity and Intergroup Relations*. Cambridge: Cambridge University Press.

Webster, C. D., Douglas, K. S., Eaves, S. and Hart, S. D. (1997). *HCR-20: Assessing risk for violence* (version 2).

Webster, C. D. and Jackson, M. A. (1998). *Impulsivity*. New York: The Guilford Press.

CHAPTER 10

Crisis/hostage negotiations
A communication-based approach

Randall Gage Rogan and Mitchell R. Hammer
Wake Forest University, Winston Salem, USA /
American University, Washington DC 20016, USA

The 1971 prison riot in Attica, New York, the 1972 Munich Olympic Games, the hostage situation in Ruby Ridge, Idaho, and the Branch Davidian standoff in Waco, Texas; these are just a few of the crisis events that will live in infamy for law enforcement, for each of these situations resulted in lost lives during a hostage-taking confrontation between police and hostage takers. As these incidents sadly demonstrate, the potential for the loss of life is an inherent ingredient in hostage-taking.

According to Muir (1977), a perpetrator effectively communicating a willingness to harm either him/herself or the hostage(s) if his/her demands are not met is a critical dimension of crisis/hostage negotiations. Undeniably, crisis/hostage negotiations are uniquely different from other types of negotiation contexts (e.g., labor/management) where parties typically come to the bargaining table in good faith and a willingness to engage in normative and equitable negotiation (Putnam & Poole 1987; Rogan 1990; Rogan, Donohue & Lyles 1990). Unlike more rational and normative bargaining interactions, crisis/ hostage negotiations are characterized by heightened levels of emotional arousal, uncertainty, and anxiety for all parties involved (Bohl 1997; Bolz & Hershey 1979; Rogan 1997, 1999).[1] The tension associated with hostage incidents is due in large part to the fact that the suspect has only two options for resolving the situation: surrender peacefully or face the consequences of a tactical assault. As such, negotiation may be a misnomer for what actually occurs as law enforcement engages in a process of seeking behavioral compliance.

More precisely, crisis/hostage negotiation is a unique form of conflict interaction in which law enforcement officers attempt to facilitate a (peaceful) resolution to an incident where an individual barricades him/herself, sometimes with a number of hostages, in an effort to elicit some desired want or to communicate anger and frustration about a personal or social concern (Hammer & Rogan 1997; Noesner 1999). These wants and concerns might include specific tangible objects (e.g., money, car), acknowledgement of the suspect's prowess, recognition of some social or political injustice, and/or undeclared help in coping with some overwhelming life stressing event (Fuselier 1986; Fuselier, Van Zandt & Lanceley 1989; Noesner & Dolan 1992).

Since 1972, much of what has been written about crisis/hostage negotiation has focused on the various motivational or psychological characteristics of perpetrators (Borum & Strentz 1992; DiVasto, Lanceley & Gruys 1992), the effects of being held captive (e.g., the Stockholm Syndrome) (Hare 1997; Ochberg & Soskis 1982), and the emotional implications of crisis management for negotiators (Bohl 1991, 1992, 1995; Havassy 1991; Mitchell & Everly 1993). Such information has been particularly helpful in increasing understanding concerning the effects of high emotional intensity and uncertainty on the participants in a crisis/hostage negotiation.

Unfortunately, however, the field and practice of crisis/hostage negotiation has developed over the years devoid of a conceptual understanding of the actual interaction dynamics involved in such incidents. Many of the guidelines used in negotiation programs tend to be derived primarily from practitioner experience rather than rigorous social science methodology (Hammer 2001; Hare 1997). Other than for a handful of relatively recent investigations (e.g., Donohue & Ramesh 1992; Donohue, Ramesh & Borchgrevink 1991; Donohue & Roberto 1993; Holmes 1997; Holmes & Fletcher-Berglund 1995; Holmes & Sykes 1993; Rogan & Hammer 1994, 1995; Rogan, Hammer & Van Zandt 1997), there exists a notable paucity in social science based research that explores the communicative dynamics of crisis/hostage negotiation. Equally important, there is an absence of work devoted to the conceptual development of crisis/hostage negotiation as an interactive social phenomenon.

The purpose of this chapter, therefore, is to advance a *communication*-based conceptualization that can function as a model for understanding the dynamics of crisis negotiation and for potentially managing the negotiation discourse of actual incidents. We begin this chapter with a brief review of traditional categorizations of negotiation incidents, followed by a discussion of three models that have been used as both descriptive and explanatory frameworks for resolving crisis situations. This is followed by a presentation of the central elements of our S.A.F.E. model (Hammer & Rogan, in progress) for crisis negotiaters. We conclude with recommendations for additional application of the model and suggestions for additional research.[2]

Categorizations of crisis/hostage incidents

The earliest attempts to conceptually define hostage negotiations involved simple descriptive categorizations (Hammer & Weaver 1998). These categorizations were grounded in a combination of psychological traits of the suspect and the contexts in which the incidents occurred. For example, during the late 1980s and 1990s, the predominant categorization scheme employed by law enforcement had four general incident classifications, including hostage takings by mentally/emotionally disturbed individuals, hostage takings occurring during the commission of a crime (e.g., bank robbery), terrorist hostage takings, and hostage takings during prison uprisings (Fuselier & Noesner 1990; McMains & Mullins 1996). Earlier, less ubiquitously endorsed categorizations delineated incidents according to particular traits of the perpetrator and his/her motivation (Cooper 1981). Seven separate types of incidents were identified, including political extremists, fleeing criminals, institutionalized persons, estranged persons, wronged persons, religious fanatics, and mentally disturbed persons (Cooper 1981). Other, psychologically based categories of terrorists are criminals, crusaders, and crazies (Hacker 1976). According to Hacker (1976), criminals engage in terrorist acts for personal gain, crusaders are oriented toward prestige and power around an identified cause, while crazies are viewed as emotionally disturbed individuals. A more recent application of this three-part categorization suggests that crusaders are "the least likely to negotiate a resolution to a crisis," (Combs 1997:57) while criminals are more likely to negotiate as "their demands are quite logical (although often outrageous), and they are based in terms which can be met" (ibid: 58).

More contemporary interpretations of incident type focus almost entirely on the perpetrator's motivation for the incident. Central to this perspective is the seminal work of Miron and Goldstein (1979) who posited that perpetrators' behavior in hostage/crisis incidents could be instrumental or expressive. According to them, an instrumental orientation denotes a primary concern for satisfying some recognizable goal that is constructively beneficial to the individual (e.g., obtaining money or the release of a fellow prisoner). Comparatively, an expressive behavioral orientation reflects a concern for fulfilling some relational desire/need that is of little substantive value (e.g., demonstration of power, communication of anger/frustration). While Miron and Goldstein (1979) believe that a suspect's behavior can be simultaneously instrumental and expressive, practitioners tend to view them as motivational/behavioral opposites (Noesner & Webster 1997). For example, Noesner (1999) recently proposed a dichotomous classification system of hostage and nonhostage situations that is grounded in Miron and Goldstein's instrumental–expressive taxonomy. According to Noesner, a hostage situation is characterized by a suspect engaging in purposeful behavior for the attainment of some concrete outcome that denotes substantive (instrumental) value for the suspect. In this context, hostages serve as true bargaining chips that can be traded for something with the police. Comparatively, nonhostage incidents are marked by suspects who engage in "emotional, senseless, and often self-destructive" (expressive) behavior (Noesner 1999:8). Any hostage that is held is as a victim to the perpetrator's anger and frustration, not as a bargaining commodity.

Historically, the value of classifying incidents has been to identify the most appropriate strategy for managing the incident and for interacting with the suspect. Over the years, three principal models have evolved from these categorizations. These models include the contending approach, the bargaining approach, and the psychotherapeutic approach. Miron and Goldstein's (1979) two-part taxonomy of instrumental–expressive behavioral motivation is a valuable heuristic for reviewing these approaches to achieving incident resolution. We now turn our attention to a brief discussion of each model.

Traditional models for managing crisis/hostage incidents

Contending model

One approach to managing conflict is contending. According to Pruitt and Carnevale (1993), this can best be understood in terms of its positioning within the dual concern model of conflict behavior. As derived from Blake and Mouton's (1964) conflict grid, the dual concern model posits two independent dimensions of individual orientation during conflict — concern for one's own outcomes and concern for other's outcomes (Rahim 1986; Thomas 1976; Van de Vliert 1997). The level of individual motivational orientation along these two dimensions ranges from weak to strong. Interaction of the dimensions produces multiple combinations of high and low self and other-concern. Within the dual concern model, contending is positioned at the high self and low other-concern ends of the continuums. Accordingly, conflict interactants who are characterized by this motivational orientation are primarily concerned with satisfying their own desires and interests while disregarding the interests of their opponent. As a strategy for dealing with conflict, contending is manifest in a variety of tactics including, threats, harassment, positional commitment, persuasive argument, and physical force (Pruitt & Carnevale 1993; Van de Vliert 1997).

Prior to 1972, the primary law enforcement strategy for resolving hostage/crisis incidents was contending, part of which involved confronting the suspect with an overwhelming show of force (Miller 1980). Two key strategies to this approach were first, to demand that the perpetrator release the hostages and surrender and second, to execute a planned assault if the suspect refused (Hammer 2001; McMains & Mullins 1996; Rogan 1999). Although a communication link might be established between the police and the suspect, little substantive negotiation took place. Further, little effort was made to understand the needs and motives of the perpetrator and no attention was given to discerning the instrumental–expressive orientation of the hostage taker. Rather, communication between law enforcement and the suspect was geared primarily to convincing him/her to surrender or face the consequences of an armed assault. Imaginably, communication in this context is highly contentious as both parties communicate threats and counter-threats.

Visible displays of weaponry, firepower, personnel, and environmental control are basic in communicating to perpetrators the disproportionate odds with which they are confronted. Often, power and utilities are disrupted while other anxiety stimulating tactics are employed (e.g., loud music, bright lights at night, helicopter fly-overs) to harass the suspect and to produce conditions of deprivation as well as heightened anxiety (Miron & Goldstein 1979). Within this framework, perpetrators are presumed to be rational and their emotionality a variable to be manipulated by the police (Miller 1980). Central to this approach is the belief that when presented with such an array of force, all of which serves to highlight the suspect's vulnerability, the perpetrator will be "rational" enough to surrender. The job of the negotiator, therefore, is to convince suspects that if they surrender peacefully, they will not be harmed (Miller 1980).

Clearly, such an approach is intended for use in situations in which the suspect's motive is instrumentally based. Admittedly, contentious tactics can be effective in forcing reluctant adversaries to rethink their position and getting them to the negotiation table or to surrender. Not surprisingly, however, contentious tactics often fail to produce the positive results desired. The principal limitation of contending is that such behaviors by one party often prompt reciprocal actions by the other. According to Pruitt and Carnevale (1993), contentious tactics often result in escalatory spirals with each party retaliating against the other, culminating in heightened reciprocal hostility. For example, if law enforcement misapplies a contending approach to a situation involving a principally expressively motivated suspect, the suspect may kill him/herself or hostages in response to the heightened pressure. As a case in point, one could argue that the fiery conclusion to the standoff between the Federal Bureau of Investigation and the Branch Davidians in Waco, Texas, was symptomatic of the misapplication of such contentious tactics as helicopter fly-overs, nighttime use of intense floodlights, the broadcasting of loud and irritating music and noise, and the use of armored personnel carriers to destroy personal vehicles and insert tear gas into the building.

September 8, 1971, and September 5, 1972, are the dates of two events that changed the way law enforcement manages hostage/crisis incidents. Attica State Prison in upstate New York and the 1972 Munich Olympic Games were the sites of two deadly hostage taking incidents in which several hostages were killed during a police assault on the hostage takers. These two events were the catalysts for law enforcement to re-examine procedures for resolving hostage/crisis situations. Since 1972, increased scholarly and practitioner attention has been devoted to exploring and demonstrating the effective role of negotiation in effectuating nonviolent resolutions to all types of crisis/hostage incidents (for recent reviews, see McMains & Mullins1996; Rogan et al. 1997). Two approaches that evolved out of this increased focus are the bargaining model and the psychotherapeutic model. We now turn our attention to a brief review of each approach.

Bargaining model

According to this model, crisis/hostage negotiations are primarily conceptualized as falling at the instrumental end of the instrumental–expressive continuum. As such, the focus is on a traditional bargaining approach to negotiation in which the efforts of each party involved in the conflict are dedicated to dictating or clarifying their individual instrumental concerns (Wall 1985). In this context, instrumentality denotes the individuals' situationally-related, substantive wants and demands. More specifically, instrumental concerns represent the commodity goals (e.g., money, goods, services) of the individual negotiator (Roloff & Jordan 1992). Basic to this approach is the presumption that individuals enter into interaction with their goals predetermined and relatively stable (Wilson & Putnam 1990). Consequently, the challenge in this type of interaction is to attempt to modify an opponent's commitment to key instrumental objectives.

An underlying presumption for instrumentally focused negotiations is that conflict is a consequence of goal interference within an interdependent relationship and that both parties to the conflict are concerned about maximizing their rewards and minimizing their respective costs (Folger, Poole & Stutman 1997; Northrup 1989). This theoretic orientation is grounded in social exchange theory that posits people's primary motivation in negotiation is self-interest (Thibaut & Kelly 1959). Briefly, this theory holds that conflict interaction is characterized by: (1) individuals who are aware of their respective costs and benefits, (2) costs and rewards that can be objectively evaluated, (3) parties who are cognitively aware of their options for various outcomes, and (4) behavioral decision making based on a rational weighing of costs and benefits (Northrup 1989; Roloff 1981). In this way, rationality assumes dominance, with bargaining and problem-solving being the benchmarks of instrumentality.

Within the context of crisis/hostage negotiation, resolution is attempted through bargaining that is typified by a quid pro quo interaction (Hammer 2001; Hammer & Rogan 1997). As noted in Greenstone (1995), this approach includes such specific negotiating tactics as making perpetrators work for everything they get, using time to one's advantage, not relinquishing too much too soon to perpetrators, and getting something for everything given. As evidenced by these tactics, concern for expressive needs is minimized. In fact, within a traditional bargaining framework, emotion is generally regarded as an addendum to the primary instrumental/rational orientation of the conflict interactants (Hammer 2001; Jones 2001). According to Hammer (2001), this represents one of the most critical limitations of the bargaining model. It is further argued that by focusing primarily on instrumental concerns, other relational and identity goals are relegated to secondary status, becoming important only when they impact on instrumental objectives (Putnam 1994).

As can be seen, a bargaining approach can be effective in those incidents in which suspects are focused on their instrumental objectives and are willing to bargain or problem-solve in order to reach an agreement. This is what Noesner (1999) would label as a "true hostage" incident. For example, negotiators might trade food and drink for hostages as they work toward the suspect's surrender. Yet, a purely instrumentally motivated hostage taker is not typical in most crisis/hostage negotiations. In a study by Head (1988), it was discovered that perpetrators made no instrumental demands in one-quarter of the incidents analyzed; while in those situations in which demands were communicated, those demands went unsatisfied 57% of the time. Further, unlike other types of instrumentally focused negotiations, participants in crisis negotiation do not usually come to the table with well-developed goals and a willingness to engage in good faith bargaining (Hammer & Rogan 1997; Rogan et al. 1990). Rather, crisis/hostage negotiations are most commonly noted for their high levels of uncertainty, anxiety, emotional arousal, and emotional instability. In fact, according to Soskis and Van Zandt (1986), most hostage negotiation incidents are the consequence of an individual failing to effectively manage a life-stressing event.

A set of recent surveys of hostage negotiation team leaders in the United States revealed that suicides, barricaded subject, domestic disputes, and criminal/high-risk situations account for a majority of the incidents negotiators actually manage (Hammer, Van Zandt & Rogan 1994; Rogan, Hammer & Van Zandt 1994). Noesner (1999) reports that 86% of all incidents can be classified as nonhostage and expressive. Similarly, McMains and Mullins (1996) note that 82% of all police negotiations deal with incidents other than actual hostage-takings. They further suggest that of the 18% that did involve a hostage, a notable percentage were "pseudo-hostage-takings" in which the suspect was more intent on making the hostage a victim than using him/her as a bargaining resource.

It is within this crisis context that volatile interaction dynamics centered around relational and identity concerns become pre-eminent. As such, traditional instrumental bargaining is not the most appropriate framework for conceptualizing the resolution process of most hostage negotiations (Hammer and Rogan 1997). It is this realization that prompted a re-conceptualization of hostage negotiation as primarily expressive interaction and crisis intervention/negotiation. This conceptual realignment is the basis for the third model of negotiation.

Psychotherapeutic model

As reflected in the name, this approach to negotiation is grounded principally in psychology and psychotherapy (Miron & Goldstein 1979; Schlossberg 1979) and human relations theory (Folger et al. 1997). Basic to this approach is the presumption that quality interpersonal relationships are critical to effective conflict management, as are the expressive needs of the parties involved. This model, therefore, focuses on the expressive end of the instrumental–expressive continuum.

According to Schlossberg (1979), a critical characteristic of expressive-based hostage incidents is that hostages do not have instrumental value to the perpetrator. Rather, the taking of hostages is done for the purpose of drawing attention to the needs or plight of the suspect. In those incidents in which no hostage is taken (e.g., suicides, barricaded subject), the goal of the suspect is to gain attention to his/her situation (McMains & Mullins 1996; Schlossberg 1979). In this way, the negotiator has nothing that the suspect wants in a material/instrumental sense. Therefore, attempts to negotiate with the suspect about substantive wants and demands (a bargaining approach) or to exert pressure (a contending approach) will be unlikely to produce the desired result of a negotiated surrender.

Clearly, this approach is best suited for nonhostage (expressive) situations (Noesner 1999). In this context, negotiators must work to elicit the concerns and feelings of the suspect and thereby convey an empathic understanding for the perpetrator's (crisis) condition (Rogan et al. 1990). According to Noesner and Webster (1997), the objective of creating an empathic relationship with a perpetrator is ultimately to enable the negotiator to reduce the perpetrator's level of emotional arousal and facilitate rational problem-solving.

Contrasted with the bargaining approach, the psychotherapeutic model emphasizes managing the suspect's emotional arousal as central to successful incident resolution (Miron & Goldstein 1979; Noesner & Webster 1997). Schlossberg (1979) contends that the heightened levels of emotional excitation that characterizes perpetrators in these incidents can negatively impact the potential for a negotiated resolution. In order to counteract these effects, negotiators need to learn and practice crisis intervention techniques that include such skills as active listening, self-disclosure, paraphrasing, and question asking (Hammer & Rogan 1997: McMains & Mullins 1996; Noesner & Webster 1997). Of these skills, listening is often regarded as the linchpin in helping perpetrators vent and dissipate pent-up anxiety, facilitating a reduction in emotional arousal and, thereby, effectuating more rational problem-solving (Noesner 1999; Noesner & Webster 1997).

Building trust between negotiator and suspect is considered a critical dimension of the relationship development process. This process is often hindered, however, by the psychological state of the perpetrator. It has been estimated that the majority of incidents that negotiators actually confront involve a perpetrator characterized by mental or emotional disorder. In fact, Fuselier (1981) claims that 52% of all negotiation incidents are perpetrated by suspects who have clinically diagnosed mental and/or emotional disorders involving antisocial personality, depression, paranoia, or inadequate personality. Consequently, a rather sizable body of literature has been devoted to understanding the psychological and personality traits of perpetrators and the most effective communication strategies for negotiating with suspects who exhibit behavior patterns consistent with specific mental and emotional typologies (e.g., Borum & Strentz 1992; Lanceley 1981; Lanceley, Ruple & Moss 1985; Strentz 1983, 1986).

The psychotherapeutic (expressive based) model of negotiation has contributed significantly to our understanding and management of crisis/hostage negotiations. As noted previously, it is argued that by developing an empathic relationship with a perpetrator, a negotiator can strive to reduce the suspect's level of emotional arousal and encourage rational problem-solving. It is also argued that by attending to and dealing with expressive issues, negotiators can guide a suspect into a "normative bargaining" mode typified by enhanced rational deliberation (Donohue & Roberto 1993). In fact, general models of bargaining and negotiation (e.g., Fisher & Ury's [1991] Principled Negotiation technique) are often advanced as appropriate frameworks for managing crisis/hostage negotiations (McMains & Mullins 1996).

Unfortunately, these presumptions simply reinforce an interactionally false bifurcation of rationality (instrumentality) and emotionality (expressiveness), wherein an expressive (psychotherapeutic) approach to negotiation is employed only in nonhostage situations to reduce a suspect's emotionality and to facilitate rational problem-solving. Such a position relegates emotion to being an addendum to rationality that must be dealt with only in those incidents noted as expressive and in which affect directly impacts instrumental issues (Hammer 2001; Putnam 1994; Rogan 1999).

Additionally, this approach does not focus sufficient attention on the identification of deeper interaction goals that emerge and define the negotiation dynamic between hostage takers and negotiators. In short, attending to the emotional state of the hostage taker is only part of the negotiation process and must be integrated with other equally salient aspects of negotiation. In this vein, several contemporary scholars posit a confluence of emotion and rationality, where emotion is a critical dimension of all decision-making and is ultimately what makes us human (Adler, Rosen & Silverstein 1998; Goleman 1995). It is this integrative perspective that serves as the basis for our communication-based model of crisis negotiation.

A communication-based model of crisis negotiation: The S. A. F. E. model

It has only been since the late 1980s that communication scholars began researching the communicative dynamics of crisis negotiation (Rogan et al. 1997). Contrasted specifically with the bargaining and psychotherapeutic models that emphasize relatively stable qualities and behaviors of the perpetrator, this communication-based approach focuses on the functional meaning of communicative symbols manifest during the conflict interaction. Situated in the social constructivist paradigm, more generally (e.g., Kelly 1963), and grounded in pragmatics theory of human communication more specifically (Watzlawick, Bavelas & Jackson 1967), the key question in this analytic model is how discourse serves to communicate and create shared meaning in such a way as to transform the contentious interaction dynamics between the conflicting parties.

This communication-based approach has its origins in interactional communication and the work of such scholars as Bateson (Ruesch & Bateson 1951), Cissna and Sieburg (1981), and Watzlawick and his colleagues (1967). Briefly, the interactional view posits that human communication is a transactional phenomenon between two individuals engaged in a mutually created interaction in which messages and meaning are conjointly operationalized. The emphasis is on the reciprocal dynamic relationship of the locutors rather than the condition or state of an individual. For crisis negotiation, this means that we engage in an interactive assessment of the communicative behavior of both the perpetrator and the negotiator rather than solely on the contextual parameters, psychological disposition, or specific behaviors of the suspect (Hammer 2001; Hammer & Rogan 1997; Rogan 1999).

Further, the interactional view of communication distinguishes between a report (content) and command (relational) level of meaning in communication (Cissna & Sieburg 1981; Watzlawick et al. 1967). The report dimension constitutes the precise information or data that is being discussed while the command level provides information about how the message content should be understood according to the communicators' relationship. More precisely, the command dimension speaks to who the communicators are, how they see themselves in relation to the other person, and how they view the other person relative to themselves in this particular interaction. In this way, command level communication is communication about report level communication; command communication is metacommunication that provides information about how a person's messages should be interpreted and also provides insight into the state of the interactants' relationship. For example, a perpetrator telling a negotiator that "It's taking too long to get the food in here!" is not merely saying that there seems to be a delay in the delivery of the food, but, more importantly, that he feels that he is being manipulated and jerked around. This presenting and responding metacommunicationally to self's and other's definitions is a continuous process in all relationships (Cissna & Sieburg 1981).

It is our contention that command (relational) communication functions as a communicative framing device for the conflicting parties (Johnson 1997). According to Putnam and Holmer (1992), framing is the communicative process whereby individuals create verbal descriptions and/or representations of an issue or relationship. As noted by Drake and Donohue (1996:301), "A frame is the particular quality assigned to an issue by the negotiator's linguistic choices." Although individuals frame events and issues in a fairly stable manner, these frames are subject to potential influence and modification based on the level of convergence with another person (Hammer 2001; Putnam & Holmer 1992). Research has demonstrated that disputing parties operating from divergent frames are more likely to engage in distributive interaction and not achieve resolution, while those operating from convergent frames are more successful in reaching a resolution to their conflict (Drake & Donohue 1996). Furthermore, individuals in conflict tend to operate from a single dominant frame as a means to express their concerns, but may change frames as a consequence of frame satisfaction through negotiation. According to Hammer (2001), negotiators can shift frames after some degree of issue resolution within the existing discourse frame has been achieved. In contrast, attempts to shift frames too early can result in conflict escalation.

The S. A. F. E. model of crisis negotiation is grounded in the pragmatics of communication and is based on four conflict concerns that constitute interpretive and discursive frames (Hammer 2001; Hammer & Rogan 1997). These frames structure and focus the negotiation discourse between negotiator and perpetrator. We now turn our attention to a brief review of the S. A. F. E. model and its four frames (see Hammer & Rogan [in progress] for the foundational theoretical and empirical elaboration of the S.A.F.E. model.

Conceptualization of the S. A. F. E. model

One way to understand frames is in terms of the functional goals individuals pursue in conflict. Three concerns (goals) that are central to conflict interactants include face (identity), substantive instrumental interests, and relational concerns (Roloff & Jordan 1992; Wilson & Putnam 1990). Briefly, identity goals denote a concern for self and/or other's projected image or face (Goffman 1967). Instrumental interests concern the relatively tangible wants and demands of the individual. Relational goals represent individual concern for the nature of the relationship with the other (e.g., power, trust, affiliation) (Donohue & Roberto 1993; Roloff & Jordan 1992). Finally, given contemporary conceptualizations of conflict and negotiation as emotional events (Adler et al. 1998; Barry & Oliver 1994; Jones 2001), we include emotion as a fourth concern (goal). These four goal concerns are the basic units of the S. A. F. E. model and represent the interpretive frames through which communicators shape their negotiation discourse. Each frame will now be briefly reviewed.

Substantive (demand) frame

Consistent with instrumentally-focused conceptualizations, an interest frame denotes individual concern for generally objective and tangible wants and demands (Roloff & Jordan 1992; Wilson & Putnam 1990). Within the context of crisis negotiation, two fundamental types of interest objectives have been identified: central substantive interests/demands and peripheral substantive interests/demands (Hammer & Rogan 1997; McMains & Mullins 1996). Briefly, central substantive interests and demands deal with situationally related wants while peripheral substantive interests and demands are wants that are not directly dependent upon the specific situation. For example, a suspect who requests a car to flee the scene of an attempted robbery with hostages is communicating a central substantive demand. On the other hand, if this same suspect requests a pizza and beer, he would be communicating a peripheral substantive instrumental demand, since food and drink are not situationally related objectives.[3]

According to Hammer (2001), the number and type of interests and demands communicated during a crisis negotiation are related to conflict escalation and de-escalation. Briefly, increased expression of peripheral substantive demands and greater expressed commitment to previously communicated central substantive demands tends to be associated with conflict escalation. Hammer further contends that an increased expression of peripheral substantive demands may be associated with escalating relational conflict dynamics involving power issues and trust between the negotiator and perpetrator. Comparatively, increased expressed flexibility toward central substantive wants and a reduction in the number of peripheral substantive demands is related to conflict de-escalation. It may, therefore, be the case that the nature of a suspect's substantive demands reflects the level of relational affiliation/attunement between the negotiator and suspect. As negotiation and bargaining research has demonstrated, successful conflict resolution will not be realized absent the management of relational (attunement) and face (identity) issues (Donohue, Lyles & Rogan 1989).

Attunement frame
Trust, power, control, intimacy, and empathic understanding are all facets of personal relationships. Within the context of crisis negotiation these qualities of interpersonal relationships are typically absent at the outset of contact between the suspect and law enforcement. In attempting to address these concerns, negotiators do not begin their interaction with a suspect along these relational dimensions at ground zero, but rather at a deficit (Rogan 1990; Rogan et al. 1990). For example, in attempting to establish trust, negotiators must often overcome the suspect's distrust of the police. The importance for negotiators to attend to such interpersonal issues and to develop a positive relationship with the perpetrator has been acknowledged as critical to incident resolution (Miron & Goldstein 1979; Womack & Walsh 1997). In fact, relational development has even been delineated as a separate phase in the negotiation process (Donohue, Ramesh, Kaufman & Smith 1991). As such, negotiators are instructed to create a trusting, empathic relationship with the suspect. Unfortunately, however, there exists little research-based knowledge about the dynamics of relationship development within the context of crisis.

One exception is a study of relational affiliation conducted by Donohue and Roberto (1993). According to Donohue (1998), affiliation denotes the extent to which individuals communicate attraction, liking, respect, trust, and a willingness to cooperate with one another. In other words, affiliation is defined as the level of relational distance between interactants. In their investigation, Donohue and Roberto (1993) found that relational patterns established early in a negotiation tend to remain fairly constant throughout the negotiation. Further, they found that in low affiliation conditions parties were less able to establish any consistent relational consensus (attunement) upon which to resolve substantive concerns, whereas in cases of high affiliation, communicators were more readily able to focus on instrumental issues rather than on relational definitions.

Face frame
In general, there is agreement among scholars that the concept of face denotes individual concern for self's and others' image, reputation, and or identity as presented during a social interaction (Hammer & Rogan 1997). Yet face is a multifaceted phenomenon that, over the years, has been conceptualized in various ways (Tracy 1990). While the origin of face is argued to be Chinese (Ho 1976), its Western roots can be traced to a seminal essay by Goffman (1955) in which he discusses the manner by which people work to present themselves during social interactions. Briefly, Goffman (1955:213) defines face as "the positive social value a person effectively claims for himself [sic] by the line others assume he [sic] has taken during a particular contact".

Accordingly, face is regarded as a concern for one's projected image within a social interaction that is inherently interwoven into the dynamics of that interaction. Individual concern for face is grounded in a desire to maintain a positive social expression of oneself, while recognizing and supporting the face of the other. In this way, face (identity) can be thought of as an abiding sense of self and self-respect in relation to the world (Northrup 1989; Ting-Toomey 1994). Consequently, face is argued to exist as part of the communication event in which a person is engaged and, therefore, is regarded as common to all social interactions (Tracy 1990) and culturally contexted (Ting-Toomey 1998).

Goffman (1967) additionally defines the processes by which individuals attempt to manage face as facework, proposing that face behaviors fall into two general types: preventive and corrective facework. Briefly, preventive facework includes actions taken to avoid and protect against loss of face while corrective facework denotes actions taken to restore face once it has been lost or threatened. Over the years, various scholars have extended Goffman's conceptualization of face and facework, applying it to various contexts of interaction (e.g., Goldsmith 2000; Tracy & Tracy 1998).

Within the context of conflict interaction, face has been acknowledged as a critical facet of the interpersonal dynamics of conflict (Northrup 1989; Ting-Toomey 1988; Ting-Toomey & Kurogi 1998). In an effort to explore facework during conflict, various scholars have proposed models to account for the types of facework strategies employed by conflict participants (e.g., Brown 1977; TingToomey 1985, 1988). Of particular interest to this chapter is Rogan and Hammer's (1994) study of facework in crisis negotiation.

Briefly, Rogan and Hammer suggest that facework strategies vary along three dimensions: (1) locus of concern: is the face act self or other directed? (2) face valence: does the face act serve to defend, maintain, attack, or honor (mitigate threats to face)? and (3) temporality: does the face act function to proactively protect against potential face threats or retroactively restore perceived face loss? Combining these dimensions produces six types of facework: (1) Defend Self Face, (2) Attack Self Face, (3) Restore Self Face, (4) Defend Other's Face, (5) Attack Other's Face, and (6) Restore Other's Face. Results from their application of the facework model to crisis negotiations indicate that Restore Other's Face was the primary behavior used by negotiators while Restore Self Face was the principal strategy for suspects. Attack Self Face was also commonly used by suspects, particularly in the suicidal incident investigated.

Additionally, two types of face that are particularly central to crisis negotiation include social/group identity and individual identity (Tajfel 1978, 1981). According to Hammer and Rogan (1997: 15–16), "Personal identity is based on an individual's unique perceptions of his/her own attributes (e.g., strong, weak, intelligent) while social identity consists of those characteristics and their emotional significance that is attached to one's membership in social group(s)" (see Chapter 1). The importance of these two types of face can vary from incident to incident as well as over time within an incident. For example, Rogan and Hammer (1994) conclude that personal identity concerns seem to be most salient in those negotiations involving a suicidal person. Comparatively, social identity seems to be of greatest concern in negotiations with members of certain social groups, cults, or particular national organizations (Hammer 2001).

Regardless of the specific face concern, communication that attacks or threatens another's face tends to escalate conflict while face honoring messages seem to result in conflict de-escalation. In sum, the publicly confrontational nature of crisis negotiation makes concern for face a constant throughout the duration of a crisis incident. In fact, Noesner (1999) contends that recognition of the basic need for respect is essential to achieving a peaceful resolution to an incident and that one of the most common mistakes for negotiators is to hurry the process toward problem resolution before establishing a strong expressive foundation.

Emotion frame
As noted in the earlier discussion about contending and bargaining approaches to negotiation, emotion was initially of little direct concern to incident resolution efforts. With the advancement of the psychotherapeutic approach, however, the

centrality of emotion to crisis negotiation was more clearly articulated. With increased attention devoted to the expressive motivation of the perpetrator, the suspect's emotional state was recognized to be a crucial ingredient in determining the success or failure of a negotiated outcome (Miron & Goldstein 1979). As discussed previously, the psychotherapeutic model requires that negotiators learn appropriate effective listening and interaction skills in order to deal with perpetrator emotion as a means for reducing the potential for negative and violent (fight/flight) reactions on the part of the perpetrator (Cannon 1929). The premise of this approach is that by reducing the suspect's emotion, the negotiator will facilitate increased rationality and normative bargaining in the interaction. In addition to focusing on the motivation of the suspect, concern for the emotional impact of intense negotiations on the police negotiator, in the form of post-traumatic stress, has also been an area of focus (Bohl 1991, 1992, 1995, 1997).

In a recent study, Rogan and Hammer (1995) explored the verbal expression of emotion in a select sample of crisis negotiation incidents. Focusing on the communicative dimensions of language (emotional) intensity and emotional valence (affect), they coded the message behavior of perpetrators and negotiators. They discovered that, across all incidents, the perpetrators' level of emotional expression was negative and intense at the outset of the interactions. This is the point at which the suspect is first confronted and forced to come to terms with the situation. Subsequent to this initial period of emotional excitation, the perpetrators' emotional expression tended to become more positively intense, resulting in a peaceful surrender. This, however, was not the case in the suicide incident analyzed. In this incident, the suspect's emotional expressiveness cycled between positive intensity and negative intensity culminating in extreme negative intensity during the final stages of the incident and his ultimate suicide. These results suggest that verbal cues of language intensity and message affect may differ dramatically between incidents that end in suicide and those that do not.

In sum, this research offers preliminary insight into the interactive dynamics of emotion and emotional expression during crisis negotiation and also highlights the potential benefit of attending to verbal message behavior to more fully understand the emotional state of the suspect as it forecasts future behavior.

Our understanding of the role of emotion in crisis negotiation and how we interact with the suspect in an attempt to manage it is still in its nascency. This is due, in part, to how emotion has been conceptualized within the context of crisis negotiation. As noted previously in this chapter, the tendency of traditional bargaining and psychotherapeutic models is to view emotion as either an addendum to instrumental incident management, or requiring reduction to facilitate increased rationality and normative bargaining (Donohue & Roberto 1993; Noesner & Webster 1997). Comparatively, the S. A. F. E. model advances a more dynamic and transcendent perspective of emotion, where emotion is regarded as a central element to conflict interaction. Consequently, it is imperative that we develop a more complete understanding of emotion and how it impacts conflict interaction in general and crisis/hostage negotiation specifically.

Epilogue

It is no understatement to claim that crisis/hostage negotiation is dramatically distinct from other more normative forms of conflict management and negotiation. Heightened levels of emotional excitation, intense public scrutiny, the possibility of physical harm — even death, mutual distrust, the likelihood of one party suffering from extreme mental and emotional stress, and the seeming intractability of the situation all converge to create a dynamic of interaction that demands the most knowledgeable and highly trained professional. Experience has clearly shown that tactical resolutions to these incidents often fail to produce the desired results, frequently resulting in the loss of life to hostages, police, and suspects. Negotiation is, therefore, the desired alternative.

Since its initial inception in the New York City Police Department in 1972 (Bolz & Hershey 1979; Hammer & Weaver 1998), crisis/hostage negotiation has evolved into an integral facet of police procedure. This maturation has been accompanied by increased conceptual clarity and sophistication in how crisis/hostage situations are defined and the preferred methods for resolving incidents. At the beginning of this chapter, we reviewed the evolution of the philosophy and practice of crisis negotiation as reflected in the three traditional models of negotiation — Contending, Bargaining, and Psychotherapeutic. Yet, as reviewed in this chapter, each of these traditional models suffers from various limitations in theoretical comprehensiveness as well as in application. Most notably, these models are limited in terms of the overemphasis on a limited set of psychological traits of the suspect and the bifurcation of a suspect's motivation as either instrumental or expressive. Comparatively, the newly-proposed S. A. F. E. model extends these existing frameworks by focusing on the communicative framing function of negotiator and suspect communication as it allows for the concomitant occurrence of instrumental and expressive needs of the parties involved. As previously described, the S. A. F. E. model is an integrative approach for discerning the functional implications of communicator discourse around four basic conflict issues including: Substantive demands, Attunement, Face, and Emotional concerns.

While various dimensions of the model have been used in analyzing authentic crisis/hostage negotiation interactions, the model, as a whole, has yet to be tested. As such, we are in the final stages of a comprehensive investigation of crisis negotiation incidents exploring the communicative manifestations of each dimension of the S. A. F. E. model and their interrelationships. Clearly, we need to more fully understand the manner in which negotiators and suspects manage each frame, shift between frames, and ultimately achieve incident resolution. Additional research efforts should delve into the relationship between message affect and suspect threatening communication to determine potential correlates with threat enactment, as well as the effect of negotiator problem reformulation on suspect frame shifting and incident resolution. Such research needs to be examined in terms of incident escalation and de-escalation. Future efforts should also seek to determine if there are particular communicative "frame markers" associated with different types of perpetrator frames (e.g., a suicidal perpetrator). Ultimately, research should further examine the initial formulation of the S. A. F. E. model in terms of its ability to elucidate specific patterns of communicative interaction between negotiator and hostage taker and to inform the development of effective strategy to peacefully manage these volatile incidents.

Although the S. A. F. E. model was originally conceived for analyzing the conflict discourse of domestic U. S. crisis negotiations, it holds significant promise for understanding the dynamics of intercultural incidents (Hammer 1997; Hammer & Weaver 1998; Weaver 1997). An informed understanding of how different cultural groups communicate in conflict contexts around the issues of demands, face, relational attunement, and emotion will better equip negotiators to manage crisis incidents involving cultural backgrounds different from their own.

Saving lives is the name of the game. The S. A. F. E. model represents a valuable heuristic for conceptualizing and analyzing the conflict dynamics of crisis negotiations. Already, the model has experienced national and international diffusion (Hammer 1999, 1998; Hammer & Rogan 1998; Rogan 1998). At the local level, Dr. Hammer has worked extensively with crisis negotiation teams in the Washington D. C. area, developing training that integrates the

S. A. F. E. model into their overall crisis response capability. In this regard, Dr. Hammer acts as the S. A. F. E. on-scene advisor to crisis negotiators, helping analyze interactional dynamics around conflict escalation and de-escalation, and collaboratively developing strategies to peacefully resolve these types of incidents. At the national level, we are working with a federal agency training their negotiators throughout the United States in using the S. A. F. E. model for negotiating critical incidents. This training involves not only presentations on the S. A. F. E. concepts, but extensive analysis of actual hostage incident audiotapes followed by indepth, realistic, crisis simulations in which participants then practice the S. A. F. E. model and associated negotiation skills. Results from these and other efforts are quite encouraging in increasing the capabilities of crisis negotiators to more accurately "read" interactional dynamics and develop effective, de-escalation strategies for peacefully resolving these most difficult, critical events. The 1972 Munich Olympic games, Attica, Ruby Ridge, Idaho, and Waco Texas; we need not add any more names to this list of failed incidents. It is our hope that the S. A. F. E. model will aid law enforcement in its efforts to realize nonviolent resolutions to future crisis incidents.

Notes

1. Throughout this chapter, we use the terms "crisis" and "hostage" negotiations interchangeably. This dual use is perhaps appropriate at this developmental stage in the field. Initial characterizations of the field termed the practice, "hostage negotiations." This is now deemed inadequate (Hammer & Rogan 1997; Noesner 1999) because many incidents law enforcement respond to involve situations (e.g., barricaded subjects, suicidal individuals) in which "hostages" are not being held against their will for the purpose of extracting concessions from the local authorities (Noesner 1999). Therefore, the more comprehensive term, "crisis negotiations" is increasingly being employed by practitioners and scholars in describing this emerging field of study and application. Nevertheless, the general public and the media continue to view such crisis events as "hostage incidents."

2. Because the goals of our communication model of crisis negotiation include both explanatory (understanding the dynamics of crisis negotiation) and applied (provide guidance for managing the negotiation discourse) concerns, we have labeled our approach with the acronym S. A. F. E., thus providing a more accessible mechanism for describing and exploring patterns of complex communication dynamics involved in crisis situations. "The acronym F.I.R.E. was used in some of our earlier writings to describe this communication model. We now refer to this model with the acronym S.A.F.E. rather than the acronym F.I.R.E."

3. Earlier work has referred to these types of demands as "substantive" and "non-substantive". It is our contention that differences in the types of demands issued by the parties reflect whether the demands are more or less situationally central or peripheral in contrast to whether the demands are "substantive" or "non-substantive". It is our view that instrumental demands and wants issued by parties are fundamentally substantive insofar as reflect communicative message "content" concerns (Watzlawick et al. 1967).

References

Adler, R. S., Rosen, B. and Silverstein, E. M. 1998. "Emotions in negotiation: How to manage fear and anger". *Negotiation Journal* 14: 161–179.

Barry, B. and Oliver, R. L. 1994. "Affect in negotiation: A model and propositions". Paper presented at the International Association for Conflict Management Conference, Eugene, OR.

Blake, R. R. and Mouton, J. S. 1964. *The Managerial Grid.* Houston, TX: Gulf

Bohl, N. K. 1991. "The effectiveness of brief psychological interventions in police Officers after critical incidents". In *Critical Incidents in Policing* (revised), J. T. Reese and M. M. Horn (eds.), 31–38. Washington, D. C.: U. S. Department of Justice, Federal Bureau of Investigation.

Bohl, N. K. 1992. "Hostage negotiator stress". *FBI Law Enforcement Bulletin* 61: 23–26.

Bohl, N. K. 1995. "Professionally-administered critical incident debriefing for police Officers". In *Police Psychology into the 21st Century*, M. I. Kurke and E. M. Scrivner (eds), 149–188. NY: Lawrence Erlbaum.

Bohl, N. K. 1997. "Postincident crisis counseling for hostage negotiators". In *Dynamic Processes of Crisis Negotiation: Theory, Research, and Practice*, R. G. Rogan, M. R. Hammer, and C. R. Van Zandt (eds), 45–56. Westport, CT: Praeger.

Bolz, F. and Hershey, E. 1979. *Hostage Cop.* New York: Rawson Wade.

Borum, R. and Strentz, T. 1992. "The borderline personality". *FBI Law Enforcement Bulletin* 61: 6–10.

Brown, B. 1977. "Face-saving and face-restoration in negotiation". In *Negotiations: Social-Psychological perspectives*, D. Druckman (ed.), 275–299. Beverly Hills, CA: Sage.

Cannon, W. B. 1929. *Bodily Changes in Pain, Hunger, Fear and Rage.* New York: Appleton-Century.

Cissna, K. N. L. and Sieburg, E. 1981. "Patterns of interaction confirmation and Disconfirmation". In *Rigor and Imagination: Essays from the Legacy of Gregory Bateson*, C. Wilder and J. H. Weakland (eds), 253–282. New York, NY: Praeger.

Combs, C. C. 1997. *Terrorism in the Twenty-First Century.* Saddle River, NJ: Prentice Hall.

Cooper, H. H. A. 1981. *The Hostage Takers.* Boulder, CO: Paladin.

DiVasto, P., Lanceley, F. J., and Gruys, A. 1992. "Critical issues in suicide intervention". *FBI Law Enforcement Bulletin* 61: 13–26.

Donohue, W. A. 1998. "Managing equivocality and relational paradox in the Oslo peace Negotiations". *Journal of Language and Social Psychology* 17: 72–96.

Donohue, W. A., Lyles, J. and Rogan, R. G. 1989. "Issue development in divorce mediation". *Empirical Research in Divorce and Family Mediation* 24: 19–28.

Donohue, W. A. and Ramesh, C. N. 1992. "Negotiator-opponent relationships". In *Communication and Negotiation*, L. L. Putnam and M. E. Roloff (eds), 209–232. Newbury Park, CA: Sage.

Donohue, W. A., Ramesh, C. and Borchgrevink, C. 1991. "Crisis bargaining: Tracking the relational paradox in hostage negotiation". *International Journal of Conflict Management* 2: 257–274.

Donohue, W. A., Ramesh, C., Kaufman, G. and Smith, R. 1991. "Crisis bargaining in hostage negotiations". *International Journal of Group Tensions* 21: 133–154.

Donohue, W. A. and Roberto, A. J. 1993. "Relational development in hostage negotiation". *Human Communication Research* 20: 175–198.

Drake, L. E. and Donohue, W. A. 1996. "Communicative framing theory in conflict resolution". *Communication Research* 23: 297–322.

Fisher, R. and Ury, W. (1991). *Getting to Yes*. New York: Penguin.

Folger, J. P., Poole, M. S. and Stutman, R. K. 1997. *Working Through Conflict*. 3rd ed. New York, NY: Harper Collins.

Fuselier, G. D. 1981. "A practical overview of hostage negotiations (Part I)". *The FBI Law Enforcement Bulletin* 50: 2–6.

Fuselier, G. D. 1986. "What every negotiator would like his chief to know". *FBI Law Enforcement Bulletin* 55: 1–4.

Fuselier, G. D. and Noesner, G. W. 1990. "Confronting the terrorist hostage taker". *FBI Law Enforcement Bulletin* 59: 6–11.

Fuselier, G. D., Van Zandt, C. R. and Lanceley, F. J. 1989. "Negotiating the protracted incident: The Oakdale and Atlanta prison sieges". *FBI Law Enforcement Bulletin* 58: 1–7.

Goffman, E. 1955. "On facework: An analysis of ritual elements in social interaction". *Psychiatry Journal for the Study of International Processes* 18: 213–231.

Goffman, E. 1967. *Interaction Ritual Essays on Face-to-Face Behavior*. Garden City, NY: Anchor.

Goldsmith, D. J. 2000. "Soliciting advice: The role of sequential placement in mitigating face threat". *Communication Monographs* 67: 1–19.

Goleman, D. 1995. *Emotional Intelligence*. New York: Bantam.

Greenstone, J. L. 1995. "Tactics and negotiating techniques (TNT): The way of the past and the way of the future". In *Police Psychology into the 21st Century*, M. I. Kurke and E. M. Scrivner (eds), 357–371. Hillsdale, NJ: Lawrence Erlbaum.

Hacker, F. J. 1976. *Crusaders, Criminals, Crazies: Terror and terrorism in our time*. New York: Norton.

Hammer, M. R. 1997. "Negotiating across the cultural divide: Intercultural dynamics in crisis incidents". In, *Dynamic Processes of Crisis Negotiation: Theory, research, and practice*, R. G. Rogan, M. R. Hammer and C. R. Van Zandt (eds), 105–114. Westport, CT: Praeger.

Hammer, M. R. 1998. "Crisis negotiation across the cultural divide". Paper presented at the SIETAR International Conference, Tokyo, Japan.

Hammer, M. R. 1999. "Using the F. I. R. E. model in crisis situations". Presentation at the annual Baltimore Hostage Negotiation Conference, Baltimore, MD.

Hammer. M. R. 2001. "Conflict negotiations under crisis conditions". In *The Language of Conflict Resolution*, W. Eadie and P. Nelson (eds), 57–80. Thousand Oaks, CA: Sage.

Hammer, M. R. and Rogan, R. G. 1997. "Negotiation models in crisis situations: The value of a communication based approach". In *Dynamic Processes of Crisis Negotiation: Theory, Research, and Practice*, R. G. Rogan, M. R. Hammer and C. R. Van Zandt (eds), 9–23. Westport, CT: Praeger.

Hammer, M. R. and Rogan, R. G. 1998. "The FIRE model of crisis negotiation". Presentation at the annual California Association of Hostage Negotiator's conference, Monterrey, CA.

Hammer, M. R. and Rogan, R. G. (in progress). *A Communication Theory of Crisis Negotiation: Discourse Analysis of Hostage/Barricade Incidents*. Westport, CT: Prager.

Hammer, M. R. and Weaver, G. R. 1998. "Cultural considerations in hostage Negotiations". In *Culture, Communication and Conflict: Readings in Intercultural Relations*, G. R. Weaver (ed.), 518–527. Needham Heights, MA: Simon & Schuster.

Hammer, M. R., Van Zandt, C. R. and Rogan, R. G. 1994. "Crisis/hostage negotiation team profile of demographic and functional characteristics". *FBI Law Enforcement Bulletin* 63: 8–11.

Hare, A. (1997). "Training crisis negotiators: Updating negotiation techniques and Training". In *Dynamic Processes of Crisis Negotiation: Theory, Research, and Practice*, R. G. Rogan, M. R. Hammer and C. R. Van Zandt (eds), 151–160. Westport, CT: Praeger.

Havassy, V. J. 1991. "Critical incident debriefing: Ritual for closure". In *Critical Incidents in Policing* (revised) J. T. Reese, J. M. Horn, and C. Dunning (eds), 139- 142. Washington, D. C.: U. S. Government Printing Office.

Head, W. B. 1988. "The hostage response". Ph.D. dissertation. The State University of New York at Albany.

Ho, D. (1976). "On the concept of "face."" *American Journal of Sociology* 81: 867–884.

Holmes, M. E. 1997. "Optimal matching analysis of negotiation phase sequences in simulated and authentic hostage negotiation". *Communication Reports* 10: 1–8.

Holmes, M. E. and Fletcher-Berglund, T. 1995. "Negotiations in crisis". In *Conflict and Organizations: Communicative processes*, A. Nicotera (ed.), 239–256. Albany, New York: SUNY Press.

Holmes, M. E. and Sykes, R. E. 1993. "A test of the fit of Gulliver's phase model to hostage negotiations". *Communication Studies* 44: 38–55.

Jones, T. S. 2001. "Emotional communication in conflict: Essence and Impact". In *The Language of Conflict Resolution*, W. Eadie and P. Nelson (eds), 81- 104. Thousand Oaks, CA: Sage.

Johnson, L. D. 1997. "A framework for interaction (FINT) scale: Extensions and refinement in an industrial setting". *Communication Studies* 48: 127–141.

Kelly, G. 1963. *A Theory of Personality: The Psychology of Personal Constructs*. New York: Norton.

Lanceley, F. J. 1981. "The antisocial personality as hostage-taker". *Journal of Police Science and Administration* 9: 28–34.

Lanceley, F. J., Ruple, S. W., and Moss, C. G. 1985. "*Crisis and suicide intervention*". Special Operations and Research Unit, Federal Bureau of Investigation, Quantico, VA.

McMains, M. J. and Mullins, W. C. 1996. *Crisis Negotiations*. Cincinnati, OH: Anderson.

Miller, A. H. 1980. *Terrorism and Hostage Negotiations*. Boulder, CO: Westview.

Miron, M. S. and Goldstein, A. P. 1979. *Hostage*. New York: Pergamon.

Mitchell, J. T. and Everly, G. S. Jr. 1993. *Critical Incident Stress Debriefing*. Ellicot City, MD: Chevron.

Muir, W. K. 1977. *Police: Streetcorner Politicians*. Chicago, IL: University of Chicago Press.
Noesner, G. W. 1999. "Negotiation concepts for commanders". *FBI Law Enforcement Bulletin* 68: 6–14.
Noesner, G. W. and Dolan, J. T. 1992. "First responder negotiation training". *FBI Law Enforcement Bulletin* 61: 1–4.
Noesner, G. W. and Webster, M. 1997. "Crisis Intervention". *FBI Law Enforcement Bulletin* 66: 13–19.
Northrup, T. A. 1989. "The dynamic of identity in personal and social conflict". In *Intractable Conflicts and Their Transformation*, L. Kriesberg, T. Northrup and S. J. Thorson (eds), 55–82. Syracuse, NY: Syracuse University Press.
Ochberg, F. M. and Soskis, D. A. (eds) 1982. *Victims of Terrorism*. Boulder, CO: Westview Press.
Pruitt, D. G. and Carnevale, P. J. 1993. *Negotiation in Social Conflict*. Pacific Cove, CA: Brooks/Cole.
Putnam, L. L. 1994. "Challenging the assumptions of traditional approaches to Negotiation". *Negotiation Journal* 10: 337–346.
Putnam, L. L. and Holmer, M. 1992. "Framing, reframing and issue development". In *Communication and Negotiation*, L.L Putnam and M. E. Roloff (eds), 128–155. Newbury Park, CA: Sage.
Putnam, L. L. and Poole, M. S. 1987. "Conflict and negotiation". In *Handbook of Organizational Communication*, F. Jablin, L. L. Putnam, K. H. Roberts and L. W. Porter (eds), 549–599. Newbury Park, CA: Sage.
Rahim, M. A. (ed.) 1986. *Managing Conflict in Organizations*. New York: Praeger.
Rogan, R. G. 1990. "An interaction analysis of negotiator and hostage-taker identity-goal, relational-goal, and language intensity message behavior within hostage negotiations: A descriptive investigation of three negotiations". Ph.D. dissertation. Michigan State University, East Lansing.
Rogan, R. G. 1997. "Emotion and emotional expression in crisis negotiation". In *Dynamic Processes of Crisis Negotiation: Theory, Research, and Practice*, R. G. Rogan, M. R. Hammer and C. R. Van Zandt (eds), 25–44. Westport, CT: Praeger.
Rogan, R. G. 1998. "F. I. R. E. model of crisis negotiation". Keynote presentation at the First European Conference on Hostage Negotiation, Arnhem, Holland.
Rogan, R. G. 1999. "F. I. R.E: A communication based approach for understanding crisis Negotiation". In *To Save Lives*, O. Adang and E. Giebels (eds), 29–45. Amsterdam, The Netherlands: Elsevier.
Rogan, R. G., Donohue, W. A., and Lyles, J. 1990. "Gaining and exercising control in hostage taking negotiations using empathetic perspective-taking". *International Journal of Group Tension* 20: 77–90.
Rogan, R. G.and Hammer, M. R. 1994. "Crisis negotiations: A preliminary investigation of facework in naturalistic conflict". *Journal of Applied Communication Research* 22: 216–231.
Rogan, R. G. and Hammer, M. R. 1995. "Assessing message affect in crisis negotiations: An exploratory study". *Human Communication Research* 21: 553–574.
Rogan, R. G., Hammer, M. R. and Van Zandt, C. R. 1994. "Profiling crisis negotiation Teams". *Police Chief* 61: 14–18.
Rogan, R. G., Hammer, M. R., and Van Zandt, C. R. (eds) 1997. *Dynamic Processes of Crisis Negotiation: Theory, research, and practice*. Westport, CT: Praeger.

Roloff, M.E. 1981. *Interpersonal Communication: The social exchange approach*. Beverly Hills, CA: Sage.
Roloff, M.E. and Jordan, J.M. 1992. "Achieving negotiation goals: The "fruits and foibles" of planning ahead". In *Communication and Negotiation*, L.L. Putnam and M.E. Roloff (eds), 21–45. Newbury Park, CA: Sage.
Ruesch, J. and Bateson, G. 1951. *Communication: The Social Matrix of Psychiatry*. New York: W.W. Norton.
Schlossberg, H. 1979. "Police response to hostage situations". In *Crime and Justice in America*, J.T. O'Brien and M. Marcus (eds), 209–220. New York: Pergamon.
Soskis, D.A. and Van Zandt, C.R. (1986). "Hostage negotiation: Law enforcement's most effective nonlethal weapon". *The FBI Management Quarterly* 6: 1–8.
Strentz, T. 1983. "The inadequate personality as hostage taker". *Journal of Police Science and Administration* 11: 363–368.
Strentz, T. 1986. "Negotiating with the hostage taker exhibiting paranoid schizophrenic Symptoms". *Journal of Police Science and Administration* 14: 12–16.
Tajfel, H. 1978. "Social categorization, social identity, and social comparisons". In *Differentiation Between Social Groups*, H. Tajfel (ed.), 61–76. London: Academic Press.
Tajfel, H. 1981. "Social stereotypes and social groups". In *Intergroup Behavior*, J. Turner and H. Giles (eds), 144–167. Chicago: University of Chicago Press.
Thibaut, J. and Kelly, H.H. 1959. *The Social Psychology of Groups*. New York: Wiley.
Thomas, K.W. 1976. "Conflict and conflict management". In *Handbook of Industrial and Organizational Psychology*, M. Dunnette (ed.), 889–935. Chicago, IL: Rand McNally.
Ting-Toomey, S. 1985. "Toward a theory of conflict and culture". In *Communication, Culture, and Organizational Processes*, W. Gudykunst, L. Stewart and S. Ting-Toomey (eds), 71–86. Beverly Hills: Sage.
Ting-Toomey, S. 1988. "Intercultural conflict styles: A face-negotiation theory". In *Theories in Intercultural Communication*, Y.Y. Kim and W.B. Gudykunst (eds), 213–235. Newbury Park, CA: Sage.
Ting-Toomey, S. 1994. "Face and facework: An introduction". In *The Challenge of Facework*, S. Ting-Toomey (ed.), 1–14. Albany: State University of New York Press.
Ting-Toomey, S. and Kurogi, A. 1998. "Facework competence in intercultural conflict: An updated face-negotiation theory". *International Journal of Intercultural Relations* 22: 187–225.
Tracy, K. 1990. "The many faces of facework". In *Handbook of Language and Social Psychology*, H. Giles and W.P. Robinson (eds), 209–226. John Wiley & Sons.
Tracy, K. and Tracy, S.J. 1998. "Rudeness at 911: Reconceptualizing face and face Attack". *Human Communication Research* 25: 225–251.
Van de Vliert, E. 1997. *Complex Interpersonal Conflict Behavior: Theoretical frontiers*. East Sussex, UK: Psychology Press.
Wall, J.A. Jr. 1985. *Negotiation Theory and Practice*. Glenview, IL: Scott, Foresman.
Waltzlawick, P., Bavelas, J. and Jackson, D.D. 1967. *Pragmatics of Human Communication*. New York: W.W. Norton.
Weaver, G.R. 1997. "Psychological and cultural dimensions of hostage negotiation". In *Dynamic Processes of Crisis Negotiation*, R.G. Rogan, M.R. Hammer and C.R. Van Zandt (eds), 115–128. Westport, CT: Praeger.

Wilson, S. R. and Putnam, L. L. 1990. "Interaction goals in negotiation". In *Communication Yearbook 13*, J. Anderson (ed.), 374–406. Newbury Park, CA: Sage.

Womack, D. F. and Walsh, K. 1997. "A three-dimensional model of relationship development in hostage negotations". In *Dynamic Processes of Crisis Negotiation*, R. G. Rogan, M. R. Hammer and C. R. Van Zandt (eds), 57–76. Westport, CT: Praeger.

Index

4th Amendment 10

A
abuse 2, 13–15, 22, 26, 29, 32, 129, 131, 132–135, 140, 141, 149, 151, 152, 155–159, 163–166, 168–172, 177, 181, 196, 197
accuracy 7, 14, 94, 101, 160, 161, 164, 166, 168
achievements 69, 71
action-oriented 12
activity 2, 36, 54, 73, 80, 93, 129, 144, 163, 178, 179, 181, 182, 203, 208, 212–214, 219
administrative 53, 54, 90, 102, 104, 105, 179
adolescents 110, 139, 212, 220
affiliation 201, 204, 207, 241, 242
African Americans 22, 23, 109, 124, 212
age 7, 31, 59, 73, 104, 105, 113, 121, 132, 145, 155, 156, 162–164, 202, 220, 221–223, 227
agenda 31, 81, 105, 118, 121, 178
aggression 11, 16, 17, 107, 112, 113, 121, 123, 125, 126, 133, 134, 136, 141, 150–153, 173, 177, 181, 200, 204, 206–211, 213–215, 217–220, 223, 224, 226–228
Air Force 9
alcohol 139, 144, 205, 208, 228
ambiguous 144, 181, 184
analysis vii, 8, 16, 18, 30, 44, 46, 48–50, 56, 59, 61, 64, 65, 68, 71, 72, 74–76, 78–83, 90, 102, 103, 108, 109, 115, 120, 122, 125–127, 133, 152, 169, 170, 190, 197, 200, 201, 203, 204, 218–220, 224, 226, 227, 248, 250, 251, 252
anger 79, 131, 141, 181, 230, 232, 249
anxiety 26, 30, 113, 177, 205, 229, 233, 236, 237
-uncertainty-manage
argument 11, 70, 75, 80, 144, 233
armed 108, 144, 195, 233
arousal 26, 144, 220, 224, 229, 236- 238
arrest 13, 34, 136, 138–141, 144, 147, 148, 149, 152, 173, 176, 189, 193, 197
arson 173
Asian 24, 206, 213, 220, 221
assailant 207, 214, 216
assault 6, 15, 60, 108, 132, 138–140, 147, 151, 152, 173, 176, 177, 181, 182, 189, 200, 206, 217, 222, 229, 233, 234
assessment 14, 17, 28, 62, 63, 85, 102, 105, 124, 157, 161, 186, 191, 192, 198, 199, 200, 217, 218, 227, 239
asymmetry 158
at-risk 13, 203
attack 18, 28, 32, 78, 178, 181, 207, 244, 253
attempted murder 108, 112
Attica 229, 234, 248
attitudes vii, 7, 8, 23, 24, 26, 34, 57, 58, 66–69, 72, 73, 81–83, 107, 115, 120, 122, 123, 141, 144, 213, 214, 225, 226, 228
attorney 35, 116, 188, 191, 192, 199
attraction 180, 242
attributional signs 16, 201, 204, 217–219, 222, 224–226
attunement 242, 247

augment 18, 46, 95–97
Australian 187, 196, 199
authoritarianism 215
autonomy 37, 42, 45, 99, 134, 140

B
bank 231
bargaining 137, 191, 229, 232, 234–239, 242, 244–246, 250
barricade 251
bashing 224, 228
battered 134, 148, 151, 177, 185, 189, 196, 197–199
battery 138, 181
bias vii, 7, 8, 16, 17, 74, 201–227
blame 140, 148
blood 184
boundary/(ies) 21, 22, 31, 40, 41, 50, 51, 53, 57, 60, 103, 118
Branch Davidians 234
brutality 25, 31, 53, 122
beaureaucracy 6, 63, 88, 104

C
California iii, 1, 3–5, 13, 15, 16, 21, 22, 29–31, 85, 104, 105, 116, 127, 174, 195, 197, 201, 202, 206, 213, 218, 227, 228, 251
campaigns 39
Captains 53, 109
care 31, 131, 147, 156, 169
cartoons 114
case vii, 11, 13–15, 17, 23, 25, 28, 30, 56, 62, 64, 65, 71, 77, 81–83, 95, 97, 103, 110, 111, 115, 118, 120, 133, 141, 144, 147, 151, 155, 157, 159, 163, 165, 166, 169, 184, 185, 187, 189, 190, 192, 203, 206, 207, 211, 216, 217, 220, 221, 234, 242, 245
celebrities 174, 194, 198
change 7, 30, 31, 33, 38, 39, 41, 42, 44, 45, 49, 57, 58, 62–64, 66, 73–75, 104, 105, 126, 130, 131, 165, 173, 183, 190, 191, 197, 212, 240
Chicano 143

child(ren) vii, 2, 10, 13–15, 29, 34, 112, 113, 123, 126, 127, 129, 132, 135, 139, 144, 145, 150–152, 155–172, 181, 228
citizen 2–4, 19, 21, 25, 34, 35, 39, 40, 46, 49, 61, 62, 66, 83, 110, 129, 131, 142, 143, 146, 147, 149, 210
civil 4, 6, 17, 25, 28, 34, 35, 64, 66, 117, 138, 140, 175, 193, 194, 199, 206
classifying 41, 202, 219, 232
cleansing 214
clichés 115, 117
clinical 169, 175, 176, 184, 198, 227, 228
codified 90, 92
coercion 130, 161, 164–166, 177, 180, 200
cognition 70, 82, 126
cohorts 184, 204, 207
collectivist 145
command level 239, 240
Commissioners 109
commitment 70, 78, 92, 180, 181, 233, 235, 241
communality 86, 87
communication i, iii, iv, vii-ix, 1, 2–12, 14, 15, 17–21, 23–33, 35, 36, 39–47, 49–52, 54–61, 63–65, 68, 70, 77, 78, 85–105, 119, 123–127, 129–131, 136, 141, 143, 145, 146, 149–152, 159, 171, 175, 183, 184, 186, 188, 195, 196, 200, 201, 206, 229, 230, 232, 233, 238–240, 243, 244, 247, 248, 250–254
community 1, i, iii, iv, vii, 1, 2, 4–9, 11, 12, 19, 21–26, 29, 30, 32, 33, 35, 36–40, 42–66, 91, 105, 107, 126, 141, 142, 146, 149, 152, 203, 204, 206, 208, 209, 212–214, 218, 225, 226
-oriented policing 5, 25, 62, 91
competence 27, 83, 136, 158, 161, 253
complementarity 88
compliance 4, 22, 23, 28, 229
computer 85, 91, 93–95, 98, 100–104, 180, 182
computer-mediated/CMC 98, 101–103

Index 257

conflict 18, 30, 63, 83, 131, 133, 137, 141, 144, 148, 152, 205, 208, 211, 213–215, 229, 232–236, 239- 244, 246–253
conformity 8, 74, 75, 78, 80, 82, 139, 149, 152
connectivity 87, 88
consensus 45, 86, 162, 242
constitutive 57, 69
constraints 86, 102, 129, 137, 141, 143, 149, 159
constructionism 70, 82
contact 2, 23–25, 29–31, 97, 101, 115, 137, 140, 145, 177, 180, 184, 186, 188, 190, 205, 212, 228, 242, 243
contagion 11, 110, 112
contaminated 164, 166
contending 190, 232–234, 237, 244, 246
content 29, 47, 48, 50, 59, 79, 108, 109, 113, 121, 122, 124, 125, 127, 145, 219, 220, 239, 249
-analysis 79, 122, 125, 127, 220
context 55, 61, 64, 73, 78, 80, 92, 93, 102, 104, 120, 121, 127, 130, 133–135, 143–146, 148, 149, 161, 177, 184, 185, 187–189, 198, 208, 212, 227, 228, 232–237, 241–243, 245
conversation(-al) 71, 72, 79, 129, 145, 146, 149, 159, 170
conviction 22, 23, 157, 166, 176
coping 15, 81, 113, 130, 168, 182, 185–187, 190–192, 197, 200, 230
cops vii, 7, 10–12, 21, 23, 31, 53, 61, 63, 67, 69, 72–75, 107, 109, 121, 125, 126
costs 12, 86, 87, 103, 131, 139, 235
counseling 9, 109, 135, 141, 147, 192, 228, 249
court 10–12, 15, 22, 23, 28, 30, 35, 71, 81, 116, 127, 131, 139, 140, 147, 151, 155, 157, 158, 169–171, 180, 194, 196, 197, 213
credibility 5, 44, 67, 169, 203
crime(s) vii, ix, 2–5, 10, 11, 13, 15–17, 20, 21, 27–29, 31, 34, 35, 37, 38, 43, 46- 48, 57, 60–66, 81, 90, 91, 97, 100, 101, 107–113, 115–117, 119, 120, 123–127, 129, 131, 133, 138, 141, 145, 147, 151, 152, 157, 165, 166, 169, 171, 173, 174, 176, 177, 183–185, 187, 188, 189–191, 195–203, 205–207, 209–221, 222–228, 231, 253
Information Center 97
criminal 2, 11, 12, 14, 17, 22, 29, 31, 32, 35, 36, 54, 62–64, 90, 91, 94, 96, 107, 108, 110, 115, 116, 119, 123–125, 127, 131, 134, 138, 140, 152, 157, 166, 172, 175, 184, 188, 189, 192–194, 196, 197, 199, 201–210, 212–215, 217, 219, 220, 226–228, 236
criminals 2, 7, 73, 91, 107, 108, 121, 202, 207, 215, 227, 231, 250
criminology 31, 61, 63, 64, 196, 197, 199, 227
cultivation 10, 31, 115, 116, 120, 122, 124–127
cultural vii, x, 4, 5, 16, 18, 20, 62, 80, 82, 126, 130, 143, 145, 146, 148, 181, 196, 201, 208, 210–216, 225–227, 247, 250, 251, 253
culture vii, 7, 8, 11, 17, 22, 26, 38, 48, 50, 54, 56–58, 61, 66–68, 72, 74–82, 92, 124–127, 130, 140, 143, 144–146, 174, 190, 201, 205, 208, 210, 211, 215, 251, 253
cyberstalking 175, 180

D

dangerous 8, 18, 67, 78, 80, 112, 116–118, 126, 129, 136, 144, 164
data iv, 2, 3, 14, 19, 27, 60, 62, 69–71, 75, 76, 78, 79, 85–87, 89–91, 94–99, 101, 102, 110, 117, 118, 120, 121, 127, 131, 157, 192, 201, 203, 218, 219, 226, 228, 239
database 99, 132
dating 133, 180, 189
deadly 118, 217, 222, 234

debates 10, 71, 132
decisions 34, 49, 51, 61, 62, 86, 87, 93, 122, 129, 193
defended 212–214, 218, 228
defuse 46
demands 18, 46, 68, 85, 93, 148, 158, 166, 195, 216, 229, 231, 234–237, 241, 242, 246, 247, 249
demeaning 149, 150
demography 107, 109, 115, 116, 121
desensitization 113
Detectives 21, 89, 109, 187
deterrent 148, 152
deviant 185, 195, 210, 211, 215
diagnostic 14, 227
dialectical 129, 142, 146, 148–150, 207
dialogue 41–44, 49, 136, 146, 171
differences 11, 14, 17, 22, 23, 36, 38, 54, 96, 98, 101, 110, 118, 120, 130, 133, 145, 146, 148, 150, 151, 178, 185, 204, 209, 217, 219, 223–227, 249
directness 145
disability 7, 202, 221, 222
disclosure 79, 80, 82, 237
disorder 37, 38, 46, 113, 126, 135, 139, 175, 177, 216, 238
dispatch 37, 89
distorted 133, 175, 185, 216
documentation 27, 202, 210, 226
domestic 2, 12, 13, 22, 32, 129, 131, 138–144, 147–149, 151, 152, 173, 175, 177, 187–200, 224, 236, 247
dominance 26, 31, 70, 214, 215, 217, 235
drama 1, 20, 108, 109, 111, 113, 114, 119, 120, 123–127
dramaturgical 123
dress 201, 204, 208, 219, 227
drug(s) 6, 104, 121, 123–125, 129, 139, 144, 191, 208
due process 15, 35
duration 57, 89, 176, 244
duties 20, 67, 78, 89, 99, 130, 141

E
economic 7, 87, 139, 140, 180, 208, 211, 213, 228
education 28, 35, 36, 57, 62, 123, 188, 206
election 38
electronic 10, 86–88, 94, 95, 97–99, 102–105, 125–127, 198, 207
elite 37
emotion vii, 8, 9, 18, 67, 68, 72, 78–82, 145, 196, 235, 238, 241, 244–247, 252
empowering 141, 167
encouraging 23, 49, 98, 248
England 125–127, 162, 171, 197, 214
environment 13, 40, 42, 43, 46, 60, 65, 89, 91, 93, 96, 98, 102, 105, 129, 138, 141, 143, 167, 173
epidemiology 112, 123
epistemology 68–70, 72, 83
equality 57, 98, 137, 167, 205
equilibrium 130, 131, 137
escalation 141, 148, 194, 202, 203, 215, 240–242, 244, 247, 248
establishment 27, 98, 148, 190
ethnic 21–23, 25, 30, 202, 203, 207, 208, 212, 214, 216–219, 220–222, 225
-ity 7, 22, 23, 29, 219–221
ethnographic 48, 208
ethnomethodological 71
European 30, 82, 103, 105, 116, 122, 123, 252
evidence 10, 14, 17, 30, 33, 46, 52–56, 58, 59, 63, 71, 82, 96, 101, 107, 110, 111, 113, 116, 117, 125, 136, 147, 151, 157, 158, 164, 166, 177, 183–188, 191, 203, 207–209, 212, 213, 217, 219, 220, 225, 226
excessive 28, 34, 57, 157, 181
exchange theory 235
expectations 4, 11, 12, 46, 80, 107, 119, 122, 130, 143, 144, 158, 161, 166, 167, 190, 197, 226

Index

experimenting 38
experts 14, 192
explanations 9, 70, 72
expressive 18, 185, 231–238, 244–247
   -ness 130, 149, 238, 245
eye 145, 184, 192, 220

F

face 15–18, 22, 32, 34, 35, 44, 53, 56, 57,
   73, 78, 98, 99, 102, 115, 119, 135,
   145, 146, 170, 177, 181, 186, 192,
   199, 205, 229, 233, 241–244, 247,
   249–251, 253
factual 48, 108, 115, 116, 225
false 168, 176, 179, 199, 206, 238
famil(y)/ies vii, 13, 129–145, 147–152,
   156, 174, 180, 181, 196, 197, 202,
   250
fanatics 231
FBI 60, 65, 105, 121, 131, 249–253
fear v, 9, 14, 38, 79, 99, 107, 113, 117, 124,
   125, 127, 134, 144, 145, 174, 175,
   184, 187, 202, 216, 249
Federal 15, 21, 31, 34, 60, 62, 97, 105, 121,
   131, 151, 174, 175, 188, 196, 202,
   203, 206, 225, 226, 234, 248, 249,
   251
feminists 13, 144
fiction 11, 12, 23, 107–116, 118–122, 126
fighting 48, 109, 115
fingerprint 97
first-order 115, 116
force 2, 4, 7–9, 25, 28, 29, 31, 34, 45, 67,
   68, 73–75, 77, 80, 160, 167, 177, 192,
   200, 202, 233
forensic 162, 169, 171, 172, 176, 184, 197,
   198
formal 50, 55, 56, 58, 59, 88, 92, 109, 144,
   155, 186, 187
framing 48, 240, 247, 250, 252
free riding 99, 100
fright 113, 123, 124
frustration 79, 230, 232
functional 6, 50–52, 54, 58, 61, 239, 241,
   247, 251

G

gangs 203, 206, 208, 209, 213, 219
gays 7, 29, 210, 211
gender 7, 13, 23, 30, 56, 80, 98, 103, 121,
   130, 133, 137, 141, 149, 178, 199,
   218–221, 223
Germany 214
ghetto 34
gifts 180, 182, 184
goal ix, 4, 18, 25, 33, 36, 41, 42, 49, 50, 57,
   87, 89, 91, 94, 96, 99–101, 144–147,
   181, 208, 217–220, 224, 231,
   234–238, 241, 252
government 1, 7, 15, 26, 29, 35, 64, 82,
   172, 174, 191, 203, 212, 251
graffiti 201, 205, 209
group(s) ix, 5, 19, 21, 22, 24, 29, 30, 34,
   41, 43–45, 56, 60, 67, 68, 77, 86, 87,
   92, 98, 102, 103, 105, 113, 116,
   120–122, 135, 138, 141, 143, 145,
   159, 192, 201–210, 212–226, 244,
   247, 250, 252, 253
guilt 17, 135
guns 97

H

harassment 7, 8, 15–17, 173–175, 180,
   181, 184, 189, 190, 194, 197, 199,
   202, 203, 211, 213, 233
harm 14, 109, 112, 142, 148, 165, 181, 184,
   185, 205, 206, 214, 222, 229, 246
harmony 1, 140, 142, 148, 152
hate vii, 2, 7, 16, 17, 21, 22, 28, 59, 63,
   201, 202–220, 224–228
HCR-20 218, 227, 228
heterosexist 210, 211
hierarchy 31, 51, 52, 58, 88, 89, 100, 105,
   130, 204
Hill Street Blues 107
Hiring 36, 214
history 6, 33, 36, 53, 65, 72, 91, 131, 138,
   143, 170, 201, 208, 209, 218
hit 76, 147, 181
homosexual 7, 73, 82, 214, 216, 227
   -ity 72–74, 82, 216

hospital 124, 131, 150
hostages 18, 230, 232–235, 237, 241, 246, 248
hostile 211, 223
hypothes(is)/-es 11, 30, 113, 115, 117, 139, 159, 163

I
identifying 12, 76, 179, 197, 225
identity 10, 21, 24, 25, 30, 31, 135, 147, 149, 201, 216, 217, 228, 235, 236, 241–244, 252, 253
ideolog(y) 16, 205–207, 209, 215, 217, 220
-ical 2, 73, 202, 204, 208, 209, 215, 227
idiographic identity diffusion 216
illegal 6, 73, 91, 104, 110, 177, 182
imitation 11, 107, 110–113, 118, 123, 127
inappropriate 167, 180, 183, 200, 209
incident 7, 36, 76, 78, 79, 138, 139, 143, 147, 148, 160, 184, 206, 220, 229, 231, 232, 235, 237, 242, 244, 245, 246–251
inconsistent nurturing as control theory 13
individual differences 130
inference 77
information iv, vii, 9, 10, 20, 27, 37, 40, 41, 45, 47, 48, 50–52, 54, 58, 59, 65, 85–105, 116, 118, 127, 130, 131, 141, 144, 147, 157–164, 166–168, 171, 180, 182, 192, 198, 203, 207, 218, 219, 225, 226, 230, 239, 240
infrastructure 86
ingroup 16, 23, 201, 204–206, 211, 212, 214- 216
inhibitions 110
injustice 74, 82, 230
innocent 74, 110, 120, 179
innovations 66, 88, 91
institutional 43, 44, 82, 83, 87, 102, 124, 191, 210, 221
instrumental 182, 185, 208, 218–220, 223, 224, 226, 227, 231–238, 241, 243, 246, 247, 249
intelligent 184, 244

intent 17, 163, 185, 202, 206, 208, 214, 236
intentional 174
interactional 71, 83, 129, 143, 145, 149, 174, 175, 186, 191, 239, 248
intercultural 20, 29–31, 148, 150, 227, 247, 250, 251, 253
intergroup vii, 3, 16, 21–27, 29–32, 151, 201, 203–205, 207, 208, 210–215, 219, 225, 228, 253
international 2, 13, 18, 29, 31, 61, 65, 66, 83, 104, 126, 150, 169, 170, 197, 213, 228, 247, 249, 250, 252, 253
interorganizational 85–88, 102, 104, 105
interpersonal 5, 21, 23, 24, 31, 32, 87, 130, 144, 152, 170, 174, 180, 186, 189, 191, 196, 197, 199, 200, 209, 216, 217, 228, 236, 242, 243, 253
interpretative repertoires 73
interrogation 20
interventions 81, 140, 164, 167, 187, 249
interview 14, 73, 79, 145, 147, 157–169, 172, 220
intimate 67, 133, 139, 151, 153, 176, 178, 181, 195, 198, 200
intimidation 132, 180, 182, 202
intoxication 205
intrusive 161
Invades 183

J
Japanese 212
judges 12, 22
jurisprudence 10, 13, 17
jury 14, 17, 30, 216
justice 9, 11, 12, 14, 30, 32, 35, 60, 62–66, 71, 97, 105, 108, 109, 115, 119, 123–125, 131, 140, 146, 151, 152, 157, 172, 174, 188, 189, 191, 192, 195–200, 209, 217, 227, 228, 249, 253

K
killed 110, 111, 114, 181, 234

L

language ix, 7, 20, 29–31, 42, 56, 59, 68–72, 81–83, 92, 145, 170, 181, 198, 201, 245, 249–253
Latinos 22, 23, 124, 213
law i, iii, iv, vii, ix, 1–21, 23, 25–31, 35, 48, 59, 61–65, 67, 68, 71, 73, 82, 83, 97, 107–110, 114–116, 119–125, 129, 137, 142, 143, 146–149, 151–153, 169, 170, 173, 176, 177, 179, 182, 183, 185–190, 192, 193, 195–203, 207, 211, 214, 215, 218, 224, 225, 226, 228, 229, 231, 233, 234, 242, 248–253
lawyer 17, 164
legal practices 15
legislation 10, 15, 16, 73, 157, 173–175, 196, 199
legitimacy 5, 11, 35, 37, 42, 44–47, 49
Lesbians 7, 210, 211, 215, 225, 228
lexicon 12, 174
life-threatening 78
liking 24, 242
listening ix, x, 4, 237, 245
literature 11, 13, 16, 18, 24, 31, 49, 57, 72, 107, 133, 151, 175, 207, 209, 213, 238
litigation 119
longitudinal 57, 112, 228
looting 36

M

mainstream 26, 34, 211, 215
management 18, 20, 26, 30, 31, 39, 40, 45, 46, 52, 56, 63, 65, 66, 68, 89, 102, 103, 104, 141, 159, 173, 177, 186, 189, 191, 192, 229, 230, 236, 238, 242, 246, 249, 250, 253
managers 36, 39, 54, 74, 88
mandatory 13, 138–141, 144, 148, 152, 173
Marine Corps 8, 9
marital 130–132, 134, 136, 137, 151, 156
McMartin Preschool 15

media 2, 3, 10–12, 25, 26, 31, 45, 47–49, 62, 63, 65, 104, 105, 107, 110, 111–120, 123–127, 129, 155, 173, 174, 178, 183, 184, 195, 196, 198, 207, 248
mentally disturbed 231
messages vii, 16, 42, 46, 47, 49, 51, 59, 114, 122, 136, 137, 143, 174, 180, 181, 201, 206, 208, 210, 212, 214, 216, 218, 227, 239, 240, 244
meta-analysis 133
  -messages 16, 201, 208, 210, 212, 214, 218, 227
metaphors 70
methodology 18, 68, 204, 218–220, 227, 230
Middle East 213
minority 34, 109, 122, 127, 138, 155, 195, 203, 204, 207, 209, 215, 225
Miranda 11, 12, 31, 61, 63, 114, 116, 118, 123, 127
mobile 85, 95, 97, 188
monitoring 8, 75, 99, 168, 180
mood 32, 113
motivation 16–18, 43, 201, 202, 204–208, 210, 217–223, 222, 224–226, 231, 232, 235, 245, 246
motives 108, 179, 185, 186, 203, 208, 210, 215, 219, 233
movies 12, 112, 116, 125
Munich Olympics 18
municipality 193
murder 6, 14, 17, 28, 60, 83, 108, 112, 131, 136, 173, 174, 181, 197, 199, 211, 216, 217

N

natural 8, 53, 65, 79, 80, 112, 126, 193
NCIC 97
neglect 132, 155, 169, 171, 172
neighborhoods 34, 36, 53, 54, 109, 209, 212, 213, 228
networks 64, 87, 97, 102–105
new technologies 2, 9, 87
New Zealand 7, 67, 73, 79, 82, 83

news 1, 7, 9, 11, 12, 21, 22, 28, 31, 34, 47, 48, 49, 51, 59, 61–63, 93, 109, 118, 121, 122, 124–127, 150
newspapers 48, 64, 71
nonverbal 4, 20, 25, 136, 145, 150
norms 30, 92, 130, 141, 143, 144

O

one-way 41, 44, 49, 91
operational 63, 85, 90, 91, 105, 203, 225, 226
orientation 7, 8, 13, 68, 69, 73, 76, 202, 208, 218, 219, 221, 222, 224, 231-233, 235
outgroup 21, 25, 202, 205, 207, 208, 210, 212, 214, 215, 217, 227

P

perceptions 4, 11, 12, 22, 23, 31, 62, 63, 99, 115–117, 120, 122, 125, 127, 198, 200, 244
prevalence 15, 79, 115, 131, 138, 151, 155, 156, 171, 172, 175, 197, 198
prevention 5, 17, 20, 27, 43, 65, 91, 169, 191, 197, 200, 203, 204
primary 34, 37, 41, 45, 51, 52, 57, 59, 89, 90, 94, 95, 97, 101, 186, 188, 220, 231, 233, 235, 244
proactive ix, 4, 38, 91, 101, 187, 228
problem(s) vii, ix, x, 5, 6, 8, 20, 30, 31, 36–39, 51–53, 56, 58, 62, 64, 73, 89, 90, 92, 95, 100, 101, 104, 105, 110, 120, 132, 136, 139, 140, 151, 155, 156, 158, 163, 164, 166, 168, 173, 185, 190, 191, 196, 198, 199–204, 208, 210, 216, 217, 235, 237, 238, 244, 247
 -solving 5, 64, 199
processes 3, 15, 21, 25, 27, 48, 50, 62, 70, 71, 85, 86, 102, 105, 117, 124, 125, 129, 131, 141, 152, 160, 183, 243, 249–254
protection 9, 10, 28, 29, 74, 75, 97, 140, 152, 158, 175, 184, 191, 193, 195, 196, 198, 200, 213, 214

R

rates ix, 35, 112, 116, 129, 131, 155, 156, 176, 195, 203, 220
reactive 38, 91, 94, 95, 100, 204, 217–219, 220, 223, 224, 227, 228
record 9, 89, 97, 100, 101, 209, 220
reduction 46, 94, 101, 155, 225, 237, 242, 246
referrals 140, 147, 148, 155
relations 4, 6, 18, 19, 23–25, 28, 29, 32, 33, 35–37, 40–46, 49, 52, 53, 57, 59–63, 86–88, 103, 144, 150, 152, 156, 195, 203, 207, 211, 213, 225, 228, 236, 251, 253
religious 146, 202, 215, 221, 225, 231
repetition 28, 114, 115
representations 109, 240
reprimands 166
research 1–3, 5, 9, 12, 15, 17–20, 22, 27–34, 36, 41, 42, 44, 46–48, 52, 56–59, 62–66, 68, 69, 71–73, 76, 81–83, 86, 102–105, 109, 111–113, 119–121, 123–127, 129, 133, 136, 138, 141, 149–151, 153, 156, 157, 167, 169, 172, 176, 177, 181, 191, 193, 195–197, 200, 205, 208, 210, 211, 216, 219, 220, 228, 230, 231, 240, 242, 245, 247, 249, 250–253
resolution 6, 131, 168, 229, 231, 232, 235–237, 240, 242, 244, 247, 250, 251
respect 40, 67, 70, 74, 80, 108, 213, 214, 242–244
responsibility 31, 36, 37, 52–54, 130, 141, 158
restricted 35, 133, 201
retaliate 140
retributional 213, 218
retrieval 27, 90, 168
rhetorical 20, 30–32, 70, 77, 78, 82, 182
ridicule 136
rights 6, 11–15, 28, 31, 34, 73, 82, 114, 116, 118, 122, 123, 130, 157, 158, 167, 204, 206, 207, 209, 211, 213
riot 229

riots 34, 36, 60, 65
risk 5, 12, 13, 27, 47, 56, 96, 116–118, 123, 124, 144, 151, 156, 166, 167, 170, 186, 195–198, 203, 205, 208–210, 217, 218, 228, 236
robbery 60, 108, 173, 231, 241
routine ix, 45, 78, 93, 101, 177
Ruby Ridge 229, 248
rule(s) 8, 28, 35, 50, 54, 56, 58, 89, 110, 117, 130, 136, 141, 143–146, 149, 159, 189, 209
 -governed 130, 145

S
safety 1, 3, 5, 8, 27, 75, 85, 115, 117, 122, 140, 141, 174, 183, 184, 187, 192, 195
scandal 6, 59
scene 77, 101, 111, 113, 139, 142, 144, 145, 147, 183, 184, 207, 226, 241, 248
school 64, 104, 161, 180, 197, 205, 206, 211
science 15–17, 19, 27, 63, 102–105, 151, 169, 171, 172, 195, 200, 230, 251, 253
second-order 115, 116, 126
secondary 52, 53, 89, 90, 95, 123, 205, 220, 235
security 27, 28, 57, 167, 177, 197
segregation 203, 214
selection 48, 73, 146, 214, 219
self-
 control 5
 defense 13, 191, 216
sensitivity 20, 30–32, 148, 150, 187
September 11, 2001 v, 2
services ix, 8, 39, 43, 49, 52, 59, 62–64, 155, 171, 172, 186, 187, 189, 191, 192, 198, 199, 234
setting 36, 57, 112, 118, 127, 163, 164, 171, 201, 251
sex 98, 103, 150, 171, 176, 178, 189, 197, 202, 216
sexual 2, 7, 8, 13–15, 17, 29, 73, 76, 134, 151, 155–158, 166, 168–172, 177,
180–182, 197, 200, 202, 216–219, 221, 222
Sheriffs 21, 101
shots 97
silent vii, 1, 11, 77, 79, 124, 166
simulators 96
situational rationality 89, 95
size vii, ix, 1, 33, 35, 63, 67, 85, 96, 107, 120, 129, 131, 155, 173, 176, 201, 229, 255, 257
skill(s) 5, 19, 30, 51, 76, 86, 88, 93–96, 144, 152, 158, 168, 178, 225, 226, 237, 245, 248
skin color 203
slack resources 89
slain 131
smuggling 6
social 1, 12, 13, 15–18, 21, 24–26, 29–34, 46, 53, 56, 57, 59, 62, 68, 69–75, 79, 81–83, 87, 89, 102–105, 109, 113, 123–126, 129, 130, 133, 138, 139, 143–146, 148, 149, 151, 152, 160, 161, 167, 169, 175, 178, 182, 195, 196, 198, 201, 204, 205, 207, 208, 210–218, 225, 226, 228, 230, 235, 239, 243, 244, 249, 250, 252, 253
sociology 124, 125, 200, 251
South Africa 112
spouse 131, 132, 141, 145, 147, 152, 189
stability 87, 130, 131, 140, 148, 225
stalking 2, 15, 16, 22, 134, 173–200
standards 4, 8, 29, 35, 55, 56, 74–76, 78, 80, 159, 184, 203, 226
statistics 108, 131, 155, 171, 197, 202, 203
stereotypes 25, 127, 173, 178, 207, 253
stigma 24, 139, 177, 228
stolen 97, 180, 224
storage 27, 90
stories 34, 47, 48, 56, 57, 62, 125, 126, 158, 160, 171, 185, 186
strategies ix, 5, 18, 20, 24, 25, 27, 36, 38, 43, 49, 58, 65, 66, 85, 86, 90, 91, 94–96, 98, 100–103, 143, 146, 150, 161, 168, 169, 192, 197, 233, 238, 243, 244, 248

street 1, 31, 40, 51, 63, 77, 95, 101, 107, 125, 129
structures 6, 44, 50–52, 54–56, 58, 62, 102, 137, 145, 187
suggestive 14, 159–164
suicide 9, 28, 117, 124–127, 177, 181, 245, 249, 251
support 4, 19, 28, 45, 46, 52, 83, 86, 94, 100, 102, 103, 105, 117, 133, 139, 161, 164, 168, 191, 205, 207, 214, 225, 226
surveillance 10, 180, 182, 184, 186
suspect 18, 28, 34, 71, 100, 138, 139, 158, 164–166, 168, 171, 186, 229, 230, 231–239, 241, 242, 245–247
SWAT 121
Swedish 155–158, 162
symmetry 41, 42, 59, 137, 151
systems 65, 86, 98, 102–105, 123, 127, 129–131, 136, 137, 140, 207, 218, 228
  theory 130

T
tactics 15, 18, 25, 120, 121, 131, 133, 134, 152, 178–182, 233–235, 250
talk vii, 2, 7, 9, 30, 39, 55, 67, 69, 71–73, 75, 76, 78–83, 125, 130, 144, 145, 152, 158, 163, 164, 166, 167, 169, 180, 186, 195
tattoos 204, 208, 218
telephone 4, 18, 22, 33, 53, 72, 101, 177, 180, 182, 191
television 11, 12, 26, 28, 31, 32, 34, 48, 107, 108–127
tension(s) 6, 36, 17, 67, 79, 80, 140, 142, 143, 146, 148, 142, 143, 146, 149, 183, 187, 205, 229, 250, 252
terrorist 97, 205, 214, 231, 250
tertiary 52, 89, 90, 95
testify 15, 147
theft 10, 15, 31, 60, 180, 182
theory 4–6, 13, 19, 21–26, 30, 31, 33, 37, 41, 43, 51, 59, 61, 65, 66, 68, 71, 83, 102–105, 112, 115, 123, 125, 126, 127, 130, 150, 172, 196, 213, 216, 228, 235, 236, 239, 249, 250, 251–253
third-parties 181
threat(s) 8, 13, 42, 13, 45, 75, 78, 80, 109, 131, 134, 173, 174, 176–8, 181, 182, 184, 186, 187, 189, 191, 192, 196, 198–200, 202, 205, 206, 213, 214, 217, 222, 233, 244, 247, 250
threshold 136, 177, 197
tolerance 74, 215
torture 211
tradition 45, 79, 174
training 3–5, 13, 15, 19, 25, 28, 29, 35, 38, 90, 96, 98, 141, 150, 152, 168, 169, 171, 172, 187–191, 196, 198, 200, 224, 228, 248, 251, 252
transmission model 117
trespass 180, 182, 189
trial 29, 82, 110, 157
trustworthiness 80
types 15, 22, 23, 31, 45, 53, 54, 89, 91, 93, 95, 101, 115, 122, 129, 130, 132, 135, 136, 158, 160, 161, 168, 170, 172, 175, 178, 179, 186, 191, 197, 229, 231, 234, 236, 241, 243, 244, 247–249
typologies 15, 135, 151, 178, 179, 238

U
unaffected 158, 159
unemployed 140
uniform 21, 62, 124, 151
unpleasant 76–78
unpredictable 78, 89, 129, 130, 195
unspeakable 78, 79, 82

V
vagueness 77, 175
values 20, 21, 24, 48, 56–58, 66, 115, 137, 141, 143, 145, 148, 159, 183, 201, 206, 211, 215, 216, 222, 228
vandalism 36, 173, 174, 181, 213, 222
variability 72, 79, 130, 170
vehicles 95–97, 234

verdict 157
vertical 6, 50–52, 86, 88
victim(s) 2, 7, 9, 12–17, 21, 28, 29, 74, 83,
    107–109, 113, 115–117, 131–134,
    137–140, 145–148, 151, 156, 157,
    163, 166, 170, 171, 174, 176–181,
    183–200, 203, 205–207, 209, 210,
    212–214, 216–222, 224–226, 232,
    236, 252
    -ization 29, 124, 125, 127, 176, 177,
        179, 195, 197, 199, 200, 203, 206,
        228
videotape 96
viewers 11, 107, 113–119, 122, 126
violence vii, 2, 3, 6, 11–13, 16, 25, 28, 31,
    36, 65, 81, 89, 107–113, 115, 120,
    121, 123–127, 129, 131–145,
    147–152, 170, 173, 175, 176, 177,
    181, 182, 184, 186–201, 203–205,
    207–219, 225–228
vulnerability 127, 161, 233

W
wants 148, 150, 178, 210, 230, 234, 237,
    241, 242, 249
weapon(s) 132, 181, 182, 184, 217, 222,
    253
wire-tapping 10
witness 13, 14, 71, 72, 114, 170, 171
written iv, 1, 18, 55, 71, 159, 181, 187, 188,
    205, 230

Y
youth 34, 129, 217